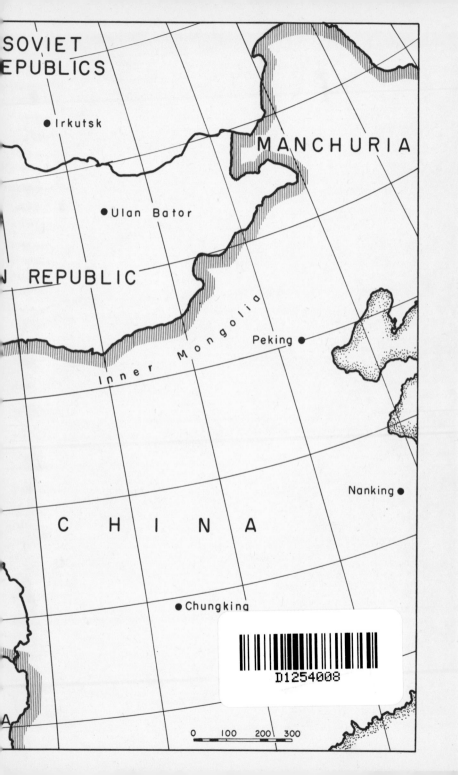

SOVIET
EPUBLICS

●Irkutsk

MANCHURIA

●Ulan Bator

N REPUBLIC

Inner Mongolia

Peking ●

Nanking ●

C H I N A

●Chungking

0   100   200 300

Sinkiang: PAWN OR PIVOT?

SINKIANG:

PAWN OR PIVOT?

Allen S. Whiting

and

General Sheng Shih-ts'ai

MICHIGAN STATE UNIVERSITY PRESS

CONTENTS

Part Two

RED FAILURE IN SINKIANG
by General Sheng Shih-ts'ai

Foreword

THIS STUDY analyzes Soviet strategy in Sinkiang from 1933 to 1949, with major emphasis upon the first ten years, when General Sheng Shih-ts'ai ruled the province. The period opens with Russian intervention in a local civil war between provincial troops under Sheng and rebellious Moslem forces, and closes with the entry of Chinese Communist armies into the area, resulting in the collapse of an anti-Chinese revolt sponsored by Moscow.

The efforts of Chinese Nationalist leaders to cope with Soviet penetration in Sinkiang cannot be considered apart from their preoccupation with Japanese invasion, first of Manchuria and then of China proper. At a later date, Chinese policies in Sinkiang were influenced indirectly by United States efforts to shape China's domestic as well as foreign policies. Similarly, Soviet actions in Inner Asia bore intimate connection with Moscow's view of Japan's intentions, as well as of China's capabilities. Postwar Russian moves in Sinkiang, as elsewhere in China, proceeded from a general policy framework which was world-wide in its focus, concentrating in particular upon actions and reactions of the United States.

Because these larger international questions encompass far more than the area being studied, they are touched upon only insofar as they directly concern Sinkiang. With this recognized limitation, however, in addition to an analysis of Soviet strategy, evidence is offered bearing on three related problems. First, previously unstudied archives of the Japanese Foreign Office throw light on Tokyo's efforts to penetrate Inner Asia, with Sinkiang as a primary avenue of entry. The interaction between Moslems and Japanese provides an intricate pattern of intrigue and infiltration within China.

Secondly, Sheng Shih-ts'ai's memoirs and personal archives fill in part of the picture of relations between the Communist centers of Moscow and Yenan during the 1930's. Sheng's provincial capital of Urumchi[1] was an important link in the line of communications between Joseph Stalin and Mao Tse-tung. Sheng's account suggests not only co-operation, but covert conflict, between these two figures. His relationship with them provides an additional perspective to an historical problem still shrouded in secrecy and uncertainty.

Finally, the study focuses upon certain aspects of Chinese Nationalist policy, domestic as well as foreign. China's handling of the Sinkiang situation reflected its approach to problems elsewhere, particularly in the turbulent postwar period. Sino-Soviet relations became increasingly influenced by provincial developments after Chiang Kai-shek extended his authority into Sinkiang in 1942, following Sheng Shih-ts'ai's swing from the Moscow orbit into that of China's wartime capital, Chung-king.[2]

These three areas of activity receive secondary attention. Perforce, Sinkiang's demographic, economic, and political development are described and analyzed in their relevance to the main theme of Soviet strategy, but no attempt has been made to give them detailed treatment. Two factors prompted this decision. First, Owen Lattimore's *Pivot of Asia* offers an excellent survey of these questions, based on materials available prior to 1950. Secondly, the impact of Chinese Communist policies in the area since that date makes problematic the usefulness of depicting the way of life in the province at the time of writing, given the likelihood of basic long-range developmental changes introduced by China's present capital, Peking.

Within this frame of reference, this book consists of two parts. The first is a chronological account and analysis of Soviet strategy from 1933 to 1949, presenting Sinkiang as a model case study with reference to borderlands adjoining the Soviet Union, from Mongolia to Turkey. By examining Moscow's policies and the reactions of target groups, parallel patterns are suggested elsewhere when similar situations emerge. The second part consists of Sheng Shih-ts'ai's memoirs for this period. As the most authoritative source for his own actions, it merits attention. Subsequent political events and the passing of time have combined to distort description as well as explanation, but this is a common fault in every autobiography which simultaneously serves as a political apologia. No attempt has been made to footnote or to comment directly upon Sheng's memoirs. Instead, it is left to the reader to form his own evaluation, facilitated, it is hoped, by the preceding analysis which draws upon other sources as well as upon Sheng's account.

In the Appendices to Sheng Shih-ts'ai's autobiography are four documents, translated from Chinese originals in his archives. The first is the so-called "Tin Mines Treaty," concluded between Sheng and Soviet representatives in 1940. The text has previously appeared, in identical form, in an official publication of the Ministry of Foreign Affairs of the Republic of China.[3] It is of interest not only as evidence of Soviet strategy in 1940, but as a precedent for the unpublished agreement concluded between Peking and Moscow in 1950, providing for joint exploration and exploitation of oil and nonferrous mineral deposits in Sinkiang.

The next three items presented by Sheng purport to be confessions of conspirators executed by his regime, following his transfer of affiliation from Moscow to Chungking in 1942. They were selected from a larger group of similar items on the basis of their relevance to the main focus of this study, Soviet strategy and Sheng's reaction to it. It is impossible to vouchsafe for the authenticity of these documents, either as to their relation with the persons to whom they are attributed, or to their correspondence with actual events. Hundreds, if not thousands, died in Sheng Shih-ts'ai's purges. Eyewitness accounts provide vivid descriptions of his torture chambers, where hot needles were systematically inserted through fleshy portions of the anatomy, and where excruciating pain preceded the extraction of a confession. The author interviewed survivors of such interrogation, in Hong Kong and Taiwan, during 1954-55. While these facts cast doubt upon the confessions, they do not necessarily disprove the allegations contained therein. At the very least, such documents offer insights on the nature of Sheng's rule.

The first confession is attributed to Mao Tse-min, brother of Mao Tse-tung. Its inclusion needs no justification. The second, although brief, was selected because of its alleged author, Tu Chung-yüan. Tu grew up in the same province as Sheng Shih-ts'ai and was his friend from childhood. Identified by some as an intelligent reformer, by others as a Communist, Tu, in 1937, published a study of Sheng's regime, which remained for many years a primary source on developments in Sinkiang. Much of it served as a basis for Western accounts of the area.[4] Sheng later claimed this work purposely "flattered" his rule, while not disavowing its praise of his educational, welfare, and nationality policies. Whatever the truth, Tu Chung-yüan's place among sources on Sinkiang makes his "confession" of particular interest.

The last document, the longest and the most detailed, is identified with Sheng Shih-ts'ai's sister-in-law. It is offered for whatever light it may throw upon the mysterious death of his brother, Sheng Shih-ch'i. This young military commander had received Soviet training, yet, according to Sheng's account, he was murdered in April, 1942, in a plot directed from Moscow. Since Sheng claims it was this event which triggered his final abandonment of a pro-Soviet policy, the evidence offered in this document merits close study.

The three confessors were executed in 1943, although the confessions are dated in 1942, well before the official *rapprochement* between Urumchi and Chungking. An historical note came almost a decade later, when Soviet and Chinese Communist representatives laid wreaths on the tombs of Mao Tse-min and Tu Chung-yüan, commemorating the "martyrs who were killed by Sheng Shih-ts'ai" in Sinkiang.[5]

Two Americans, personally acquainted with Sheng, offer differing but related estimates of the validity of these accusations of plots against Urumchi. The first observer noted critically, "Sheng is patently a man possessed of a spy mania. This is not to say that there were no intriguers or spies or would-be assassins in Sinkiang. It is only to say that, if one reads Sheng's 'Eight Points' and 'Six Policies,' or even if he limits himself to a study of Sheng's immediate and automatic reactions upon meeting a new personality, he appreciates that Sheng fancied himself beset by all sorts of modern demons— imperialists, Trotskyites, KMT and Japanese agents, Turki nationalists, and just plain assassins."[6]

The other comment came from Wendell Willkie, who met Sheng briefly in Urumchi, yet his limited acquaintance may make it meaningful for the reader who, in these pages, is encountering Sheng for the first time. Willkie, defeated Republican candidate for president of the United States in 1940, remarked after visiting Sinkiang in 1942, "The stories he [Sheng] told me of murder, intrigue, espionage, and counterespionage sounded like a dime thriller and would have been incredible to an American were it not for the evidence all about of suspicion and mystery."[7]

It is not the purpose of this work to pass moral judgment upon Soviet strategy or upon Sheng Shih-ts'ai's actions. Such evaluations, whether of foreign or domestic policy, are made difficult by the wide gap, both in time and custom, which separates Sinkiang from observers in the Western world. To say that the populace benefited or suffered during this period is to assume a common and perceptible scale of values and preferences, shared by the various groups of the province. The complexity of the actual scene, however, as will become evident in the following pages, makes identification of such values extremely hazardous at this distance.

Therefore, where evaluation is offered, it is in terms of the success or failure of policies which set out to achieve perceived objectives. Various groups contested for control of Sinkiang during the period 1933-49. From Tokyo, Moscow, and Chungking, influence was brought to bear upon the center of the struggle, Urumchi. Means of policy are weighed in terms of their effectiveness in attaining ends of policy. If the study achieves the modest aim of laying bare the way in which the competing groups succeeded or failed in their objectives, it will have justified the efforts of the many persons whose contributions made this book possible.

Sources and Acknowledgments

Sinkiang has existed, until recently, beyond the reach of all but the most adventurous travelers. Its atmosphere of rumor and intrigue challenges confirmation of facts and precision of analysis. Written accounts and firsthand observations are scarce. Moreover, later tailoring of evidence to fit the official garb of leading parties in Sinkiang politics compounds the problem of source evaluation.

From the start of this study, such matters have plagued the research to a degree which requires consideration, if the subsequent analysis is to be properly evaluated. In 1954, while in residence in Taiwan, the author learned of the presence there of General Sheng Shih-ts'ai, celebrated war lord of Sinkiang from 1933 to 1944. Two weeks after requesting an interview, he was informed officially that the general's whereabouts was "unknown." This seemed incredible, considering Sheng's inactive rank in the armed forces and his prolific articles in the local press. Further investigation resulted in a third party arranging clandestine meetings between Sheng Shih-ts'ai and the author, doubtlessly known to the authorities yet not receiving official sanction.

Similarly, secrecy was imposed in February, 1954, on a resolution introduced in the second session of the National Assembly of the Republic of China, attended by more than 1,500 delegates. This statement demanded punishment of Sheng for alleged crimes against residents of Sinkiang, as well as for his pro-Soviet policy pursued from 1933 to 1942. Both it, and Sheng's lengthy rejoinder, remained officially classified secrets, their existence being learned through well-informed Hong Kong newspapers.

In addition to secrecy, the difficulty of establishing available evidence as bona fide was compounded by the checkered careers of firsthand observers. Necessity compelled those involved in Sinkiang politics to cross opposing lines without hesitation, if they were to survive the rapid shifts of power in Urumchi. Kuang Lu, now attached to the Ministry of Foreign Affairs in

Taipei, illustrates this problem. Gifted in Russian and Manchu, as well as Chinese, Kuang played a critical role in 1934, as an intermediary between Sheng Shih-ts'ai, and the Soviet consul general, Garegin A. Apresoff. Subsequently assigned by Sheng as Chinese consul in Tashkent, he was identified by Japanese intelligence sources as "a Soviet agent." In 1938 Kuang visited Urumchi at Sheng's invitation, when the general's pro-Soviet orientation was clearly established. Whatever may have been his sympathies with that orientation, however, he fell victim to a purge of "Trotskyite-imperialist plotters," instituted by Sheng with the assistance of Soviet advisers.

Jailed until 1942, Kuang won release when Sheng transferred his affiliation to Chungking. Yet apparently the Kuldja rebels, acting under Russian direction in the western part of the province in November, 1944, found Kuang Lu sufficiently acceptable to offer him a post in the insurgent regime. Kuang chose Chungking at this point, remaining a trusted adviser on Sinkiang since that time. Thus, while his political preferences display some consistency, Kuang's choices of action seem to have been dictated by more immediate, pragmatic considerations.

His career is not unique in its apparent identification with conflicting political camps. Sheng Shih-ts'ai is an outstanding example of this phenomenon. Protective coloration, resulting from such changes of affiliation, makes evidence from firsthand observers in this situation particularly difficult to evaluate.

Furthermore, unintentional error follows from the frequent confusion of rumor and fact. For instance, estimates on the number of persons executed during Sheng's purges range from several hundred, by his own account, to more than one hundred thousand, stated by responsible Chinese sources.

Another point of dispute concerns that of alleged treaties concluded between Urumchi and Moscow. A rumored pact of 1935 purportedly pledged Soviet assistance to Sheng in case of outside attack, excluded all other foreign influence, and offered Russian support should he declare Sinkiang independent of China. Japanese intelligence sources reported various versions of this treaty, while public accounts appeared in secondhand sources at the time. Yet investigation has failed to confirm existence of the pact, at least as summarized in Western studies.

This is not to claim that every statement in the following chapters has been irrefutably established as fact. Were all unverifiable information to be rigidly excluded, only the shadow-iest outlines of the Sinkiang scene would remain. On the contrary, material with a high degree of probability, albeit without certainty, is included and so identified, so as to provide guidelines for further research and analysis. It is hoped that circumspect handling of the sources will add substantially to understanding of Soviet strategy in Sinkiang, as well as to determining the motivations of other groups subject to or allied with that strategy.

Sheng Shih-ts'ai himself, of course, is a primary source for this study. His autobiography, comprising the second part of this book, was written in retirement on Taiwan and translated in 1954 under the auspices of The Asia Foundation. The original, considerably longer than the published version herein, has been reassembled, edited, and provided with transitional material culled from interviews with Sheng and from his other writings. The purpose of this revision was to facilitate reading of Sheng's account by a non-Chinese audience, the original version containing personal as well as political references un-familiar or irrelevant in the present context. Such additions as have been made come from written answers provided by General Sheng to the author, based on questions submitted after study of the original manuscript. Sheng's many articles, including a condensation of "My Ten Years in Sinkiang," published serially in Taiwan, also provided material inserted in editing. The author wishes to express his appreciation for the opportunity to make such revisions, and to accept the responsibility for any injustices or shortcomings which the manuscript may have suffered in the process.

A second major source is the archives of the Ministry of Foreign Affairs (Wai-chiao Pu) of the Republic of China, portions of which were made available through the courtesy of the Ministry of Foreign Affairs, George C. Yeh. While such records were not examined in the original Chinese, English paraphrases of selected items provided a basis for further research. Additional documents appear in official publications or in authorized accounts by Sinkiang specialists resident in Taipei, granted access to official archives.

Thirdly, co-operation from informants in Taiwan, Hong Kong, and Japan provided eyewitness accounts of principal events and negotiations concerning Sinkiang from 1933 to 1949. Although such evidence suffers inevitable distortion through recollection, it adds a dimension of reality to written materials. Unfortunately, most of those interviewed requested that their contributions be anonymous. Out of deference to this request, such persons are identified in the general listing of sources below, but only where permission was granted is specific information attributed to the source in subsequent pages. Naturally, every effort was made to establish the accuracy of these accounts.

Finally, a supplement made by the Ford Foundation to its original grant enabled the author to delve into the archives held by the Ministry of Foreign Affairs of Japan. These archives contain more than 40,000 pages of materials pertaining directly to Sinkiang, with additional volumes covering Sino-Soviet relations in general. The documents range in reliability from patent forgeries, passed through police files and intelligence sources, to telegrams intercepted in passage between the Commissariat of Foreign Affairs (Narkomindel) and Soviet diplomats on the one hand, and the Wai-chiao Pu and Chinese officials on the other. These telegrams, intercepted by Japanese agents, provide ample evidence of authenticity. In addition, Japanese analysis benefited from friendly Chinese sources, sometimes holding official positions and acting as agents for Toyko, as well as for Chungking. Among the more valuable dispatches were those from trained personnel in the Japanese foreign service, notably Minister Masamoto Kitada, stationed in Kabul.

Russian sources proved disappointing. A scanning of *Pravda* for the years 1931-35 indicated insufficient material to warrant continuation in this direction. Nor do Chinese Communist writings throw much light on this period, confined mostly to general denunciations of Sheng's allegedly reactionary rule and eulogies to the "martyrs" executed after his change of policy in 1942. Sheng's earlier "progressive" period is explained as a product of circumstances over which he had no control.

Among specific acknowledgments, two, in particular, head the list. The author is extremely indebted to General Sheng Shih-ts'ai for his generosity and patience. The first quality granted free examination of his voluminous files of original documents, letters, and photographs. The second aspect, patience, enabled General Sheng to tolerate endless hours of questioning, much of it based on confusion and ignorance, probing into his personal, as well as his political, views. Without the impetus provided by his friendly and willing help, this study would not have been possible.

Another individual whose efforts enhanced this work is O. Edmund Clubb. Now retired from the foreign service of the United States, he served in Sinkiang in 1943, opening the first American consulate in Urumchi. His interest in the research for this book and his direct, but encouraging, criticism provided a ready source of inspiration during the tortuous process of writing it. As a consultant, his reservoir of knowledge about China in general, and about Sinkiang in particular, proved most helpful.

In addition, many persons gave generously of their time and insight to sharpen the analysis and to clarify the thinking of the author. Special mention should be made of those on Taiwan, both in official and unofficial capacities, including the Minister of Foreign Affairs, George C. Yeh; Lieutenant General Chiang Ching-kuo; Dr. Lo Chia-lun; Chu Hsin-min; Wang Yun-wu; Kuang Lu; Pu Tao-ming; Prince Wang Ming; and Dr. Shen Nai-ch'en. The Asia Foundation co-operated in providing the translation of General Sheng Shih-ts'ai's autobiography. Ward Smith, of that organization, counseled the author and helped to provide the initial contacts which made possible research on this subject.

In Hong Kong, Henry R. Lieberman, of *The New York Times,* Frank Robertson, of *The Christian Science Monitor,* and A. Doak Barnett, of the American Universities Field Staff, all kindly made available their notes on trips into northwest China after the war. Mr. Robertson lent the author his unfinished manuscript describing a visit to Sinkiang in 1947, including valuable material on the Kuldja uprising. Additional help came from James Ivy, of The Asia Foundation, and his associates. The Union Research Institute generously opened its unique clipping files of Sinkiang newspapers and offered personal assistance, as well as critical comments. Robert Burton kindly arranged interviews with Chang Kuo-t'ao, who offered firsthand observations on relations between Urumchi and Yenan during the 1930's, when Chang was still in the Politburo of the Chinese Communist Party. Personal reminiscences from Vincent Shuei and Huang Chen-hsia filled in details on Sinkiang events of 1944-45.

The Ministry of Foreign Affairs of Japan permitted un-limited access to its archives, for which the author is deeply grateful. The gracious assistance of Ken Kurihara and his staff saved many hours of searching and directed research into re-mote areas of the archives. Their patience was unflagging, despite language shortcomings of the author. Dr. Chihiro Hosoya and the Honorable Arita Aoki assisted in translation work. The Honorable Masamoto Kitada and his associate, S. Saitoh, helped to reconstruct the situation as viewed from Kabul in the midthirties, and offered critical evaluation of archival documents. Shigehiru Matsumoto, of The International House of Japan, provided introductions to key figures in the study. P'eng Chao-hsien and Miao Chien-chu gave freely of their time in personal interviews pertaining to experiences con-cerning Sinkiang developments.

Few foreigners know Sinkiang as does Professor Owen Lattimore. His books, as well as the writings of his wife, Eleanor, provided valuable and imaginative perspectives, based on extensive travel through the area. Conversations with him added still another dimension of understanding. Another special-ist on China, Professor Howard Boorman, kindly made avail-able a draft of his manuscript on Sinkiang and commented critically on part of this manuscript at an early stage of writing. Dr. Chaucer H. Wu similarly provided draft portions of his forthcoming study, based on his role as Special Commissioner for Foreign Affairs in Sinkiang during 1943-44. Personal dis-cussions with him helped to clarify this complex period, although a detailed account is omitted from this book in view of the imminent publication of Dr. Wu's firsthand account.

Dr. Sun Fo granted an interview at his home in Anaheim, California, during which he offered observations based on his negotiations with Stalin in 1939, at which time he spent several days in the Sinkiang capital en route to Moscow. Dr. William Su-ting, while conducting research at the University of Califor-

nia, Los Angeles, provided information based upon his supervision of geographical and geological surveys in Sinkiang during
1943. Miss Anna Louise Strong kindly opened her files to the
author at her home in Los Angeles, pertaining to her trip
through Sinkiang in 1940 and her interviews with survivors of
Sheng Shih-ts'ai's anti-Communist purge who returned to Yenan.
These interviews were obtained during her visit to the Chinese
Communist capital in 1946.

The author wishes to express his gratitude to the Ford
Foundation, which provided a generous grant, making possible
travel to Formosa, Hong Kong, and Japan during 1953-55.
Without this assistance, none of the research for this book
would have been possible. Writing up the findings was facilitated by time made available to the author while a member of
the Department of Political Science at Michigan State University.
A research grant from that institution facilitated supplementary
research and consultation. Final editing and revision took place
after the author had joined the research staff of The RAND
Corporation, Santa Monica, California. That organization's
co-operation is gratefully acknowledged. None of the sponsoring
institutions, however, bears any responsibility for the views expressed herein, and their sponsorship does not constitute endorsement of the author's findings.

Invaluable research assistance was rendered by Yoshihiko
Sasaki. His diligence and painstaking care in indexing, para-
phrasing, and translating relevant portions of the voluminous
archives of the Ministry of Foreign Affairs in Tokyo made available quantities of material in a short period of time. His advice
helped to smooth the way in interviews as well as in research.
In Taiwan, General Sheng's son, Sheng Keh-hsin, kindly acted
as interpreter in some of the interviews with his father. As
tutors in the Chinese language, Messrs. Chao and Ting equipped
the author with necessary research tools while checking his

translation of Sheng Shih-ts'ai's published writings. Miss Chou Kuang-mei, as a research assistant at Michigan State University, assisted in translation and summaries of additional Chinese sources. Finally, Alice C. Whiting deserves more than the inevitable tribute paid a writer's wife for her patience during the many evenings and week ends sacrificed to this study. During a brief bout with polio on Taiwan, the author found her help and her counsel an inestimable support at a time when it was most badly needed.

None of the persons named above shares the blame, exclusively the author's, for whatever shortcomings or errors appear in the following pages. All, however, deserve the reader's commendation for their contribution to the completed study.

By titling this book, *Sinkiang: Pawn or Pivot?*, the author wishes to place a different emphasis upon the role of the province in recent history, compared with that offered by Professor Lattimore and others. A synthesis of the two approaches was suggested by a chess expert, who noted that in certain situations a pawn may prove to be pivotal in importance.

A. S. W.

Santa Monica, California

Notes

1. The Wade Giles system of transliteration has been used throughout the text for the spelling of Chinese names. Towns in Sinkiang are known by two, and sometimes three, designations. Official usage has vacillated between the native, or Turki, appellations and their Chinese counterparts, depending upon policy at the time. Because the People's Republic of China employs Turki nomenclature, its use in the present text facilitates reference to

contemporary maps. Thus, the capital of Sinkiang is identified as Urumchi throughout the analytical portion of the book, although Sheng Shih-ts'ai identifies it in his memoirs, according to Nationalist practice, by its Chinese name of Tihua. Where conflicting transliterations occur, the spelling of the National Geographic Society has been followed.

2. The capital of China during the Manchu Dynasty, and in the first years of the Republic of China which succeeded it in 1911, was Peking. The National Government, under Chiang Kai-shek, overthrew the Peking regime in 1927 and named Nanking as the new capital. Ten years later the Japanese attack forced the Chinese to retreat inland, with Chungking becoming the wartime capital in 1937. Thus, the reference to the three cities in the text are synonymous with the seat of central government at the particular time.

3. *Su lien tui Sinkiang ti ching chi ch'in lüeh* (Soviet Economic Aggression Against Sinkiang) (Taipei: Ministry of Foreign Affairs, 1950); hereafter cited as *Soviet Economic Aggression.* Photocopies of the Chinese and Russian texts are included, together with an English translation.

4. Tu Chung-yüan, *Sheng Shih-ts'ai yü hsin Sinkiang* (Sheng Shih-ts'ai and the New Sinkiang) (Hankow: 1938). Martin R. Norins in *Gateway to Asia: Sinkiang* (New York: The John Day Company, 1944), includes a lengthy paraphrase and summary of Tu's book, pp. 141-51. Owen Lattimore, *Pivot of Asia* (Boston: Little, Brown and Company, 1950) draws upon Tu's study to a lesser extent.

5. New China News Agency report from Urumchi, April 7, 1954. The ceremonies were held on April 5, 1954. Mao Tse-min was identified as an "elite Chinese Communist Party member," while Tu Chung-yüan was termed "a democratic progressive personage."

6. Confidential letter to the author.

7. Wendell L. Willkie, *One World* (New York: Simon and Schuster, Inc., 1943, paper edition), p. 86.

SOVIET STRATEGY IN SINKIANG:

1933-49

ALLEN S. WHITING

PART ONE

1

Sinkiang: Its Domestic & International Background

IN SIZE, Sinkiang ranks among the largest of China's provinces, but among the lowest in its population density. More than 650,000 square miles in area, it has less than five million people, fewer than the city of Shanghai. Virtually cut off from much of China and the outside world by towering mountain ranges, the province has remained outside the main stream of civilization since the days when the ancient caravans, which once traversed the area, were replaced by water transport.

To a degree unparalleled in modern China, except perhaps for Tibet, physical features have shaped the history of Sinkiang. The Tien Shan splits the province in two, with the Tarim Basin in the south and the Dzungaria Basin in the north. Continuing along the Soviet border in the west, this range merges with the Pamir on the Afghanistan boundary. On the south, the Kunlun range separates Sinkiang from Kashmir and Tibet; while along the eastern frontier the Altai Mountains separate it from Mongolia, and the Altyn Tagh, from China proper.

While these mountains tend to isolate Sinkiang from India and China, they have provided a less formidable barrier to Russian contact. During the czarist expansion in the nineteenth century, the Ili River Valley, in particular, and several mountain passes, afforded easy access for Russian traders and settlers. Completion of the Turkistan-Siberian Railway (Turksib) in

1930 furthered this orientation of Sinkiang toward the Soviet Union. No railroad from China proper has yet crossed the area, although by 1960 a new line will facilitate integration of Sinkiang's economy with that of China.

In addition to mountains, Sinkiang has vast areas of arid depressions. More than half of the Tarim Basin, 850 miles long and 350 miles wide, is desert. Around this wasteland runs a line of oases, containing almost three fourths of the total population, mainly in Khotan, Yarkand, Kashgar, and Aqsu. Likewise, a desert belt lies in the center of the Dzungaria Basin to the north of the Tien Shan, although this area enjoys more moisture than does the south. Here, too, the trade avenue from east to west, known since ancient times as the Silk Road, is dotted with oases, such as Kitai, Manass, Wusu, and Urumchi, the provincial capital.

Most striking are the cultural differences between north and south Sinkiang. A slight majority of the province's population is Uighur, a Turki-speaking people concentrated in the Tarim Basin oases, where they pursue a settled life of farming. In recognition of this group's predominance, in September, 1955, Sinkiang was renamed the Sinkiang Uighur Autonomous Area.

The next largest ethnic group, totaling about ten percent of the population, is Kazakh. These nomadic herdsmen frequent the Dzungarian steppes, and are noted for their horsemanship and fighting abilities. The Chinese, ranking third, comprise only six percent of the inhabitants, with Kirghiz, Mongols, Tadzhiks, and Sibo forming small but identifiable minorities scattered throughout the area.

Chinese efforts to rule Sinkiang encountered many obstacles, not the least of which was the insignificant percentage of Chinese inhabitants. Religious as well as ethnic hostility to Peking's domination came from the Moslems, who represent an overwhelmingly large proportion of the population. Even those Chinese, chiefly along the northeast border adjoining Kansu province, who became Islamic converts, seldom enjoyed the full confidence of fellow Uighur and Kazakh worshipers. Known as Tungans, these converts frequently joined forces with other Moslem rebels against central government authority. However, schisms invariably split the coalition apart, as racial animosities took precedence over religious identification.

It would be misleading to identify local aspirations toward self-rule as nationalism in the sense that that term is commonly used in the West. An amalgam of Uighur, Kazakh, and Kirghiz rebels periodically proclaimed a so-called "Eastern Turkistan Republic," complete with cabinet officers and star-and-crescent flag. But genuine nationalism was precluded by the heterogeneity of the peoples, in marked contrast with near-by Mongolia. Pan-Islamic and pan-Turki movements repeatedly won short-lived success, only to fragment before conflicting claims of rival ethnic groups. Those rebellions which proved successful, as under Yakub Beg in the nineteenth century and the Kuldja revolt during World War II, temporarily fused Uighur and Kazakh through anti-Chinese sentiment. No lasting sense of unity was achieved, however, and the symbols of common identification did not provide the cohesive power customarily associated with nationalism.

In addition to racial animosity, Chinese control of Sinkiang faced difficult physical barriers, which served to orient the province, economically at least, toward the Soviet Union. During the 1930's the province's trade center nearest to China proper was Hami, roughly 1,200 miles from the railhead at Pao-t'ou.[1] For caravans, this meant a three-month trip at best. For motor vehicles, the two weeks of arduous passage over rough roads and through treacherous passes made only passenger goods and luxury traffic feasible. By comparison, less than two hundred miles lay between the Turksib railway and either Chuguchak or Kuldja. Good roads facilitated cheap transportation westward. Kashgar, in the Tarim Basin, was only twelve days from Soviet rail contact, but at least 2,500 miles from a similar point in China.

Militarily, this logistical pattern left local authorities in Urumchi at the mercy of marauding rebels for weeks, perhaps months, until central government forces could make their way across the mountainous passages of northwest China. Meanwhile, Russian forces could cross the border at several points, arriving at Kashgar or Urumchi within days. Thus, provincial authorities were confronted with the dilemma of relying on foreign arms to quell local revolts, while attempting to maintain Chinese sovereignty over an area which lay beyond the control of the central government.

Reinforcing these immediate factors, distant political developments increased the disparity of Russian, as opposed to Chinese, influence in Sinkiang. Czarist expansion into Central Asia coincided with the declining years of the Manchu Empire. While the Bolshevik revolution temporarily interrupted the steady increase of Russian pressure in Inner Asia, the respite soon ended. Within a decade, the new Soviet leaders added fresh impetus to political and economic development of Kazakhstan, Kirghizia, and Tadzhikstan, adjoining Sinkiang. In contrast, the founding of the Republic of China, in 1911, had failed to create a strong, stable central government. The ensuing civil war and foreign encroachment perpetuated disorder, jeopardizing Chinese control of peripheral areas. Soviet penetration of Outer Mongolia in 1921, and Japanese invasion of Manchuria ten years later, provided graphic evidence of this weakness.

Still another complication beset consolidation of Chinese power in Inner Asia. The line of political demarcation, so clearly drawn on maps, defies identification in reality because of the similarity of peoples residing on both sides of the Sino-Russian border. Furthermore, few natural phenomena provide unambiguous marking of international boundaries in this area. Nomadic groups, following the vagaries of weather and water, show little concern for rival jurisdiction claimed by remote capitals. Similarity of race, religion, and custom make Kazakhs on either side of the border essentially one people, as is true for the Mongols, Kirghiz, and other groups which straddle thousands of miles of the Sino-Soviet border. At the very least, this has permitted misunderstanding, saddling China with the responsibility for maintaining order in areas of dubious jurisdiction, far from its centers of power. At the worst, it has offered the opportunity for piecemeal Russian encroachment and subversion along endless stretches of unguarded, ambiguous boundary.

The first instance of this latter threat arose with the Moslem revolts of the 1860's, sweeping across Sinkiang as through Shensi and Kansu provinces. When Yakub Beg led his rebel legions into Urumchi and looked to Delhi for British support, Russian concern manifested itself in military movements down the Ili Valley in 1871. St. Petersburg appeared anxious for its expanding trade benefits, jeopardized by British competition. It was also concerned by the possible spread of Moslem uprisings into its newly acquired Central Asian holdings. At the time, it mattered little that the area occupied by czarist troops was claimed by China. Not until after the defeat of the uprising by Manchu forces in 1877, aided in part by Russian supplies, did St. Petersburg evacuate most of the disputed territory.

The initial agreement covering this withdrawal granted to Russia western portions of the Ili area, including Kuldja, the valley of the Tekes River, and strategic passes. In addition, China was to provide extensive trading privileges, as well as to pay an idemnity to defray occupation costs. However, Peking quickly denounced this draft, imprisoning the envoy who had agreed to it. A new treaty in 1881 narrowed the territorial cession considerably, while leaving intact the economic provisions. Thus, military means had won for Russia a slice of Chinese territory and had opened the door to extensive commercial penetration.

Formally organized as a province in 1884, Sinkiang passed under the rule of successive generations of Chinese bureaucrats. Collapse of the Manchu dynasty in 1911 coincided with the overthrow of the local governor in Urumchi, but otherwise the revolution in China proper left the remote province untouched. Yang Tseng-hsin, succeeding the deposed governor, ruled Sinkiang with a firm hand from 1912 until his assassination in 1928.

By certain actions during the Bolshevik revolution, Yang established himself as a friendly but independent political neighbor of the new Soviet state. When more than thirty thousand White Russians fled into Sinkiang in 1920-21 before advancing Red units, he invoked a threefold strategy. He disarmed and interned some refugees. He offered a safe return to Russia to others, provided they went peacefully, as established in terms he had negotiated with Bolshevik representatives. In co-operation with Red troops provided at his request, he pursued those who fled into the Altai Mountains, along the Outer Mongolian border.

His foreign policy frankly recognized Russia's dominant economic role in Sinkiang. With the closing of the Russian-Sinkiang border in 1918 and the resultant impact upon the province's economy, Yang, in 1920, was prompted to conclude a provisional trade pact with Soviet authorities in Tashkent. This provided for two Chinese consulates, at Semipalatinsk and

Verkhne-Udinsk, with reciprocal Soviet establishments in the Ili Valley. Although the Peking government publicly denied implications of recognition of Moscow attending this local agreement, it subsequently approved its terms. An incentive to such acceptance undoubtedly was Russian renunciation of extraterritorial privileges held by czarist representatives.

Peking's approval was merely a formality for Yang. Actual power lay with the governor in Urumchi, just as Chang Tso-lin held sway over Manchuria and Sun Yat-sen's Nationalist forces ruled areas of south China. China remained a fiction insofar as the term connoted control from a single, central government. War lord rule, commonplace throughout the border provinces, operated in Sinkiang as elsewhere. Thus, Yang concluded agreements with Soviet officials precisely as though he were the Wai-chiao Pu in Peking. In 1924 he extended Soviet economic opportunities by a new treaty which established Russian consulates in Urumchi, Kuldja (Ining), Chuguchak, Sharasume, and Kashgar. In return, he appointed Chinese consular officials in Semipalatinsk, Tashkent, Alma-Ata, Zaisan, and Andijan. In 1927 these officials refused to follow Nanking's lead in breaking relations with Moscow, pursuing instead a policy of "friendliness," as ordered from Urumchi.[2]

According to the canons of international law, Yang lacked authority to conclude such arrangements. Practice established precedent, however, and his successor, Chin Shu-jen, followed in his footsteps at a quickened pace. In 1931 Chin agreed to Soviet trade agencies at the eight cities of Urumchi, Chuguchak, Kuldja, Kashgar, Aqsu, Kucha, Yarkand, and Khotan. He lowered customs duties on Soviet goods, and placed telegraph and radio communications under "joint management," which in practice meant Soviet control of these facilities. The free movement granted Soviet trade representatives throughout Sinkiang, coupled with customs and tax privileges, afforded

Russia unrivaled economic advantages. Following this pact the Soviet-Sinkiang Trading Agency, or Sovsintorg, endeavored to spread Soviet commercial ascendancy throughout the province.

Chin's motivations in concluding the pact are not clear, but probably paralleled those later suggested by Sheng Shih-ts'ai, who claimed that Russian military assistance was guaranteed Chin in secret annexes. Chin needed such help, as revolt, occasioned by his maladministration, corruption, and abuse of non-Chinese groups, spread through the province between 1931 to 1933. However, no deliveries of Soviet equipment arrived, and Chin proved unable to cope with the unrest, being ousted in a *coup d'état* in April, 1933.

Unlike Yang Tseng-hsin, Chin Shu-jen had kept Nanking ignorant of the 1931 trade pact. When the central government learned of its contents, it repudiated the agreement. Nonetheless, Sovsintorg continued operations, with all provisions of the 1931 pact regarded as valid by Chin's successor, Sheng Shih-ts'ai.

Whether or not Chin had sought Russian military help, he had carried the independent policy of his predecessor still further. Essentially, however, he had pursued a similar line as had Yang, pledging nominal allegiance to the central government while encouraging closer economic ties with the Soviet Union, cemented by formal agreements. Soviet authorities, on their part, had taken advantage of this opportunity to extend their influence in Sinkiang. The Turksib railroad added strength to the economic position of Russian traders, already active in the northwestern districts of Sinkiang. Chin's concessions had bolstered their position to the disadvantage of traders from central China, as well as from British India.

Just as the foreign policies of Yang and Chin provided an important backdrop for the rule of Sheng Shih-ts'ai, so did their domestic policies establish the pattern of things to come. From the inception of his rule, Yang remained alert to the danger of local revolt. Immediately after winning power in 1912, he dealt vigorously with a separatist movement in Ili, headed off Moslem unrest in Hami and Komul, and suppressed secret society activities throughout the province. An eyewitness account tells of his quelling a plot by subordinates from Yünnan, in 1916, hoping to co-ordinate their activities with political events in China proper. Yang questioned the suspects, who denied all charges of conspiracy. He then killed his intelligence agent to demonstrate belief of the suspects' disclaimers. Then, at a ceremonial banquet to which he invited the accused, Yang's bodyguards murdered two of the suspects at the table, imprisoning or banishing the rest.[3]

Through a combination of bribery, force, and nepotism, Yang repeatedly suppressed incipient intrigue and revolt. His extreme caution manifested itself in rigorous censorship of all Chinese and foreign periodicals, prohibition of newspapers in Uighur or Kazakh, and personal control of important documents as well as of the provincial telegraph headquarters. To prevent non-Chinese from uniting against him, he shrewdly pitted one group against another, in traditional divide-and-rule fashion.

Seventeen years of tenure bear witness to Yang's successful use of political tactics, customarily associated with a bygone period. His practices contrasted with verbalized aspirations for reform elsewhere in China, marked by experiments at parliamentary rule and fumbling attempts at party development. No counterpart of Sun Yat-sen's Kuomintang penetrated Sinkiang, nor did western intellectual currents, visible from Peking to Canton, break through the mountain vastness separating the remote province from China proper. For Sinkiang, time stood still. The clock seemed stopped several centuries back, when cunning and force provided the political combination for successful rule. However anachronistic this pattern might appear from a later, more distant viewpoint, its prevalence on the eve of Sheng Shih-ts'ai's assumption of power is of crucial importance for understanding his regime.

It should be noted that Yang's suspicions, while appearing exaggerated to foreign observers, were not without justification. Dramatic proof of their validity came on July 7, 1928. Yang's Commissioner of Foreign Affairs, Fan Yao-nan, gave a celebration dinner, commemorating graduation exercises of the Government Law School in Urumchi. Yang arrived, with an escort of two hundred soldiers supplementing his regular bodyguards. His precautions were of no avail, as Fan's henchmen, disguised as waiters, whipped out concealed pistols and assassinated Yang and his supporters. Fan called upon Chin Shu-jen, head of the Political Department, to become governor. Chin countered by seizing Fan, killing thirteen of his bodyguards. The next day Fan and his accomplices were executed. Such was the pattern of violence in the provincial capital.

Nor did Chin fare much better than his predecessor. Resentment against his rule led to open revolt in 1931. Carnage spread, as marauders sacked villages. In reprisal, government troops laid waste to whole areas. The tempo of fighting increased the following year when rebel forces attracted the support of Ma Chung-ying, member of a family renowned for its fighting prowess and Tungan commander of the Thirty-Sixth Division in Kansu. When Ma's legions sacked the countryside and threatened the capital in April, 1933, local forces in Urumchi moved to oust the corrupt and inefficient governor. White Russian units, which had been armed by Chin, turned their guns against his headquarters, killing his younger brother, head of the Military Bureau. Chin fled, reportedly disguised as a woman. Whatever the details, he made good his escape to Russia, whence he returned to Nanking to be tried and imprisoned for his 1931 concessions to Moscow.

Into this chaotic situation stepped the young Manchurian officer, Sheng Shih-ts'ai. Eschewing the formal position of governor, he headed the provincial garrison with the title of commander, or *Tupan*. Regardless of title, Sheng governed the fate of Sinkiang for at least the following decade. On the surface, his policies followed those of Yang and Chin, regarding Russia as the dominant power in the area and meeting domestic unrest with ruthless repression. However, neither his foreign nor his domestic policies were mere copies of his predecessors. Because of these fundamental differences, which will become apparent later, Sheng merits attention as a unique figure on the Sinkiang scene.

Born in 1895 in the province of Liaoning, in southern Manchuria, Sheng Shih-ts'ai came of a moderately wealthy family. His subsequent military and foreign training provided a background typical of many rising young officers in the new Republic of China.[4] Routine education culminated in his enrollment in the Provincial Forestry and Agricultural School at Mukden, at the age of fourteen. Three years later he moved to Shanghai, where he studied politics and economics. There he came in contact with teachers and students of radical inclination, opposed to the conservative rule of Yuan Shih-k'ai in Peking. Upon their advice, Sheng visited Japan after graduation in 1915.

There he attended Waseda University for one year, but the ferment in China drew him back home. After advanced military training in the southern province of Kwangtung, another center of liberal and reformist views, Sheng returned to his native province of Liaoning, to serve as company commander under Marshal Chang Tso-lin. His commendable performance won him an assignment to further military study in the Imperial

War College of Japan in 1924. Three years later he completed this course, with a minor interruption in 1925, when he became involved in the complexities of Manchurian military politics.

Upon his return to China in 1927, the rising young officer won the rank of colonel under Ho Ying-ch'in, Chief of Staff to Chiang Kai-shek. It was rumored that, while in Japan, he had gained Chiang's favorable attention and even his financial support. Whatever his political connections, he soon proved his worth on the Northern Expedition, serving in various command staff capacities with recognized ability.

However, the favored clique within the New Nationalist regime was composed almost exclusively of Whampoa Military Academy graduates, widely regarded as intimates of Chiang Kai-shek. Accounts vary as to the sequence of events which catapulted Sheng from the ranks of the Northern Expedition to supreme command of remote Sinkiang. The most reliable version appears to be that of one of Sheng's intimate associates at that time. In 1928 or 1929 Chin Shu-jen sent emissaries to Nanking to receive formal approval of his position as governor of Sinkiang. This associate of Sheng's claims to have recommended Sheng as a reliable and experienced officer, well suited for settling the incessant turmoil and for raising the low morale which plagued the provincial garrison.

Shortly thereafter, Sheng arrived in Urumchi, where he was assigned to Chin's staff and made responsible for officer training. As Chief of the General Staff Office of the Frontier Army, he coped skillfully with Ma Chung-ying's initial offensives in 1931 and 1932. His reputation as a military leader soon rose, as it became increasingly apparent that without Sheng's leadership of the provincial forces, Chin Shu-jen's regime would topple.

Were Sheng merely a military figure, he might have become simply another of the many war lords who wielded local power during the first two decades of the Republic of China. The step from control of provincial troops to political control was easily taken at this time, but few officers who aspired to such positions of power had demonstrated any ability commensurate with the attendant responsibilities. Sheng's interests had long ranged beyond the military training and experiences he had received, however. As he later recalled, "I became a Marxist in 1919. At that time, I read with interest a book published in Shanghai called *The Economic Interpretation of History*. I considered that the economic point of view explained the past, present, and future history of man's society in terms of its origins, development, and changes. Later, I read *The ABC of Communism, The Philosophy of Feuerbach, The Philosophy of Hegel,* and *Dialectical and Historical Materialism*. Although at that time I had no opportunity to enter the Communist Party, my ideas, personal outlook, and world view had already become those of a believer of Marxism. . . . Although I served on the staff of Chiang Kai-shek in 1927-29, I did not join the Kuomintang because of my belief in Marxism."[5]

One perspective on Sheng's attitudes and political beliefs of the time comes from the aforementioned associate who recalls him as a devoted, if not profound, student of radical ideas. He identifies Sheng as one of a group of young officers, increasingly dissatisfied with the political orientation of the Nationalist movement as it moved into the financial strongholds of Shanghai and Nanking. This group felt a betrayal of the initial purpose of the revolution, as landed and vested interest groups appeared to play a more prominent role in determining policy. According to this source, these "progressives" looked to the remote areas of northeast and northwest China as bases for building power which could later be utilized in a "second revolution."

In Sheng's case, the circumstances which opened the door to such power were so circuitous as to cast doubt upon the accuracy of this analysis. Japan's invasion of Manchuria, in 1931, drove from two to three thousand northeastern troops, commanded by General Su Ping-wen, across the Russian borders. There they won refuge, despite Tokyo's protests.[6] While Moscow parried requests for guarantees as to their future disposition, these units moved on Soviet rail lines to Sinkiang, where they re-entered China. Now, however, they came under the command of Sheng Shih-ts'ai, a fellow northeasterner, who quickly employed them in the tumultuous months of 1933.

This proved to be merely the first in a series of Soviet steps taken to support Sheng. Moscow had good reason to strengthen his hand in Urumchi, assuming that peace in the province would be enhanced thereby. Bolstering China's rear served Soviet interests, regardless of Nanking's coolness toward Moscow. As a characteristic *Pravda* analysis pointed out, with some alarm, in May, 1933, "The seizure of Chahar is regarded as the beginning of Japanese aggression to the *north, northwest, and west* [*sic*]. It is more than likely that Japan will not meet the opposition from the United States and Great Britain in this direction which it would encounter and already has encountered in moving to the southwest [from Manchuria]."[7] Although the Russian writer foresaw "preparations for a major war for Asia's markets and for war with the United States," he viewed the immediate portent of Japan's drive into northwest China as ominous. Given the vulnerability of Soviet holdings in the Far East, Siberia, and Central Asia, his concern was well founded.

The juxtaposition of events, including the spreading unrest in Sinkiang, the White Russian coup against Chin, and the arrival of northeastern units predisposed to serve loyally under Sheng, presented the Manchurian officer with propitious circumstances for seizing power. Much more than favorable timing was necessary, however, to maintain that power. Insight into the situation confronting Sheng comes from the observations of Owen Lattimore, who visited the province in 1928. His analysis of anticipated problems proved so prescient, it bears examination in detail as background to the main theme of this study.

Obviously impressed with Yang Tseng-hsin's rule, Lattimore wrote, "Only the death of the old Governor and a scramble for power among his successors, or the invasion of Sinkiang from China proper in civil war, is likely to rend the province. Once the artificial cohesion of the province were destroyed, however, it could hardly be restored again except by Russian occupation of dominant positions along the frontier and an extension of Russian influence almost up to the borders of China proper."[8]

In addition to this forecast of foreign penetration, Lattimore commented pessimistically on internal prospects for the area. "A pointed racial superiority is publicly maintained by the Chinese. At any sort of public reception, the subject races, if they are seated at all, are separately seated. Very often they are not seated at all. . . . On the streets also the Chinese take precedence. Even children may have to look lively. . . . There is . . . hardly a Chinese in Chinese Turkistan who would not say that the only way to rule the Turki and the other 'natives' is high-handedly."[9]

In defense of the cruelty and suspicion evident in Yang's behavior, as well as in explanation of general Chinese attitudes, Lattimore concluded, "Since the Chinese Revolution, the Chinese in Turkistan have had in China only a background and a memory without any general support; with, in fact, an increasing danger of civil war and the breakdown of Chinese rule in the New Dominion [Sinkiang] through an attack, from China, on the ruling faction. Thus, the Chinese in this province have, during recent years, become even more isolated. Nor have they been in a position to emphasize their military control of the subject races. Any attempt at importing arms through China would be futile as they would be confiscated long before their arrival and possibly used in an attempt on the province. As for importing arms from other countries, either the other government would refuse, or would demand privileges of trade and exploitation which the Chinese would not be willing to grant for fear of losing their economic control."[10]

Yang Tseng-hsin's solution to this dilemma foreshadowed in surface respects that later followed by Sheng. As Lattimore described it, "It is true they have played off one group of their subjects against another, in order to frustrate any revolutionary coalition against them and have deliberately retarded economic development in certain directions, lest the pace of development get beyond their control. On the other hand, they have encouraged in many ways the general prosperity of the mass of the people. . . . This policy of fostering general contentment and strictly limiting the control that could be exercised by any one group was consistently developed by the old Governor."[11]

One last line must be drawn to complete this background sketch of Russian, Chinese, and Sinkiang forces operating on the eve of Sheng Shih-ts'ai's assumption of power. It is difficult to depict adequately the degree of savagery and the intensity of fighting which periodically swept over the province. In the twentieth century, as in the nineteenth, revolts and their suppression involved the systematic destruction of entire villages, wholesale massacres, and despoilation of farm lands and irrigation systems. Chin Shu-jen's vengeance against resistance to his customs and tax enforcement in Hami led to the leveling of the town and its near-by fields of world-renowned melons and grapes. In like manner, Ma Chung-ying's forces executed hundreds of fleeing refugees, and fired "infidel" settlements at will.

Neither political assassination nor scorched earth are peculiar to Sinkiang. But their commonplace occurrence there, and the absence of sanctions against such violence, sets the area apart from China proper, where different standards prevailed. It is noteworthy that from 1911 to 1942, no Sinkiang administration completed rule without the death of the governor or of an immediate member of his household. In the field, fame went to the warrior, not on the basis of strategy, but on the basis of cruelty against his foe. It is against this domestic and international background that the rule of Sheng Shih-ts'ai and its relationship with Soviet strategy in Sinkiang must be examined.

Notes

1. Owen Lattimore, *Inner Asian Frontiers of China* (New York: Capital Publishing Co., 1931).
2. According to *Izvestiia,* January 8, 1928, the consul general and the consulate secretary in Semipalatinsk notified a local newspaper on December 28, 1927, ". . . we judge it our duty to explain that the Consulate of Semipalatinsk has nothing in common with Central China and is not able, consequently, to take upon itself the responsibility for events which have occurred recently in Central China. This consulate is dependent upon *Western China* which does not wish, in any case, to sever its friendship with the U.S.S.R. . . . relations with whom are so dear and are so necessary for us, from the point of view not only of commerce but also of politics. . . . These mutual relations and the friendship between *Western China* and the U.S.S.R. should be eternal and immortal"; translated in Martin Norins, *Gateway to Asia: Sinkiang, op. cit.,* pp. 65-66.
3. Lattimore, *Pivot of Asia, op. cit.,* pp. 52-53.
4. This information was provided in an interview with Sheng Shih-ts'ai.
5. In an interview with the author.
6. *Pravda,* December 21, 1932, reported Deputy Foreign Commis-

sar Karakhan as informing Japanese authorities "some days ago" that 2,890 troops and 1,200 civilians had entered the Soviet Union from Manchuria. All allegedly remained interned near Tomsk. *Ibid.*, January 12, 1933, quoted *Rosta* from Khabarovsk to the effect that 3,150 Chinese troops had been interned.

7. *Ibid.*, May 26, 1933. This article, complete with map and lengthy summation of Japanese accomplishments and goals, reviewed eighteen months of events since the Manchurian invasion in 1931. Its theme paralleled statements from prominent Soviet officials, who alternated between expressions of alarm over Japanese aims, and guarantees of Soviet ability to repel all attacks.

8. Owen Lattimore, *High Tartary* (Boston: Little, Brown and Co., 1930), p. 67.

9. *Ibid.*, pp. 300-301.

10. *Ibid.*, pp. 302-303

11. *Ibid.*, p. 304.

2

Sheng Seeks Soviet Aid: 1934–36

RUSSIAN ECONOMIC and military influence, which had sporadically penetrated Sinkiang from the middle of the nineteenth century, had generally affected only the area immediately adjacent to Russia, and was without political influence *per se*. However, between 1934 and 1936 Soviet intervention in the province increased extensively, while Sheng Shih-ts'ai's political orientation introduced an ideological aspect not present during earlier periods of Russian influence.

To be sure, this new penetration came at Sheng's invitation, as part of his effort to restore order and to preserve Chinese rule. His memoirs trace his initial appeal to Moscow, carried by Ch'en Te-li and Yao Hsiung, culminating in Red Army assistance against his Moslem opponent, Ma Chung-ying. Yet the dispatch of Russian troops to Sinkiang, albeit at Chinese request, supported Moscow's own interests, just as had intervention from St. Petersburg in the nineteenth century during Yakub Beg's rebellion. Another precedent had been established by Red Army intervention in 1921 in Outer Mongolia, which had given victory to one faction in the civil war, defeating White Russians hostile to Bolshevism and establishing a new regime immune to either Chinese or Japanese influence. So, too, in 1934, did intervention in Sinkiang counter the specter, conjured up by Soviet writers, of Japanese agents working among discontented White Russian and national minority groups who might spread dissatisfaction among related peoples in Soviet territory.

Sinkiang, however, unlike Outer Mongolia, was not fated to become a full-fledged satellite. Instead, Soviet military, economic, and political controls were gradually extended, and Moscow superseded Nanking's authority, while officially leaving Sinkiang within the Republic of China. Sheng Shih-ts'ai's willing participation in this process transformed his rule from that of a traditional, independent war lord to a voluntary, disguised satellite of the Soviet Union.

Although Chin Shu-jen's ouster in April, 1933, jeopardized Soviet economic influence won in the secret treaty of 1931, *Pravda* offered no comment on the coup. Not until several months later, when Ma Chung-ying's Tungan-Turki coalition threatened the provincial capital of Urumchi, did the Russian press warn of imperialistic infiltration into Sinkiang.[1] *Pravda* charged Britain with supporting pan-Islamic rebels in the southern area, and described Japanese "special schools for studying Sinkiang and for preparation of 'the propagation of Japanese ideals.' "[2] From these schools came "agents working with Ma [Chung-ying]." British as well as Japanese conspiracies allegedly aimed at "Soviet Central Asian republics."

There was cause for Russian concern with these republics. Collectivization in these Soviet areas had left chaos in its wake, as herdsmen slaughtered their livestock rather than submit to collective state ownership. Militant Bolshevik atheism alienated Moslem groups there. Racial animosities pitted Uighur, Kazakh, Tadzhik, and Kirghiz against what appeared to be renewed Russian interference with traditional native societies. In this turbulent context, slogans of pan-Turki or pan-Islamic union sounded from Sinkiang might add still another complicating factor to impede sovietization.

Nor could Moscow remain disinterested in the struggle for

power within Sinkiang. White Russians, quiescent under Yang Tseng-hsin, had staffed Chin Shu-jen's military forces. Their potential as anti-Bolshevik allies of Japan had been proved in Manchuria. Japanese agents, already at work among the Mongols of north China, might arm dissidents in Sinkiang so as to extend a sphere of influence from Mukden to Kashgar, flanking Outer Mongolia and threatening the Soviet Union's vulnerable Central Asian regions.

Always alert to "imperialist plotting," Russian fears received surface reinforcement when Sheng's forces captured a Japanese, Tadashi Onishi, attached to Ma's headquarters. Nanking immediately queried Tokyo for an explanation, but the Japanese Foreign Office denied knowledge of Onishi's activity.[3] Whether a lone adventurer or one of the many agents from Kwantung Army headquarters in Manchuria, Onishi provided *Pravda* with a provocative footnote to its running commentary on Japanese imperialism.[4] The shot was not wide of the mark. At this very time, Sinkiang insurgents appealed to Japanese consular establishments in Turkey and Egypt for "leadership" and assistance.[5]

Russian readers learned of additional Japanese interest in Sinkiang when a trio of noted civilian and military figures from Tokyo attempted to visit the province in late 1933.[6] After getting permission from Nanking, the group ran afoul of conflicting conditions imposed on their itinerary by Sheng and Ma, acting separately.[7] Meanwhile, in Moscow, the Deputy Foreign Commissar, Leo Karakhan, rejected Ambassador Ota's request for travel into the area by the Japanese consul in Novosibirsk, noting, "The Soviet Government does not approve such travel because of the unsettled situation in Sinkiang."[8] This rebuff frustrated Tokyo's efforts to learn more of conditions in the province, efforts already limited by inadequate sources of information in Novosibirsk and Semipalatinsk.[9]

Of lesser magnitude was Soviet concern for British economic

competition spreading northward from India. Exclusion of British interests would facilitate integration of Sinkiang with the burgeoning Central Asian economy following completion of the Turksib railway in 1930. Not to be overlooked, in addition, was the possibility of British political activity in southern Sinkiang, where the apocryphal "Eastern Turkistan Republic" cropped up recurringly in time of trouble, fostered by rebel leaders of great vision but of limited power. Its reappearance in late 1933 was attributed by Sheng, as well as by Soviet analysts, to "British imperialism." Whether assisted by Britain or not, the "Republic" held brighter promise for empire-building than did the volatile Mongol and Kazakh warriors in the north.

Against either British or Japanese penetration, Nanking offered no protection so far as Moscow was concerned. The central government had never controlled its generals for long in Sinkiang; neither Sheng nor Ma proved an exception. Furthermore, it remained divided over the degree of opposition or accommodation with which to meet Japanese advances. Sino-Soviet relations remained at low ebb, despite re-establishment of official contact in 1932. Finally, maneuvering by personal cliques in Nanking impeded development of a consistent, predictable policy.

Nanking's interest, although impotent, manifested itself in the mission of General Huang Mu-sung in June, 1933. The details of this trip are murky, and complicated negotiations among Tungan, Turki, and Sheng factions cloud the picture. Japanese reports identified Huang as an ally of Wang Ching-wei, seeking to overthrow Sheng.[10] Sheng's earlier accounts corroborate this, although his memoirs do not repeat the charge. Certainly his reaction at the time was hostile, placing Huang under house arrest and executing three prominent officials in Sinkiang for allegedly plotting with the Nanking emissary.

While Tokyo's informants saw this as a move by Wang

Ching-wei against Chiang Kai-shek, whose earlier ties with Sheng were known, they also attributed anti-Soviet intent to the plot, which might redound to Japan's benefit. At the same time, *Pravda* reported negotiations between Sheng and Ma for a division of influence in Sinkiang, upset only by a new coalition of General Chang P'ei-yuan in the Ili region with Ma Chung-ying, directed against Sheng's forces in Urumchi.[11]

Given this complex skein of intrigue against the threatening backdrop of growing Japanese influence and interest in north China, it is small wonder Russian strategy designed a cautious but forward policy. This policy was threefold. For Moscow, the most pressing need was military intervention to end the civil war which had opened the door to Japanese infiltration. Next, economic stabilization had to bolster the provincial administration so as to remove the immediate cause of discontent. Finally, political developments would have to cope with racial tensions and the deep-seated hostility to Chinese rule which made Sinkiang's nationality groups responsive to foreign intrigue. Fortunately for Soviet Russia, this policy coincided, almost to the letter, with the thinking of Sheng Shih-ts'ai.

Following the mission to Moscow of Ch'en Te-li and Yao Hsiung, the two emissaries returned to Urumchi in the fall of 1933, accompanied by a new Soviet consul general, Garegin A. Apresoff.[12] Swiftly moving events required an on-the-spot study to fill in the details of Moscow's general strategy. Apresoff's earlier activities as Soviet consul in Meshed and his work there with the Iranian Communist Party stood him in good stead for coping with matters in Sinkiang.

Apresoff approached Sheng clandestinely, discussing conditions for granting military and economic assistance. Perhaps concerned about his reliability or to test the extent of his support, Apresoff then secretly offered similar support to one of Sheng's associates, provided he would overthrow Sheng.[13] Rebuffed, he settled on Sheng for the present, although, as will be seen shortly, not without plans for exploiting other alternatives later should Sheng prove difficult.

In January, 1934, Red troops and planes crossed the Chinese border to smash Ma Chung-ying's siege of Urumchi, and, in conjunction with Sheng's troops, drove Ma's forces southward. Discreetly garbed in uniforms without insignia or identifying markings, the Red forces mixed with White Russian units already in Sinkiang as "the Altai volunteers." A Soviet emigré later recounted Moscow's intervention from his vantage point as director of the department in charge of military deliveries to foreign countries, "The Politburo ordered two brigades of G.P.U. troops with air units of the Red Army to clear the roads and liquidate the rebellion. Meanwhile, on the order of the Politburo, we shipped a number of planes and bombs to the borders of Sinkiang. There they were stuck for some time, as the road to Urumchi . . . was blocked by the rebels. Finally, the command of the Red Army Air Force operating there took charge of this shipment. They 'delivered' our cargoes, consigned to the governor, by dropping the bombs on the rebel forces gathered round the capital, and by landing the planes right on the airfield of the besieged fortress. I was instructed to send the bill for the bombs, as well as the other goods, to the governor."[14]

Although Moscow withdrew its forces after victory was assured, it did not lose interest in the civil war. The Soviet consul in Kashgar quietly granted refuge to the same Ma Chung-ying, who only a short while before had fled under fire from Russian planes. Ma, accompanied by his personal retinue and a sizeable store of weath, crossed the Soviet border to receive political asylum. Sheng Shih-ts'ai immediately demanded

Ma's extradition through Apresoff, but "the Soviet Government, acting in the spirit of the Soviet constitution, did not find it possible to accede to the request of the Sinkiang Provincial Government."[15] Sheng's protest was more than mere formality. Ma's brother-in-law, Ma Hu-shan, took over the rebel forces in southern Sinkiang, where Turki hostility to the provincial government remained strong. By giving asylum to the celebrated Tungan warrior, Moscow held a powerful alternative should circumstances call for another change in regime.

This sequestering of Ma highlighted the uncertainty plaguing relations between Moscow and Urumchi. Foreigners in the Sinkiang capital noted coolness between Apresoff and Sheng, marked in countermanding of provincial orders on the part of the Soviet consul general.[16] Later, the retiring Red troops exchanged their old cannon for new ones scheduled for Sheng. His prompt accusations of bad faith by the Russians were assuaged by Moscow's discounting the price of the equipment.[17]

On Stalin's part, there was reason to placate feelings in Sinkiang. The only alternative to Sheng Shih-ts'ai was Ma, yet the latter's suspected relations with Japanese agents made him a less certain ally. As further evidence of Soviet support, Moscow equipped "10,000 Sinkiang troops completely, from boots to Kuomintang insignia . . . A commission headed by Stalin's brother-in-law, Svanidze, was sent to Sinkiang to draw up a plan of reconstruction for the province."[18] The aforementioned Soviet emigré noted that such largesse was not available to all Chinese: "At this same time, 1935, Chiang Kai-shek addressed a request to us through his air ministry for a delivery of airplanes. I was instructed to refuse. Stalin did not want to strengthen Chiang Kai-shek's government."[19]

Sheng had good cause for ambivalence about Soviet support, in view of the precarious nature of his rule. The same military intervention which had awarded him victory might turn against

him should he prove hostile to Soviet interests. Nor could Nanking be relied upon for help, distant and divided as was the
central government. To be sure, relations with the capital had
improved somewhat when Huang Mu-sung finally recommended
acceptance of Sheng despite, or perhaps because of, Huang's
witnessing the triple execution of his alleged "co-plotters."
Formal installation of both Acting Chairman Liu Wen-lung
as governor and Sheng as commander of the provincial armed
forces, or *Tupan,* came in September, 1933. Almost immediately, however, Sheng charged Liu with "plotting" and
replaced him with Li Yung, senile but compliant. This move
won him no friends in Nanking, and symbolized the insecurity
which was to impel Sheng to repeated purges of the provincial
government in later years.

Within this framework, Moscow, Urumchi, and Nanking
played a circumspect, and at times confusing, game with
respect to the second aspect of Soviet penetration, economic
assistance. Rumors of an impending Russian loan to Sinkiang
prompted the Chinese Ambassador in Moscow, W. W. Yen,
to protest to the Narkomindel in October, 1933, asserting
Sheng's lack of competence to conclude foreign agreements.[20]
It had been precisely such negotiations for which Sheng's
predecessor, Chin Shu-jen, had been tried and sentenced by
Nanking only four months earlier. The following June, the
Wai-chiao Pu filed a similar protest with Ambassador D. V.
Bogomoloff, warning that any loan contracted by another
agency would be "invalid unless previously authorized by the
Central Government."[21]

Sheng observed the fiction of Nanking's authority by cabling,
in concert with Li Yung, to the Executive Yuan in July, 1934,
reporting negotiations with Soviet officials over the exchange
of Sinkiang produce for a five-year loan. He denied any political

implications attended this move, and requested prompt approval for the projected agreement, although no text accompanied his report.[22] The amount of the loan was stated as four million gold rubles; negotiations the previous winter had mentioned three million. This increase, boosted in the end to five million rubles, suggests that Sheng may have used his communications to Nanking as a stall, bargaining with the Russians for the highest amount possible despite his limited leverage. Whatever his motivations, the fact remains that although he exchanged cables with the central authorities for more than eight months, at no time did he accede to their requests for a copy of the loan agreement. On May 16, 1935, he signed the Soviet draft without authorization from Nanking.

Soviet representatives maintained a firm position throughout, dodging or delaying discussion in Moscow and Nanking. The dispersal of political power in China had long afforded opportunity for dealing directly with local military leaders in violation of central authority. Thus, in 1923, Moscow had negotiated with Sun Yat-sen's regime in Canton, while offering recognition to the government of Peking. In 1924 Soviet negotiators had signed an agreement with Marshal Chang Tso-lin in Manchuria concerning the Chinese Eastern Railway, in direct violation of a treaty concluded in Peking four months before.

Similarly, in Sinkiang, ample precedent existed in the negotiations with both Yang Tseng-hsin and Chin Shu-jen to suggest the course of events. Initially, the Narkomindel fell back on an excuse employed in these earlier cases, dismissing Chinese protests on the pretext that only local trade matters were involved.[23] Hoping to exploit differences within the Nanking regime, Ambassador Bogomoloff visited Chiang Kai-shek in search of "understanding" among pro-Sheng circles.[24] While this bypassing of the Wai-chiao Pu initially weakened its position, it did not have favorable results for the Russians. In heated discussions between the Russian ambassador and Chinese officials, conflicting versions of Chiang's views were exchanged. Bogomoloff finally offered a threefold refusal of Wai-chiao Pu demands for negotiation, insisting (1) no text had as yet been agreed upon and therefore none could be forwarded to Nanking, (2) negotiations had been initiated by the Sinkiang authorities and not by Moscow, and (3) it was purely a local affair concerning commercial problems.[25]

Despite these subsurface tensions, appearances were preserved on all sides. When Sheng informed the central authorities of his final signature of the pact, he added a lengthy defense in terms of Sinkiang's economic plight. He praised the nominal interest rates, the ease of payment, and the absence of any political conditions.[26] At least this was more co-operation than Chin Shu-jen had shown Nanking in 1931. Chinese officials, such as Ambassador Yen, for their part, consistently denied all Japanese assertions of growing Soviet influence in Sinkiang, claiming the province remained loyal and subservient to the central government.[27] Although Ambassador Yen may have been discouraged by Moscow authorities from visiting the area, as instructed by the Wai-chiao Pu in July, 1935, his military attaché won Russian co-operation for the trip. Yen informed a Japanese diplomat that this trip and the information gained therein proved the absence of Soviet bad faith.[28]

Yet, these formal appearances did not conform with reality. The entry of Russian troops and aircraft into Chinese territory without authorization from Nanking, as in Outer Mongolia in 1921, set a dangerous precedent in Sinkiang. Furthermore, the provincial economy remained tied to a Soviet loan for five years. Only the third form of Soviet penetration, political influence, received little implementation at this time. Caution in this area was dictated by the danger of offering Japan any pretext for further advances into Central Asia, as well as by the risk of arousing nationalities that were suspicious of Russian as well as of Chinese rule. Religious sensitivities in particular demanded delicate handling of any pro-Soviet orientation. As a final brake, Sheng himself may have been reluctant to destroy all lines to Nanking, so long as his archrival, Ma Chung-ying, remained alive by Soviet sanction.

Thus, while Red military and financial experts examined Sinkiang's needs during the summer of 1934, Sheng prominently displayed Nationalist flags at victory celebrations in Urumchi.[29] To be sure, more than a thousand troops marched down the streets in new uniforms with Soviet rifles, under banners in Russian as well as in Chinese and Turki. Yet nowhere in Sheng's speeches did he praise Soviet assistance. On the surface, at least, Sinkiang remained a loyal province of the Republic of China.

Sheng's propaganda did not coincide with that of the central government, however. In part, his greater emphasis upon Japanese imperialism stemmed naturally from the intense regional loyalty expressed by all "Tungpei" or "Northeast" natives, hailing from Manchuria. While the August 1, 1934, celebration ostensibly focused on the defeat of Ma, slogans called for "Down with Imperialism! Down with Japan!" This cry echoed that of a more renowned Northeasterner, the famous "Young Marshal" Chang Hsueh-liang, of Manchuria, who rankled under Nanking's failure to fight for his home province.

More significant were the hundreds of pamphlets which rained upon Urumchi from newly acquired Soviet aircraft. Their content differed sharply from Nanking policy in three main themes, maximizing the Japanese threat, minimizing central government strength, and interpreting world events in terms of a crude Marxist analysis. As one pamphlet proclaimed:

> The advance guard of imperialism has been defeated, but imperialism itself still lives and is trying to overrun our

Sinkiang in order to conquer the province and the whole of China. In such circumstances the standard-bearers of imperialism will fight against one another and then the new world war will be in full swing. . . . Ma Chung-ying is our executioner, but our real enemy is imperialism, especially the Japanese . . .

We must understand why imperialism attacks us. It is because capitalism has turned into imperialism. To solve the insoluble [*sic*] problem, the imperialists will fight among themselves and the new world war will begin. . . . To make a new world war impossible, and to exterminate all imperialists, we must fight against them. When we have crushed them we shall have a peaceful existence in our country, as in all the world.[30]

It is doubtful that the various nationalities in Sinkiang felt concern about a "new world war," as these words implied. Nevertheless, the Marxist approach to international events continued to dominate speeches and writings commemorating the third anniversary of the fall of Mukden, September 18, 1934. Here criticism of Nanking neared the surface:

> The Government abandoned Manchuria without resistance and allowed thirty millions of our countrymen to be crushed by the imperialists. . . . But a war will break out between the imperialists one fine day as a result of the unequal distribution of colonies. . . . When all the different races of Sinkiang are welded together into a firm whole, placed on the same level and treated in the same way, it does not matter what secret conspiracies imperialism directs against Sinkiang. We shall be able to crush them. We must be resolutely on our guard every moment against the imperialists and give them *one* answer only: that is, *blood*. Down with imperialism![31]

Sheng gradually shifted to the left in his political propaganda. By 1935 his "Six Great Policies" had supplemented his earlier "Eight Points," marking increased parallelism with Moscow. Adopting a symbolic red six-pointed star, of obvious inspiration,

Sheng proclaimed a foreign policy based on "pro-Sovietism" and "anti-imperialism." While his autobiography offers his present defense of this policy, contemporary Sinkiang publications indicated more fully the degree to which he leaned toward Moscow and away from Nanking.

A major statement of Sheng's program appeared in May, 1935, printed in Alma-Ata under Soviet auspices.[32] Entitled "Major Duties of the Sinkiang Provincial Government," it outlined domestic and foreign policy. Declaring the world to be divided between roughly one and a quarter billion "oppressed peoples" and two hundred and fifty million "oppressors," Sheng concluded that, "No single race can overthrow its oppressor without support from the other oppressed races." Sinkiang fortunately enjoyed such support from the Soviet Union, as evidenced by its agricultural assistance program, its gradual financial stabilization, and its improvement of living standards. Among the consequences of Soviet aid cited by Sheng was "protection of religion."

After a detailed blueprint for developing industry and agriculture, Sheng emphasized Sinkiang's isolation in the face of Japanese aggression. His remedy was clear: "The Government of the U.S.S.R. intends to check the aggressive ambitions of the oppressors by supporting and protecting weak minority races and thereby maintaining world peace. We desire to protect the safety of the people and therefore request the Central Government to have closer relations with the Soviet Union." While his program remained fixed within the larger context of loyalty to Nanking, his loyalty appeared diluted by repeated protestations of Soviet innocence abroad.

This theme continued in his warning against the "conspiracy to separate Sinkiang in its relations from Soviet Russia." Explaining Russian interest in Sinkiang as motivated solely by fear of Japanese aggression, Sheng concluded, "The fact that the Soviet Union has no political ambition can be clearly seen in her relations with Iran, Afghanistan, and Turkey." His careful choice of Moslem countries aimed at stilling fears of antireligious consequences stemming from a pro-Soviet orientation.

One point should be noted, however. Neither in this nor in any other publications of the time did Sheng call for communism in Sinkiang. As he explains in his memoirs, whatever discussions may have taken place with Russian advisers about the ultimate desirability of making Sinkiang into a model Soviet republic, too radical policies in those years could only have led to renewed civil war and chaos. This prudence was to stand Sheng in good stead later, for it kept open the way to reconciliation with the central government, a way Sheng eventually chose.

In view of the evidence, it may be wondered whether Ambassador Yen's reassuring statements concerning Sinkiang's loyalty were given in good faith. An informed observer has claimed that the visit by Yen's military attaché to the province in 1935 was so severely restricted by Sheng as to preclude any valid estimate of the situation.[33] Even if the ambassador knew the full extent of Soviet penetration, he had good reason to withhold this information. As he obliquely remarked in his conversations with the Japanese chargé d'affaires, Sakawa, "I know that Japan would not feel pleased to see Sino-Soviet friendship develop."[34] By implication, Yen recognized Japan's vested interest in furthering rumors of Soviet influence in Urumchi.

Tokyo's efforts to keep Moscow and Nanking divided, documented in well-informed dispatches from Nanking, made little concrete progress. All that could be hoped for was playing upon divisions within the central government so as to strengthen anti-Soviet forces. Encouragement for this may have followed from an interview in November, 1934, wherein Councilor Wakasugi pressed Chiang Kai-shek for an explanation of Russian influence in Sinkiang.[35] Chiang conceded that, "The situation in Sinkiang is an international problem in which communization will cause serious effects on other nations. I am trying to separate this district from Soviet influence, but unfortunately my country is too occupied with Japanese relations." With this thrust, Chiang reminded Wakasugi of how "a Japanese army officer pressured the Chinese Government to issue a visa for Sinkiang, only to be prevented from entering by the Soviet Government, much to the embarrassment of our Sinkiang policy." He apparently was referring to the mission blocked by both Sheng and Ma in 1933.

The only alternative for Japan lay with potential anti-Soviet forces in Sinkiang itself. Tokyo increased its attention in this direction as accurate reports on the progress of the Soviet loan negotiations came into the Foreign Office in 1935.[36] One avenue of approach lay through Kabul. There Minister Masamoto Kitada, previously in Cairo, and deeply interested in all aspects of Islamic culture as well as of Central Asian politics, tapped sources of information funneling into Afghanistan. In January the Afghan foreign minister informed him that Soviet moves in Sinkiang stemmed from spreading Moslem unrest in Russia, proved by a flood of 600,000 refugees crossing into Afghanistan during the previous five years.[37] Although he felt Britain reluctant to support "an independent government of Moslems in Sinkiang because it might instigate Moslems in India," Kitada noted the hopes of Afghan leaders that such a government could be formed.

In May, Kitada forwarded an appeal from "a leader of a Sinkiang nationalist movement and former head of the Kashgar government," which claimed that, "Moslems in the vast area east of Kashgar to Hami have anti-Soviet, pro-Japanese senti-

ment which may enable Japan to make an ideological drive
into Sinkiang. For this armed invasion is unnecessary. Such
an ideological drive might disturb the situation in Soviet
Turkistan, the weak point of Soviet Russia."[38] Almost simultaneously with this dispatch came approval from the Japanese
Foreign Office in support of an army-sponsored agent to attempt
entry into Sinkiang, via Tibet, through co-operation from the
Dalai Lama.[39] As with other similar efforts, the agent was
apprehended soon after entering Chinghai province, and the
Foreign Office subsequently negotiated his release.[40]

Kitada's informant, one Ahmed Tewfik Sherif Pasha, so
interested him that in June, 1935, the minister issued a certificate for Pasha to visit Japan "to study culture and religion."[41]
That more significant results might follow was suggested by
Kitada's accompanying dispatch, which claimed that Pasha
was "widely known in Turkey, Egypt, and India; went into
Sinkiang twice for the Moslem movement . . . and still has a
large influence in Sinkiang. Is highly respected by the Uighurs."

A second Moslem leader visited Kitada's office at this time,
identified as the Emir of Khotan.[42] Paralleling the proposal by
Pasha, the Emir submitted a detailed plan for establishing
an "Eastern Turkistan Republic" under Japanese sponsorship,
with arms and money to come from Tokyo. Preparation for this
called for "(1) anti-communist propaganda, (2) unifying the
Moslems, (3) enlightenment of the people, (4) working jointly
with other races, and (5) establishing Mahmud Sidjan as our
leader." Following Japanese penetration, armed revolt would
"disturb the rear, assisting the advance of Japanese troops."
The Emir's ultimate goal was an "independent" Sinkiang, with
special economic and political privileges for Japan.

It is quite possible that Soviet authorities learned of these
clandestine contacts through their extensive intelligence net in
Asia. Double agents dotted the espionage systems of the Soviet

Union, China, and Japan, affording likely access to such information. At the very least, the known record of Japanese efforts to reach Sinkiang and the shadowy contacts between Moslems and Tokyo's representatives warranted intensified Soviet attention to Sinkiang. At the most, this may have played a role in the purges of the midthirties against Moslem groups in the Soviet Union, designed as a safeguard, if not as deserved punishment, against conspiracy with Japan.

Further study of the Foreign Office archives as well as of army documents, particularly those of the chief of staff in Tokyo, is necessary to trace the implementation of such proposals as Kitada forwarded. It is unlikely that his dispatches went unnoticed, especially one optimistic prognosis sent in mid-1935, entitled "Japan's Spiritual Advance Into Sinkiang."[43] Its compatibility with the enthusiasm current in certain Japanese circles for a "positive policy" on the mainland warrants study of this document.

Kitada began by noting the prevalence of Moslem faith in parts of "the Soviet Union, India, China, the Near East, and the Dutch East Indies. Therefore Sinkiang will furnish a point of advantage to Japan against Britain and the Soviet Union if coalition with the Moslems is secured." The most favorable area for Japanese penetration was northeastern Sinkiang where, according to Kitada, "the majority of the inhabitants are . . . stubbornly anti-Soviet and anti-communist (Hami, Turfan, and Kuchengtze districts). . . . Closer to Manchukuo, from these districts we can have spiritual advancement and predominate over all Sinkiang." The report saw no need to challenge British influence in the southern sector for the time being, or to "touch on the problem of China's sovereign rights." Instead of overt military action, Kitada advised construction of a motor road from Manchuria to northern Sinkiang, facilitating contact with local groups.

The Japanese diplomat was not blind to the strategic implications of his advice, despite his emphasis on "spiritual" and "ideological" tactics. In another note, he declared, "In time of war, the Sinkiang situation might permit Japan to disrupt the Turksib railway and might permit linking with military preparation now under way in Singapore [*sic*] to the disadvantage of either Russia or Britain. Examination of the Sinkiang problem is believed necessary in considering matters such as conclusion of a nonaggression pact with the Soviet Union."[44]

Many obstacles lay in the path of Kitada's proposal. The Japanese government was by no means of one mind on foreign policy at this time. Few military or civilian figures could be found in Tokyo with Kitada's depth of understanding and access to information on Inner Asia. The gap between plan and accomplishment is evident in the repeated frustrations of Moslem leaders, on the one hand, pleading for assistance from Japan. Such help was slim, when it was forthcoming at all. On the other hand, Japanese efforts to break through the barriers imposed by Moscow, Urumchi, and Nanking seldom won success, as attested by dispatches from the field to Tokyo.

Thus, Tewfik Sherif Pasha's trip "to study culture and religion" proved a failure. According to his final interview at the Foreign Office, "My spending three months in Japan did not bring any desired results, contrary to my expectations. I understand that at present Japan is unable to do anything in Central Asia, but Sinkiang remains the key to this area and I still hope that Japan will be with us to solve the problem of Moslem independence. Japan lacks two points in its continental policy: (1) scientific research on Asia, and (2) private diplomacy through merchants."[45] The Japanese spokesman merely replied that his government had "no practical program at present, although it has some interest in Sinkiang."

Meanwhile, in Moscow, General Ma Shao-wu, from Kashgar, excited Japanese journalists by publicly extending an invitation to visit Sinkiang.[46] Ambassador Yen promised to recommend entry to the Urumchi authorities, and Soviet officials disclaimed any objections. However, Sheng Shih-ts'ai's refusal to grant visas "because political unrest still exists" blocked still another effort by Tokyo to acquire firsthand information. This was interpreted by Japanese officials as the result of Russian pressure. Similarly, in Nanking, talks between Bogomoloff and Suma found the Soviet ambassador adamant in denying cause for Japanese concern about Sinkiang, insisting the only Soviet interest there to be "normal trade relations."[47]

Nor did Japanese efforts to smoke out Russian intentions fare any better at the open level of official exchanges. Thus, in January, 1935, Foreign Minister Hirota expressed anxiety over "reports of the Sovietisation of Sinkiang."[48] Within a week Molotov took up the challenge, speaking to the Seventh All-Union Congress of Soviets:

> It remains for me to say a couple of words on the slanderous rumours about the Sovietisation of Sinkiang. One is struck by by the fact that special efforts to spread this slander against the U.S.S.R. are being made in Japan, whose policy in relation to China is known to everybody and cannot possibly be covered up by the spreading of inventions. I consider it necessary to emphasize the real Soviet policy towards China: the Soviet Union considers as incompatible with its policy the seizure of foreign territories, and is an absolute adherent of the independence, integrity, and sovereignty of China over all her parts, including Sinkiang.

Molotov's words to the contrary notwithstanding, by the end of 1936 local initiative from Sheng Shih-ts'ai and external pressure coming largely from Japan had combined with Soviet strategy to advance Russian influence in Sinkiang well along its triple path of military, economic, and political penetration. That penetration fell far short of complete control. Nevertheless, it afforded Moscow unprecedented leverage over Sinkiang affairs at relatively little cost, simultaneously excluding rival influence from both Nanking and Tokyo. The chain of external events, plus the added means of ideological penetration, found the Soviet leaders extending their sphere of influence further into inner China than had ever been achieved by their czarist predecessors.

Notes

1. *Pravda,* August, 1, 1933, #210(5736); August 15, 1933, #224 (5750).
2. *Ibid.,* August 15, 1933.
3. *Miscellaneous Documents Relating to the Political and General Situation in Sinkiang* (in Japanese), A.6.1.3:4, Vol. II, June, 1930-December, 1933, Japanese Foreign Office archives; hereafter referred to as *Documents*. Minister Ariyoshi in Shanghai to Hirota, November 20, 1933. Ariyoshi requested "information as to whether he has connection with the Japanese Tientsin Army."
4. *Pravda,* December 8, 1933, #337(5863).
5. *Documents, op. cit.* See dispatches of September 13, 1933, from the military attaché at the embassy in Ankara to Headquarters, Chief of Staff, Tokyo; also from Consul General Kitada in Alexandria to Foreign Minister Hirota, October 3, 1933. Kitada was visited by "Prince Mahmoud Chevket, accompanied by General Wahb [?] Pasha, formerly of the Turkish Army . . . The Prince entrusted a letter to be forwarded to the Japanese military attaché in Berlin."
6. *Ibid.* Minister Ariyoshi to Hirota, October 21, 1933. Ariyoshi was to have been accompanied on this trip by "Major Imada of the Japanese Chief of Staff." *Prava* referred to the mission on October 18, 1933, #280(5806) and November 5, 1933, #306(5832).

7. *Ibid.* Sheng insisted the Eurasian plane bearing the mission could not stop in Ma's territory; Ma refused to "guarantee its safety" if the plane did not land at his headquarters.

8. *Ibid.*, Ota to Hirota, November 16, 1933.

9. *Ibid.*, Ota to Hirota, November 29, 1933.

10. *Ibid.*, consul general in Nanking to Uchida, September 12, 1933; minister in Shanghai to Uchida, November 3, 1933.

This plot is referred to in Sheng's memoirs but is not attributed to Nanking; instead Sheng claims it was a Russian plot. Highly illogical, his explanation may have been prompted by deference to his compatriots on Taiwan.

For an authoritative and suggestive account of this period see Aitchen K. Wu, *Turkestan Tumult* (London: Methuen, 1939). Wu quotes a telegram from Liu Wen-lung and Sheng to Nanking of July 20, 1933, which illustrates Sheng's circumspect observance of protocol, despite his ruthless handling of Nanking's subordinates. As the wire put it, ". . . News of our humble intentions has doubtless reached you from our representative at Nanking and his Excellency the Envoy Huang Mu-sung has sent you news of the happenings in Sinkiang and has expressed his relief that the mission on which he departed by your esteemed commands is successfully terminated. His good work has contributed greatly to the calming of the province and a difficult situation has been dealt with through his good work among us which has won for him universal esteem. We, Liu Wen-lung and Sheng Shih-ts'ai, now acknowledge our debt to your wise advice which we have done all in our power to follow . . . Great as is doubtless our ignorance we have wisdom enough to know that only by obedience to our National Government can we be saved. This obedience we hereby promise and have sworn in the presence of the Omnipotent God. We will do as you ask us and dare not in any matter run counter to your will. Accept in these matters our whole-hearted pledge of loyalty, of which this message is a humble token." Sheng notes in his memoirs having executed T'ao Ming-yüeh, Li Hsiao-t'ien, and Ch'en Chung in what he calls the "Ch'en-T'ao-Li plot."

Wang Ching-wei was one of the few political figures whose reputation rivaled that of Chiang Kai-shek. Prominent in the United Front between the Kuomintang and the Chinese Communists in the twenties, he tended to side with radical and liberal elements against the conservative forces grouped around Chiang. In 1940 he headed a puppet government under the Japanese aegis. Although his political choices suggested inconsistency of principle, his changeability and aspirations for power seemed constant.

11. *Pravda*, August 24, 1933, #233(5759); December 10, 1933, #339(5865). Russian press comment appears to have avoided detailed reference to Sheng, the only description of his rule at this time being anonymous reference to "a new Chinese provincial government . . . declaring a whole series of administrative reforms and satisfying certain demands of nationalities which enables this government to win agreement with various leaders of the insurgent movement in Dzungaria," *ibid.*, August 15, 1933, #224(5750).

12. Apresoff was a Soviet specialist on Central Asia and was acquainted personally with the important Chinese in these negotiations.

13. Interview with participants in Taiwan and Japan, 1954-55.

14. Alexandre Barmine, *One Who Survived* (New York: G. P. Putnam's Sons, 1945), p. 231. Barmine headed the "Auto-Motor-Export," a camouflaged organization which supervised secret deliveries to foreign nations.

15. *Izvestiia*, July 14, 1934, in Jane Degras, ed., *Soviet Documents on Foreign Policy, 1917-1941* (London: Oxford University Press, 1953), Vol. III, p. 85.

16. Sven A. Hedin, *The Silk Road* (New York: E. P. Dutton and Co., Inc., 1936), pp. 145 ff. Hedin's departure from Urumchi had been forbidden by the provincial government, but Apresoff telephoned Ch'en Te-li and personally ordered reversal of the decision.

17. Barmine, *op. cit.*, p. 232. Barmine's immediate superior, Rosen-

golz, Commissar of Foreign Trade, authorized the discount to avoid difficulty with the G.P.U.

18. *Ibid.*, p. 231-32. Barmine's assertion of Svanidze's role may be correct, but his nephew makes no reference to this in his memoirs, *My Uncle, Joseph Stalin* (New York: G. P. Putnam's Sons, 1952).

19. *Ibid.*, p. 232. No record of this request has been found in Chinese sources. Soviet rejection would have been likely, given the lack of agreement over the proposed nonaggression pact and Soviet uncertainty of Chiang Kai-shek's determination to resist Japanese advances.

20. *Soviet Economic Aggression, op. cit.*, pp. 32-36.

21. *Ibid.*, Wai-chiao Pu to Bogomoloff, June 12, 1934.

22. *Ibid.*, Li Yung and Sheng Shih-ts'ai to Executive Yuan and Military Affairs Commission, July 16, 1934.

23. *Ibid.*, Narkomindel to Yen, August 2, 1934.

24. *Ibid.*, Narkomindel to Yen, August 2 and August 20, 1934.

25. *Ibid.* Although the Chiang-Bogomoloff conference took place in July, the Wai-chiao Pu disclaimed any knowledge of it before being informed by the Narkomindel on August 20, at which time the Russians claimed that Chiang had already approved the agreement. In response to an inquiry from the Wai-chiao Pu, however, Chiang denied this, stating he had made clear to Bogomoloff the necessity for examination of the text. Bogomoloff, in a lengthy discussion with the Vice-Minister of Foreign Affairs, Hsü Mo, on August 29, modified the Narkomindel version somewhat, but insisted that Chiang had implied approval was forthcoming.

26. *Ibid.*, Li Yung and Sheng Shih-ts'ai, to the Executive Yuan, Ministry for Foreign Affairs, and Ministry for Industry, May 25, 1934. Despite the statement in this message that a full text of the agreement would follow, no copy was received by the Wai-chiao Pu. So far as the author could determine, the full contents of the loan agreement have never been ascertained conclusively.

27. Typical was Ambassador Yen's statement to the Chargé d'Affaires, Sakawa, "It is impossible to believe that the Soviet Union

intends sovietization of Sinkiang or support of the Chinese Communist Party . . . Most of the people there are Moslems who hate the Soviet regime." Ota to Hirota, November 3, 1935; see *Documents, op. cit.,* Vol. V.

28. Yen's trip was reported in a dispatch from Ota, referring to the "Wai-chiao Pu monthly bulletin at the Chinese Embassy," Ota to Hirota, August 23, 1935, *Documents, op. cit.,* Vol. V. Yen later told Sakawa he had decided against the trip because of his age and health, *ibid.,* August 26, 1935. Yen's summary of the military attaché's report was made to Sakawa on November 3, 1935.

29. Hedin, *op. cit.,* pp. 182 ff.

30. *Ibid.,* pp. 183-84.

31. *Ibid.,* pp. 197-98.

32. *Documents, op. cit.,* Vol. IX; this pamphlet, although printed in May, 1935, was not translated into Japanese from Arabic until 1939, at which time it reached the Foreign Office archives.

33. Interview given the author by a reliable source in 1955.

34. *Documents, op. cit.,* Vol. V; Ota to Hirota, November 3, 1935.

35. *Ibid.,* Vol. III, Councilor Wakasugi in Peking to Hirota, November 2, 1934.

36. For instance, a report of October 8, 1934, from the Japanese minister to China summarized negotiations, noting, "Contract of this loan will be made anyway, no matter whether the Nanking Government approves it or not," *ibid.,* Vol. III; a month later the military attaché in Shanghai cabled to Headquarters, Japanese Chief of Staff, "Sinkiang is not replying to the request from the Central Government," *ibid.,* dispatch of November 15, 1934.

37. *Ibid.,* Vol. IV, Kitada to Hirota, January 19, 1935; Kitada's grasp of the complex political picture in Sinkiang was unrivaled in Japanese military and diplomatic circles, as evidenced in the volumes of reports on file in the Foreign Office archives.

38. *Ibid.,* Vol. IV, interview with Tewfik Sherif Pasha reported by Kitada to Hirota, May 7, 1935.

39. *Ibid.,* Vol. IV, memorandum of the First Section, East Asia Bureau to Hirota, approved by Hirota, May 17, 1935.

40. *Ibid.*, Vol. III, Ambassador Kawagoe in Shanghai to consul general in Nanking, September 10, 1936, requesting assistance on behalf of Japanese Military Intelligence Service; Consul General Suma in Nanking reply of September 19, 1936.

41. *Ibid.*, Vol. V, Kitada to Hirota, June 12 and August 1, 1935.

42. *Ibid.*, Vol. IV, Kitada to Hirota, undated but among reports of June, 1935. Although no further identification is given in this dispatch, and titles were used loosely by claimants for prestige, it is likely that this person was Sabit Mullah, religious leader at Khotan in Sinkiang. In 1933 he was named "Emir" or prince. In the "Eastern Turkistan Republic" proclaimed later that year, he was appointed Prime Minister, with Khodja Niaz as President. The movement collapsed several months later. Although identified by Sheng as under British inspiration at the time, it would have been logical for its followers to cast in all directions for help, including Tokyo.

43. *Ibid.*, Vol. V. Kitada to Hirota, June 10, 1935.

44. *Ibid.*, Vol. V, Kitada to Hirota, June 1, 1935.

45. *Ibid.*, Vol. VI, interview of Arita and Tewfik Sherif Pasha, Foreign Office record, July 3, 1936.

46. *Ibid.*, Vol. V, Ota to Hirota, November 11 and November 17, 1935.

47. *Ibid.*, Vol. V, Consul General Suma in Nanking to Hirota, November 19, 1935.

48. Max Beloff, *The Foreign Policy of Soviet Russia, 1929-1941* (London: Oxford University Press, 1947), Vol. 1, pp. 237-38 quotes Hirota's remarks and Molotov's rejoinder from *Documents on International Affairs, 1934,* Royal Institute of International Affairs.

3

The United Front Begins: 1937

A NEW ERA in Sino-Soviet relations began in 1937, when Japanese troops, on July 7, attacked at Marco Polo bridge in an "incident" which was to last more than eight years. In casting the die for war, Tokyo triggered a chain of events which was to throw Russia and China into a quasi-alliance of mutual benefit, with the Soviet Union providing material aid for China to use against Japan. On August 21 Chinese and Russian representatives signed a nonaggression pact, which had far-reaching military and economic consequences for beleaguered China. And the Chinese Communist Party (CCP), in a declaration of September 22, signaled acceptance of Chiang Kai-shek's terms for ending the civil war and for inauguration of a "united front" against Japan.

Consistent with Soviet support for China, the suspension of hostilities between Communist and Nationalist forces sought to ensure unity in defense. Comparison of the external situation as it affected Sinkiang before 1937 makes clear the importance of these developments for both Sheng and the province.

On the diplomatic front, China had proposed a nonaggression pact to the Soviet Union as early as May 10, 1933.[1] Hoping to block Soviet recognition of Manchukuo and to settle the question of Moscow's relations with the CCP, Nanking drafted nine guarantees: (1) mutual respect of territorial sovereignty, (2) renunciation of war and aggression as instruments of policy, (3) a detailed definition of aggression, (4) no assistance to a third party attacking either of the signatories, (5) non-recognition of the results of aggression, (6) nonintervention in domestic affairs, (7) no hostile propaganda or agitation, and (8) no support of organizations hostile to either side. As a ninth and final proviso, the proposed treaty was to have no effect on other agreements signed by both sides, referring to the 1924 pact of recognition signed by Russia with the Peking government.

Five months later a Soviet counterproposal sidestepped most of these pledges, offering: (1) neutrality in case of third-party aggression, (2) renunciation of aggression as an instrument of policy, (3) nonparticipation in hostile alliances, whether political, military, or economic, (4) no support for organizations seeking overthrow of the signatories, and (5) settlement of all conflicts by peaceful means. No further exchange followed, Chinese negotiators being dissatisfied with Soviet refusal to define aggression more fully and to pledge nonintervention in China's domestic affairs. In addition, they feared ambiguity in the reworded pledge concerning aggressive third parties and saw "nonparticipation in hostile alliances" as a veiled effort to tie China unconditionally and exclusively to the Soviet Union.[2]

In subsequent years, Moscow avoided a clash with Tokyo, while maintaining correct but distant relations with Nanking by mutual consent. In 1935, in their sale of the Chinese Eastern Railway, the Russians beat a careful retreat in the face of Japan's *fait accompli* in Manchuria. Chinese protests of the illegality of the sale were of no avail. Similarly, in 1936 Chinese criticism proved futile when Russia made known, by a formal treaty, its guarantees to protect Outer Mongolia. Both actions violated the Sino-Soviet pact of May, 1924, and both actions frankly recognized Nanking's lack of power to enforce authority within its claimed limits of territorial sovereignty.

Sinkiang, together with Outer Mongolia and Manchuria, played a small but perceptible part in preventing a *détente* between Russia and China. Considerable friction attended Soviet extension of economic aid to Sheng Shih-ts'ai in open flouting of Wai-chiao Pu protests. In November, 1935, Ambassador Bogomoloff complained to a Japanese official that negotiations for a trade pact with China had dragged on for six months, impeded in part by repeated Chinese demands for cessation of Soviet activity in Sinkiang.[3] Meanwhile, in Moscow, Ambassador Yen won no favorable response from the Soviet foreign minister, Litvinoff, to Yen's request for a review of all outstanding issues, including "discussion of spheres of influence in Sinkiang and Mongolia . . . and readjustment of the Sinkiang boundary."[4]

Although effectively excluded from exercising its jurisdiction in Sinkiang, Nanking kept a watchful eye on developments there. Reports from the Chinese consul general in Novosibirsk, for instance, provided a fairly accurate picture of increasing Soviet influence during 1935-36. These reports also found their way into the files of the Japanese Foreign Office, apparently with the connivance of the Chinese consul.[5]

The Japanese attack at Marco Polo bridge in July, 1937, brought fresh pressure on both parties to repair past relations. The desperate bargaining power of the two sides, however, is evident in comparing the new exchange of drafts with that of 1933, and, in turn, with the final agreement.[6] While the initiative now seems to have come from the Soviet Union, the Russian text differed only in part from that offered in 1933. It conceded Chinese wording with respect to nonassistance to third-party aggressors, and deleted the pledge forbidding participation in pacts "hostile" to the signatories. These concessions came easily, in view of the changed circumstances. There was now far less likelihood of Russia wishing to assist Japan against

China, while China would now be bound not to seek an end to hostilities by joining the anti-Comintern coalition.

Similarly, while Russia permitted inclusion of favorable reference to previous treaties signed by both parties, it steadfastly refused all Chinese counterproposals relating to interference with internal affairs. Nanking officially interpreted the previous treaty reference to preclude such interference as that covered in Article 6 of the 1924 agreement. Moscow's stickiness, however, could only imply unwillingness to tie its hands on either Sinkiang or the Chinese Communist Party. Events were soon to prove the validity of this analysis.

At first glance, it would appear that China had gained little by delaying acceptance of the Soviet draft offered four years earlier. Actually, substantial changes were made in the final version. In addition, secret pledges of Soviet economic and military assistance made the pact palatable in a way that had not been possible previously. It may have been these tangible benefits which dissuaded Chinese negotiators from pressing the Sinkiang issue at this time. On the one hand, far greater concerns confronted them with the Japanese attack. On the other hand, Sinkiang, regardless of its orientation, provided the principal avenue of supply for China's sole source of help. The subsequent flow of Soviet planes, trucks, and ammunition through the province, construction of military highways there, and the training of Chinese pilots served not only to bolster the war front but to stabilize the rear against Japanese penetration.

Nevertheless, the pact left unsettled the question of Soviet interference in a province clearly within Nanking's jurisdiction. It brought favorable consequences for China insofar as it enabled central government authorities to move more freely in Sinkiang, implementing transfer of Soviet material assistance. However, it relieved Sheng of whatever embarrassment he may have felt in working with Soviet advisers. The presence of these advisers in Urumchi now had official blessing, because they were rendering support for China's war effort. Any protests from besieged Chungking would have even less leverage than before the August agreement. In sum, Sinkiang increased in importance but not in subservience to the Republic of China.

Military and political events in 1937 provided added proof of continued Soviet penetration. Once again a coalition of Tungan-Turki warriors raised the banner of revolt, this time in southern Sinkiang. Under the leadership of General Ma Hushan, brother-in-law of Ma Chung-ying, the rebellion had begun late in 1936 and had fanned outward from Kashgar. As the "Eastern Turkistan Republic" reappeared on the Sinkiang scene, local leaders such as Mahmud Sidjan, Yollbars Khan, and Khodja Niaz flocked to its colors. Sheng Shih-ts'ai faced a fresh challenge, similar to that of 1933-34.

As before, both Sheng and his Soviet advisers attributed the uprising to a mixture of Japanese and British intrigue. Other sources, hostile to Sheng, explained the rebellion in terms of rising Moslem resentment against Soviet influence. Whatever the cause, the effect of the revolt was to create a crisis permitting, if not necessitating, the return of Russian military power to the province.

There is reason to believe that without this new intervention Urumchi had little prospect of success in quelling the uprising. According to Sheng, he commanded "more than 10,000 infantry, cavalry, and artillery troops, with more than ten planes and one company of tanks and armored vehicles."[7] Against him stood perhaps 15,000 troops of recognized fighting ability, weakened only by recurring friction between Tungan and Turki.[8] Sheng claims that he did not even request help from Nanking, so involved were Nationalist forces against Communist guerrillas. His only alternative, as he defined the situation, lay with the Soviet Union.

Thus, Red Army units moved across the border in May, adding some 5,000 fresh troops as well as an air unit and an armored regiment to the provincial garrison.[9] Between the combined assault of the Soviet-Sheng forces and rising dissention within the rebel ranks, the revolt collapsed. By 1938 order was restored. The participation of Russian military units in a purely civil war within Chinese territory did not arouse official protest from the central government at this time, faced as it was with the more serious concern of a Japanese invasion.

Sheng has little to say concerning this affair in his autobiography. However, in an interview with the author, he admitted that Red Army intervention "had received my agreement previously."[10] Apresoff informed him that the "Kuei Hua Chün," the term which had formerly applied to the White Russian troops in Urumchi and was now used for the Soviet forces, would remain in Sinkiang "indefinitely." It appears from Sheng's account that while part of the intervention force returned to Russia, a self-contained task force remained as what was later known as the "Red Army Eighth Regiment," stationed at Hami. Uncertainty arises from the changed composition of the unit based at Hami and from its general association, both in Chinese and Western analyses, with Sino-Soviet co-operation against Japan. In support of Sheng's version, however, was a later Chungking protest against continued presence of "uninvited" Red troops in Sinkiang, lodged in 1940 at a time of strained Sino-Soviet relations.[11]

The garrisoning of Russian soldiers in the province, in contrast with their withdrawal in 1934, did serve to bolster a vulnerable part of China against Japanese encroachment. Yet Red intervention began well before the Japanese attack of July, and particularly before the Sino-Soviet pact of August.

As such, it did not serve to maintain Chinese control as opposed to Japanese control, but rather to safeguard, and perhaps extend, a Soviet sphere of influence in this critical area.

Although no evidence has been uncovered linking Tokyo with the Kashgar revolt, it was followed closely in Japanese reports. Minister Kitada cabled from Kabul of rebel belief in Sinkiang that "Japan would support Tungan and Turkish Moslems by sending Inner Mongolian troops."[12] He concluded, "It is felt that the Soviet Government adopted positive measures at this time, feeling threatened by Japan's advance into Inner Mongolia and probably into Sinkiang." It may well have been only Japan's decision to strike at China proper which emptied that advance of all immediate threat to Inner Asia. Added signs of Soviet insecurity, according to Afghan analyses, appeared in the sweeping purges of non-Russian groups in republics bordering Sinkiang. Meanwhile, Kitada entertained fresh pleas for assistance from the Emir of Khotan and Mahmud Sidjan, the latter having fled Kashgar before advancing Red units.[13]

Nanking continued to be without political power in the area, as demonstrated by its confessed inability to intercede on behalf of foreigners detained by Sheng and by its referral of protests to Soviet authorities.[14] Dramatic proof of Moscow's political penetration came in the extension of Soviet police controls and purges to Urumchi. In his memoirs, Sheng tells of his execution of "Trotskyite-fascist conspirators" in the spring of 1937, justified in terms of "evidence" produced at the Moscow trials. Further proof of the Russian role was Sheng's admission, in an interview with the author, that "in order to study the facts, the Soviet Government sent officers to Sinkiang to take part in the investigation." Among the victims was Apresoff, subsequently recalled to Russia to be tried and executed for "Trotskyite conspiracy."

The evidence in support of Sheng's allegations of international conspiracy is scanty. One report in the Japanese archives described "anti-Soviet White Russians, Grunkov (Colonel) and Medzhinin in Urumchi. . . . Army officer Ivanov is issuing secret instructions from Semipalatinsk. Shevagin joined the GPU in order to infiltrate its apparatus. Yusoff, Navieff, Niasvakiev, Harimov, and others are working to contact leaders of Moslem movements."[15] However, this dispatch warned that "the majority of White Russians . . . have compromised and are working with the Red Russians because of religious differences between themselves and the Moslems."

Whatever may have been the basis for Sheng's suspicions, one effect of the purge was to weaken his ability to resist Soviet penetration. Leadership was already scarce in Sinkiang. A purge decimated the ranks of those trained during the first three years of his new regime. Most of those executed for allegedly plotting with Germany and Japan were non-Chinese, in marked contrast with Sheng's rapid promotion of these persons in accordance with his self-proclaimed nationality policy. Thus, the purge may have served Sheng, as it did Stalin, to destroy rival centers of potential power. In addition, Sheng seems to have shared the Georgian dictator's paranoid tendencies. Seen in this light, the purge of 1937 appears as an extension of Stalinism into Sinkiang, with Sheng acting as the willing executioner of both policy and people.

One final aspect of Sinkiang's relationship to Soviet strategy in 1937 remains to be noted: relations with the Chinese Communist Party. As one consequence of the "united front" in China, the CCP established a clandestine line of communication with Moscow by way of Urumchi. At the same time introduction of CCP members into the provincial administration brought a new element into the already complex picture of Sinkiang politics.

Prior to the Sino-Soviet pact and the parallel establishment of CCP-KMT co-operation, the Chinese Communists played no part in Sheng's regime. In fact, Stalin seems to have kept them ignorant of Soviet influence there. Chang Kuo-t'ao, prominent in the CCP Politburo during this period, claims that Sheng's pro-Russian orientation became known only in 1936-37.[16] Chang apparently did not contemplate Sinkiang as an alternative base of operations during the celebrated Long March, arguing instead for Sikang and Szechwan during the Moukung conference debating CCP strategy in July, 1935.[17] Sheng's memoirs implicitly corroborate this impression of Moscow's monopoly of influence prior to 1937.

The relationship between the Russian and the Chinese Communists at this point is an elusive one, clouded by struggles for power within the CCP and by absence of evidence revealing the positions of participants, and of Mao Tse-tung and Stalin in particular. It seems certain, however, judging from the elliptical references to the period made by later CCP historians, that Mao's ascendancy came without Stalin's blessing, if not actually against the Kremlin's wishes.[18] If this analysis is correct, Stalin's strategy with respect to Sinkiang takes on added interest.

Certainly, Stalin did not advise the CCP to retreat into Sinkiang in 1934-35, when pursued by Chiang Kai-shek's forces. Instead, he appears to have recommended a point in northwest China, close to Russia and far from Chiang's main bases. This move had much in its favor. Sinkiang's predominantly non-Chinese population and its remoteness from China proper did not enhance it to the CCP. However, more than strategic logic may have dictated Stalin's secretiveness concerning Sheng's pro-Soviet posture. By keeping the CCP out of the area, he could enhance Russian Communist influence to the exclusion of Chinese Communist influence. While there is no direct evidence on this point, later events provide indirect substantiation for this hypothesis.

If this were Stalin's intent, formation of the "united front" on both an international and a domestic line in China changed circumstances considerably. Now Sinkiang's pivotal role in Sino-Soviet communications precluded maintaining it as a closed sphere of influence. Furthermore, a direct Moscow-Urumchi-Yenan route served both Russian and Chinese Communist interests. Late in 1937, for instance, Sheng forwarded money from Moscow to Yenan. Mao Tse-tung acknowledged this service in a profuse letter of thanks, sending a fur-lined coat as a token of appreciation.[19] This action, so soon after the Sino-Soviet pact, underscored Soviet refusal to pledge noninterference in China's domestic affairs.

In addition, Moscow sent Chinese Communists from Russia to act as Sheng's advisers, including, among others, Mao Tse-min, brother of Mao Tse-tung.[20] Their responsibility for such matters as fiscal reform indicated Sheng's willingness to cede positions of power, which he had refused Nanking's representatives, to CCP members. In fact, Sheng's drift leftward was accelerated by the more favorable environment provided by the "united front." Yenan's representative in Urumchi, Teng Fa, cabled that Sheng now desired formal membership in the CCP.[21] Such prominent Communists as Ch'en Shao-yü (Wang Ming), K'ang Sheng, and Jen Pi-shih visited the provincial capital in 1937, traveling from Moscow to Yenan. According to Sheng, they endorsed his application to become a full-fledged party member.[22]

The importance of Sheng's decision to join the CCP at this time cannot be overstressed. First, as a logical consequence of his previous ideological and political development, it signaled his refusal to allow Kuomintang ascendancy in Sinkiang. While continuing to give official obeisance to Chiang Kai-shek as titular leader of China, Sheng recognized Mao Tse-tung as his desired superior.

Secondly, acceptance of Sheng as a subordinate in decisions taken at Yenan necessarily lessened his subservience to Moscow. This would have increased Chinese, as distinguished from Russian, influence in Sinkiang. At the high level of generalized slogans and oaths to international solidarity, this might appear as a routine matter, logical enough given Sheng's Chinese status. At the practical level of politics, however, it carried implications which threatened to be disadvantageous for Moscow. The appearance of CCP members in Urumchi, both as visitors and as men of provincial authority, symbolized one way in which Sinkiang might become less of a Russian sphere of influence, thereby facilitating Chinese, albeit Communist, control over its affairs. To anticipate somewhat, Sheng's application for membership in the CCP, apparently approved in Yenan, later ran afoul of Stalin's personal veto. Consistent with his previous pattern, the Soviet dictator enrolled Sheng in the Russian Communist Party.

Thus, 1937 brought new forces into play in Sinkiang and altered the path of old ones. *Rapprochement* between the Soviet Union and the Republic of China spotlighted Sinkiang as a pipeline for valuable military and economic aid to Chungking. Simultaneously, a *détente* between Chiang Kai-shek and Mao Tse-tung resulted in Nationalist sanction for Communist activity. On the one hand, this freed Yenan from its blockaded position as a rebel capital. On the other hand, it encouraged Sheng Shih-ts'ai to seek membership in the Chinese Communist Party.

Finally, revolt inside the province and fears of aggrandizement outside it combined with Sheng's sense of insecurity to permit Soviet intervention on an expanded scale. Quantitatively, the size of Russian military forces and the duration of their stay surpassed in importance the intervention of 1934. Qualitatively, the accompanying political purge of the provincial administration, paralleling that in Moscow and assisted by Stalin's agents in Urumchi, signaled an extension of Russian influence unparalleled in Sinkiang's history. Behind the façade of the "united front," Soviet strategy continued to work to the disadvantage of China.

Notes

1. Information pertaining to negotiation of the Sino-Soviet non-aggression pact was obtained from unpublished archives made available through the co-operation of the Ministry of Foreign Affairs of the Republic of China in Taipei, Taiwan, 1954-55. Such data will be referred to hereafter as *Wai-chiao Pu archives*. More specific citations are impossible, since only copies or paraphrases of original documents were available, none with file or code number.

2. This summary of negotiations is corroborated by information given a Japanese diplomat by Chinese sources at the time; see *Documents, op. cit.*, Vol. III, p. 1398.

3. Consul General Suma in Nanking reporting a conversation with Bogomoloff of November 18, 1935, in *Documents, op. cit.*, Vol. V.

4. *Ibid.*, Vol. V, intercepted telegram of Yen to the Wai-chiao Pu, forwarded by the Japanese consul in Novosibirsk. Yen's cable perceptively commented, "It is suspected that Japan is intercepting mail and telegrams between China and the Soviet Union. . . . It is desirable to establish direct cable in order to maintain secrecy. Soviet Government has given informal approval but technical plan is yet to be made."

5. Some of his dispatches may be found, in the original Chinese, in the Tokyo archives. For a sample of his reporting, see *Documents, op. cit.*, Vol. VI, Consul Kayanagi in Novosibirsk to the

Foreign Office, in January, 1936: "Mr. Li Fang, Chinese consul general who came here in September 1935, has access to Sinkiang information. We came on very good terms and I owe him much in obtaining information." According to this report, Sheng choked off Nanking's sources of information by replacing Chinese consuls in Tashkent, Alma-Ata, and Semipalatinsk, with loyal appointees. One of his appointees, Kuang Lu, is here identified as "a Soviet agent." Subsequent independent evidence adds weight to this statement. For another dispatch of July 10, 1936, from the same Li Fang, see the official Wai-chiao Pu publication, *Soviet Economic Aggression, op. cit.,* pp. 138-39.

6. *Wai-chiao Pu archives, op. cit.* The Soviet draft came on August 5, 1937. The Chinese counterdraft of August 8 paralleled that of 1933. On August 12 Russian response rejected this *in toto,* adding only the reference to earlier treaties.

7. Interview with the author, May, 1954.

8. Hedin, *The Silk Road, op. cit.,* pp. 300-301, based on "Swedish sources."

9. Sheng interview, *op. cit.*

10. *Ibid.* Sheng added that he did not request the crossing at this particular time, nor did he request help from Nanking either, "since the Central Government was still engaged with the Chu-Mao Red Armies and help could not come quickly."

11. *Documents, op. cit.,* Vol. IX, intercepted telegram from the Soviet ambassador in Chungking to the Narkomindel, October 10, 1940, relayed by the Japanese consul general in Harbin to Foreign Minister Nomura. According to this telegram, the Soviet representative rebuffed Nationalist protests over the presence of Soviet troops in Sinkiang by claiming that "the expedition of Soviet troops was made in compliance with the direct request of the Chinese Government." Since the Sino-Soviet Nonaggression Pact had not been signed at the time of crossing, this seems improbable. The note further explained the troop activity as "solely to secure the safety of the supply route of war materials to China and to support the local government in the promotion of trade in accordance with the Sino-Soviet trade pact." The

protest specifically concerned the unit at Hami, usually identified as having entered Sinkiang in 1938.

12. *Documents, op. cit.*, Vol. VIII, Kitada via consul in Bombay to Hirota, October 27, 1937; Kitada's reports on south Sinkiang were based in part upon information from the French consul general who had visited the area.

13. *Ibid.*, Kitada to Hirota, dispatches of August 24 and 31, and September 7, 1937.

14. *Ibid.*, Vol. VII, Japanese consul in Novosibirsk to Foreign Minister Sato, May 31, 1937. According to information given the Japanese consul by the German consul, a well-known German explorer, Wilhelm Filfnel, was detained at Khotan, while holding a Chinese visa. When the German Embassy at Nanking requested action, "the Nanking Government gave the unusual reply that Germany might better approach the Soviet Government for release of the German scientist, because the influence of the Chinese Government does not extend that far. The German consul also stated that according to his information the Soviet Union is sending 10,000 troops from Kazakhstan into Sinkiang."

15. *Documents, op. cit.*, Vol. V, consul general in Shanghai to the Foreign Office, September 10, 1935. Spelling of Russian names is based on Japanese transliteration and is quite likely erroneous.

16. Interview with Chang Kuo-t'ao in Hong Kong, August 1, 1955. Chang said he did not learn of Sheng's policies in detail until the end of 1936.

17. According to Robert C. North, *Moscow and Chinese Communists* (Stanford: Stanford University Press, 1953), p. 164, Chang informed him in an earlier interview that "Moscow's telegrams at that time [1934] were routed through Sinkiang or Outer Mongolia." However, Chang specifically denied this in a later discussion with the author. While recollection of things past suffers with time, corroboration for the present analysis may be seen in materials gathered shortly after the event in Edgar Snow's *Red Star Over China* (New York: Random House, 1944), pp. 212-13, and Agnes Smedley's *The Great Road* (New York: Monthly Review Press, 1956, p. 329.

18. For an analysis of Mao's rise to power and his probable relations with Stalin during this period, see Benjamin I. Schwartz, *Chinese Communism and the Rise of Mao* (Cambridge: Harvard University Press, 1951), supplemented by his article, "On the 'Originality' of Mao Tse-tung," *Foreign Affairs*, Vol. 34, No. 1, October, 1955.

19. Chang interview, *op. cit.* Rumor placed the amount as $300,000 CNG. This seems rather small, since the first Soviet loan to the Republic of China concluded the same year came to $100,-000,000 CNG, or about $50,000,000.

20. *Ibid.* Chang said this occurred in 1936, but he probably erred in his recollection of the precise year. According to information given Anna Louise Strong by Chinese Communists in Yenan in 1946, a number of CCP advisers went to Sinkiang in 1938 from Yenan at the request of Sheng. Mao Tse-min was identified as "in charge" of the group, although it is unclear from the context whether he made the trip from Yenan or Moscow. His wife was placed in charge of a middle school for girls and was interviewed by Miss Strong in 1946. Notes from personal files of Anna Louise Strong, examined in January, 1958.

21. *Ibid.* Sheng asserted that Ch'en Shao-yu (Wang Ming), K'ang Sheng, and Teng Fa visited Urumchi "as early as the beginning of our war of resistance" and learned of his desire to join the CCP at that time; see his letter to Chiang Kai-shek of July 7, 1942, quoted in *Soviet Economic Aggression, op. cit.*, pp. 67-68. Although Sheng and Chang, interviewed independently, corroborated one another's recollections, additional sources for checking this period are not readily available. Most of the participants have remained silent as either loyal Communists or Nationalists.

22. Chang Kuo-t'ao remembered several of Sheng's visitors as having reported him to be "ambitious and suspicious . . . unreliable." Ch'en Shao-yü, in particular, claimed that Sheng requested considerable amounts of arms, money, and equipment from the Soviet Union.

4

Soviet Influence Increases: 1938–41

DURING THE NEXT few years Sinkiang occupied a paradoxical position. On the one hand, it was the scene of intense activity implementing Russia's agreement to assist China in the war with Japan. On the other hand, it fell increasingly under Moscow's economic and political influence, further removing it from control by Chungking.

The province played a prominent role in sustaining Chinese resistance against Japan. Measured in sheer numbers, the Soviet aid is not impressive. However, the qualitative impact of Russian help, particularly in the air, afforded critical assistance when China stood alone. A reliable Nationalist official later recalled that Soviet deliveries of approximately two hundred fighters "proved very helpful against the Japanese Zeroes . . . Pilots to fly them were signed on an individual contract basis, with the Soviet Union acting as guarantor."[1] Subsequently, he claimed, the program fell short of expectations. Although the pilots originally contracted to fly for six months' combat, this was pared down by Moscow first to three, and then to one month. Since Chungking paid all transportation and salary expenses, this rotation system proved expensive for China, while giving Russian pilots valuable combat training.

The air route entered China by way of Sinkiang and the northwest cities of Lanchow and Sian.[2] Approximately five hundred Soviet pilots served as "volunteers" in China, flying fighters and bombers in successful forays against the Imperial Air Force. When losses rendered the initial shipment unusable, additional deliveries were made to newly trained Chinese pilots, schooled in Ili, northwest of Urumchi.[3] Whether because of their inexperience, or because of increased Japanese familiarity with Soviet aircraft, gained both in China and in the Nomonhan affair of 1939, heavy losses were sustained in subsequent engagements.[4] As a result, no further deliveries were accepted by Chungking.

Of the 885 aircraft to arrive from Russia, almost all came via Sinkiang.[5] To maintain them, Moscow provided an airplane assembly plant, disguised under the name of the "Agricultural Implements Factory." Although Chungking requested construction in Kansu province, it was built instead in Urumchi, on Soviet insistence. Heavy fortifications surrounded it, bolstered by a score of tanks and more than 1,500 troops.[6] Additional Red soldiers at Hami, apparently remaining from the May, 1937, intervention, guarded the 1,700-mile motor route linking Russia with Lanchow via Hsinghsinghsia, on the Kansu-Sinkiang border.

Chungking faced a dilemma with respect to these Russian forces in Sinkiang. On the one hand, the benefit of Soviet aid was manifest. An American journalist reported hundreds of Red trucks, carrying ammunition, bombs, and guns, through the mountain passes into Lanchow. Fuel for these convoys traveled picturesquely, on the backs of two thousand camels.[7] In 1940 a Chinese official claimed that, "China is now using 20,000 camels to carry military supplies across Chinese Turkistan from the Soviet Union."[8]

On the other hand, the presence of these troops and tanks in Sinkiang impeded assertion of Chungking's authority. Although the National Government had little direct information on conditions in Urumchi, Dr. Sun Fo's sojourn there in March, 1939, enroute to negotiations in Moscow for further loans and military assistance, furnished fresh evidence of Soviet influence.[9] He noted Sheng's repeated visits to the Russian consulate for consultations and, in subsequent discussions with Stalin, raised the question of Moscow's intentions in Sinkiang. Stalin reassured Sun, recounting the familiar charges of Japanese backing of Ma Chung-ying and of Soviet response to Sheng's appeal for assistance. Disclaiming any interests in the province which might clash with Chungking, Stalin described all Soviet activity there as "indirectly helping the Chinese Government."

Yet such reassurances did not remove the grievance nor the troops. Of minor interest at first, especially with more demanding problems on the military front, the matter became of growing concern to Chinese officials as Russo-Japanese relations improved after signing the Nazi-Soviet pact, in August, 1939. Official protests to Moscow called for settlement of the matter in 1940, in vain. Not until Russian reverses in World War II strained Soviet resources to the utmost, was Chungking able to force withdrawal of Red units from Sinkiang.

To be sure, Russian interest in the strategic northwest communications line served Chinese interests as well, insofar as it acted to exclude Japanese penetration. Tokyo exploited all avenues of approach, without success. In 1937 and 1938, Japanese agents contacted Ma Pu-fang, nominally loyal to Chungking yet independent in his military control of Chinghai.[10] His friendly but guarded reaction gave no promise of support until Japan conquered Nationalist armies elsewhere and proved itself ready to fight Russia. As a Foreign Office evaluation remarked somewhat acidly, "Ma may not have too much enthusiasm for joining hands with Japan. He seems too preoccupied with securing his own province and his influence. He will continue his ambiguous 'non-separation, non-coalition' attitude toward Chungking and the Central Government will tighten surveillance around him."

Another approach came through Mahmud Sidjan, formerly of the ill-fated "Eastern Turkistan Republic." After finally winning Tokyo's confidence in early 1939,[11] he proceeded to China the following year. There an extensive tour ended in Suiyuan province in October, 1940.[12] His grandiose schemes aimed at a pan-Moslem movement under the auspices of a "Japan-Islam Society, recently established in Tokyo for cultural and economic mutual enhancement between Japan and Moslems." In addition, he planned a "Sinkiang Uighur Society," with headquarters in Tokyo and branches throughout Inner Asia.

Japan's efforts came to naught. Dispatches from Japanese listening posts on the periphery of Sinkiang revealed a growing tone of bitterness and frustration, as reports of increased Soviet influence filtered into Tokyo, seldom offset by firm evidence of counter gains. Given the amount of attention awarded Sinkiang and Moslem groups, the incidental instances of infiltration appear surprisingly insignificant.

Thus, China had reason to question the degree to which Soviet troops in Sinkiang were necessitated by the Japanese threat. When a cooling of relations permitted official protest over these forces in 1940, Chungking took the opportunity to rebuff Moscow's request to open a consulate in Lanchow.[13] While offering visas to Soviet officials for travel there, Chinese authorities refused to sanction permanent Russian residence at this important junction on the route from Sinkiang into China proper.

In only one instance were Nationalist negotiators able to win an extension of their power through Soviet co-operation in Sinkiang. Discussion of joint operation of a Sino-Soviet air line through the province began in 1938. Flights actually preceded by five months the final pact, concluded in September, 1939.[14] Under a Chinese chairman, a board of directors, based in Alma-Ata, gave equal participation to both sides, while a Russian general manager headed the company offices in Urumchi. Capital was equally contributed, with no third party participation permitted in either financing or operating the air line. Chungking controlled operations from Hami to the war-time capital, while Soviet pilots flew the Moscow-Alma-Ata-Urumchi-Hami sections. In addition, the pact pledged maximum training opportunities for Chinese pilots and technical personnel. This agreement struck a more favorable balance for China than similar "joint management" enterprises, and survived subsequent friction over Soviet moves in Sinkiang.

Russian economic activity was not merely designed to assist China against Japan, however. These years saw Soviet tactics drive out British competition in Sinkiang both by fiat and by special pricing. In 1938 Urumchi banned all trade with India, ostensibly on grounds of British intrigue during the 1937 re-volts.[15] Meanwhile, Russian goods in plentiful supply and at cheap prices flooded the oases markets, although across the border, the Soviet cities of Samarkand and Tashkent experi-enced acute shortages of consumer goods.[16]

The major economic goal was not trade, but exploitation of Sinkiang's resources. Although Sheng is elusive on this matter, it appears that Soviet geologists began surveys of the province shortly after Red Army intervention in 1934. A large Russian map in Sheng's archives shows manganese, copper, lead, tin, wolfram, oil, and other mineral deposits in Sinkiang. Drawn in 1935, the map indicated few of these resources then in produc-tion, but many deposits were identified "on the basis of survey."

A particularly rich cluster of minerals lay in the northwest section of the province near the Soviet border, in the vicinity of Wusu. According to later Chinese Nationalist investigations, Russian oil drilling began here in 1935, with daily production of small amounts reported by 1939.[17] Soviet sources claimed "an oral agreement" from Sheng authorized exploitation of the Tushantze fields.[18] Sheng's silence on this point may stem from the absence of revenue accruing to Urumchi from the Soviet venture.

The full amount of Soviet exploitation may never be known, since the provincial government had no access to production facilities nor were any reports provided Sheng on output. In view of Soviet assessment of annual capacity of the Tushantze refinery as 50,000 tons of crude oil, it is possible that expected, if not actual, output far exceeded Nationalist estimates made later when the field was inoperative.[19] Observers in Sinkiang later claimed that production increased markedly after the Nazi attack upon Russia of June, 1941, with constant truck convoys traveling between the fields and the Soviet border.[20] In addition to oil, large amounts of tungsten came from well-engineered mines located along the northwestern frontier, just within the Chinese border. This provided sufficient amount to enable a cutback in Soviet imports of the valuable material from other parts of China. Yet none of the geological surveys conducted by Russian teams was made available to Urumchi, information on these operations coming only from rumor or in surveys conducted from Chungking in 1943.

That exploitation of Sinkiang's resources brought few returns to the provincial government is attested by the so-called "Tin Mines Agreement," signed between Sheng and Soviet representatives on November 26, 1940. This document, included in the Appendices, merits analysis as an example of Soviet designs for a closed sphere of political as well as economic influence. Valid for fifty years, the agreement granted Moscow privileges in Sinkiang so extensive as to constitute a state within a state, immune from control by Urumchi or the central government.

In Article One, the Soviet Union won "exclusive rights for the prospection, investigation and exploitation of tin and its ancillary minerals." With this monopoly came the right to build all power lines, transportation media, and communications networks necessary to the project, without interference from outside authorities. In view of the paucity of provincial funds for such facilities, this clause promised Russia virtual control of principal roads, railroads, telegraph, and radio stations in the area. Soviet personnel received unlimited entry privileges and enjoyed unrestricted movement within Sinkiang. Land was to be given the exploiting corporation, "Sin-tin," upon demand "without delay," and all persons residing there were to be removed. Armed guards controlled by the corporation closed the premises and activities from outside examination, including that of the provincial police.

Economic provisions offered Russia extremely favorable terms. All exports of produce were to be duty free, compensated for only by a two per cent *ad valorem* charge. Rent for land and facilities was to be paid in kind at the rate of five and six per cent of production. This was then to be sold to the Soviet Union at prevailing world prices. No share in net profits and no participation in management was given either the provincial or the central government. Moreover, Urumchi was expressly forbidden to "inspect, supervise, investigate, or audit the various operations of production, finance, and commerce of 'Sin-tin'." In return, Sinkiang was to receive all facilities without compensation at the close of the fifty-year period. Prior to that time, its only tangible reward, apart from the nominal rent, would be the training of an unspecified number of local citizens in the technical operation of the corporation. Nowhere did the pact provide for consultation with the central govern-

ment. It entered into effect upon signature by Sheng and his
Soviet negotiators.

Conflicting evidence attests to Sheng's reaction at the time.
His autobiography asserts resistance to Soviet terms and
describes his subterfuge to keep open a legal loophole, in-
validating the agreement. Sheng had good cause to fear criticism
for accepting the pact, even under duress. For this reason, he
apparently kept it secret from his immediate associates, as well
as from Chungking. Its fifty-year duration and its unilateral
benefits to the Soviet Union exacted more onerous concessions
from a Chinese negotiator than at any time since Japan pressed
its famous "Twenty-One Demands" in World War I.

Sheng's defense of his actions, however, must be placed
against his political perspective of the time. It seems doubtful
that he settled on an exclusive Soviet orientation as early as
1935, as alleged in rumored treaties.[21] Yet there is no reason
to question Sheng's own account of his trip to Moscow, in 1938,
in pursuit of membership in the CCP, and his subsequent
acceptance of Stalin's decision to enroll him in the Russian
Communist Party. That action sharply revealed the intentions
of both autocrats. For Stalin, it meant refusal to facilitate
Chinese encroachment, whether Nationalist or Communist,
upon a Russian sphere of influence. For Sheng, it signaled his
willingness to accept Soviet discipline, as clearly defined in
Party membership. That discipline ultimately was invoked
during negotiation of the 1940 pact.

Further evidence of his political stance came in Sheng's
second major purge, shortly before signature of the "Tin
Mines" agreement. His present account conforms neither with
explanations offered for the purge in 1940, nor with the logic
of events. There is little evidence that the alleged conspirators
were any more vulnerable to Soviet blandishments, his present
charge, than were their successors. Nor are accusations of "im-

perialist-fascist plots," made at the time, borne out by any evidence of increasing Japanese pressure.

One probable cause of tension, however, is suggested indirectly by Sheng's memoirs. The atmosphere of intimidation and insecurity which it reveals may have aroused resentment against his rule. Further disillusionment among more idealistically or radically inclined groups in Urumchi also may have followed the Nazi-Soviet pact of 1939. This event led to a visible downgrading of Japanese aggression in Sinkiang propaganda, coupled with renewed emphasis on Great Britain as the main imperialist threat. If such discontent occurred, Sheng's paranoia, feeding on doubts occasioned by these sources of opposition, readily triggered a new wave of arrests and executions. As in 1937, his emasculated regime became ever more dependent upon Soviet advisers and police controls.

Final proof of the political context within which Sheng signed the 1940 contract comes with a review of slogans, speeches, and articles appearing in Sinkiang before and after the pact. Conveniently assembled in a "study guide" by Sheng in January, 1942, these materials point up the degree to which his political tie with Moscow excluded virtually all favorable reference to Chungking.[22] In view of his later protestations of anti-Soviet attitude throughout this period, his contemporary utterances merit examination in some detail.

A six-pointed red star dominating a map of Sinkiang on the cover of this compilation set the tone of its contents. Numerous quotations from Marx, Lenin, and Stalin opened the study, asserting capitalism to be the root of imperialist conflict. Sheng followed with an attack upon British policy, which aimed "not to intervene against aggression but to actually help it." In contrast, the Soviet Union held the hope of oppressed nations throughout the world:

> . . . At a time when the democratic countries adopt a policy
> of neutrality and tolerance toward the fascist aggressive bloc's
> invasion of weak and small countries, when fascist bandits
> actually plot war, when the great Chinese masses are engaged
> in their mighty task of struggling for national liberation . . .
> it is the Soviet Union which can protect the interests of weak
> and small nations, can utilize every method to preserve world
> peace, can actually help the Spanish and Chinese wars of re-
> sistance, thereby helping other small nations in their fight for
> liberation—the only fortress protecting world peace! [23]

This material, written one week after the Nazi-Soviet Pact
of 1939, evidenced a radical departure from the cautious references to Russia which characterized earlier statements. Notice-
ably absent was any mention of Chiang Kai-shek or the
Nationalist government.

Not only did Sheng see the Soviet Union as beneficial to
lesser nations, but he called for assistance by "small nations"
to build Soviet power, declaring Russia to be "the Fatherland
of the world proletariat . . . of the world peace camp for
colonies, semicolonies, and oppressed nations. . . . To strengthen
the Soviet Union is to strengthen the interests of weak and
small national revolutions." Sheng described at length what
he termed the basic differences between the "new world" and
the "old world," employing familiar "statistical comparisons"
to demonstrate the dynamic growth of socialism contrasted with
depression-ridden capitalism. For him, victory of the "new"
over the "old" was inevitable "because the Soviet economic
system is superior to the capitalist system."

Addressing himself to political problems in Sinkiang, Sheng
took up first the question of Soviet forces stationed in Hami.
He addressed himself to challenges against their usefulness while
Japanese troops continued to advance throughout China:

> Within the countries of the new world, the troops trained in
> the Red Army are troops to reinforce Soviet power, to protect

the peace not only of the Soviet Union but of the entire world, to help the oppressed peoples and oppressed humanity struggling for liberation to safeguard peaceful livelihood and to prepare for world revolution. One day they will rise in sacrifice on the field of battle with valor and glory, to defend peace, to protect the workers' fatherland, to protect security, to resist aggression and to use war as a means of ending war.[24]

Would these troops merely further Soviet ends, making Sin-kiang a Communist satellite? Sheng countered this criticism:

. . . Taking the Soviet Union as our close friend and ally is misunderstood among nationalities of economically backward and culturally backward areas. Especially in semi-colonial and semi-feudal China, old-fashioned and backward-thinking peo-ple misunderstand this . . . as risking "communizing" and "Bolshevizing" the situation (this happens in Sinkiang). But this is misunderstanding and rumor. . . . In the past, Persia, Afghanistan, and Turkey were all countries which received Soviet help, just as Sinkiang's pro-Soviet policy for the past six years has received vasts amounts of Soviet spiritual and material aid. But these countries, as with China's Sinkiang, are today still not "Red" or "communist." Recently all of China adopted a pro-Soviet policy but we see no danger of it becoming "Red" or "communist." These things happen because of other reasons and not from adoption of this policy—they come from more basic causes than a pro-Soviet attitude![25]

As before, Sheng attempted to quell Moslem fears of anti-religious persecution by reference to Islamic countries border-ing Russia which had not suffered that fate.

One portion of the book, written in October, 1939, consisted of a long panegyric to Lenin and Stalin and the significance of the October Revolution. In this section, devoted primarily to the problems of colonialism, nationality development, and liberation movements, Sheng made no reference to Sun Yat-sen or Chiang Kai-shek, to the vaunted Three People's Principles of Sun, or to similar Nationalist figures and symbols. In writing on China's struggle against Japan, among the groups on his united front honor role he again omitted any mention of the Kuomintang.

This implicit shift of loyalty evoked a curious analysis of the "greatest victories of the Soviet Union's peace policy," evidencing Sheng's admiration for Stalin's sagacity. First on his list was the Sino-Soviet nonaggression pact of August, 1937. Among the reasons for terming this a victory, Sheng claimed that it "put down the backward thinking of Chinese Russophobes and struck a heavy blow at the traitors and Trotsky bandits who would divide China from Russia." But it was also a victory "because it reduced Japan's threatening force against Russia and reinforced the power of the peace camp centered in the Soviet Union." Certainly this was to be applauded from a Russian point of view. But Chinese interests would have been better served by increasing Japanese involvement with Russia, thereby lessening Japan's pressure on China. Sheng pursued precisely the opposite line of reasoning, regardless of its implications for China.

His citations for Russia's foreign policy victories included the Nazi-Soviet pact of August, 1939, for allegedly defeating Anglo-French schemes to force war between Hitler and Stalin. Sheng also applauded the "mutual assistance pacts" concluded by the Soviet Union with the Baltic states, which purportedly "saved them from danger and preserved their peace, and moreover established a firm and peaceful frontier on the Soviet northwestern borders." As for the Nazi-Soviet partition of Poland, this "helped the White Russian and Ukrainian peoples inside the Polish border, saving them from falling under German fascist oppression . . . bringing them over from the dark camp of the old world to the bright new world." This invasion he praised as the "glorious mission of the great and courageous Red Army."[26]

It would be difficult to find a more full-throated approval of Soviet policy, outside of official Russian pronouncements than that penned by Sheng Shih-ts'ai. In 1940, he saw the struggle as an imperialist war. Moscow deserved credit for having managed to stay clear of the conflict, despite the plotting of British and French capitalists. Soviet invasion and intimidation of the "weak and small nations" of Eastern Europe and the Baltic area was specifically condoned as "liberation." The Soviet-Finnish war had been instigated by Britain and France, with United States connivance. Therefore, the peace between Helsinki and Moscow was another "victory," praised by Sheng on April 12, 1940, because it defeated the imperialists' scheme to involve the Soviet Union in war. Similarly, in the Far East, the three capitalist powers sought peace between China and Japan, so as to free Japan for an anti-Soviet war. This would simultaneously divert Japan from their colonies and weaken the socialist homeland.[27] Again, Sheng argued for Chinese resistance against Japan in terms of its value to the Soviet Union. At the very time he voiced this plea, the Trans-Siberian railway carried strategic supplies between Berlin and Tokyo. Simultaneously, Soviet shipments to China suffered a marked decline.

Against this review of Stalin's omniscient foreign policy, Sheng painted a dark picture of "defeatism, reaction, and compromise" in the highest Chinese circles.[28] In addition to the Wang Ching-wei "puppet government" sponsored by Japan, he also attacked "internal forces" tending toward surrender policies. Without mentioning the Nationalists directly, he condemned Chungking by lauding "progressive" groups, "friends of the Soviet Union," and those "determined to fight." He concluded that defeatist elements were stronger in China proper than in Sinkiang. Only in the ritualistic slogans issued in commemoration of such events as the "April Uprising" and the "Marco Polo Bridge Incident" did Sheng pay lip-service to the patriotic theme of "Unite KMT & CCP! Eliminate Friction!" Even here, prominence was given to "Defend Perpetual Friendship of China and Russia!" and "Eliminate Trotskyite Traitors!"

The one change of note came in June, 1941, with the Nazi attack upon the Soviet Union. For Sheng, as for all who up to the attack had faithfully followed the Soviet foreign policy line, this immediately transformed the "imperialist war" into a "war against fascism." He demanded that Britain "use land, sea, and air forces in their full power, particularly land and sea power, to attack and threaten the German rear, ceaselessly bombarding Germany, thereby allowing the Soviet Red Army to smash to dust easily and quickly the German invading force."[29] China likewise was to act valiantly in support of Russia, as Sheng called for unity "against the diverse elements, the defeatists, compromisers, etc." The "counterattack" which he outlined "must in foreign policy be pro-Soviet Union and help the Soviet Union in its war against Germany . . . In Sinkiang we must root out the counter-revolutionary remnants . . . and help the Soviet Union to win victory in war." His last entry in this book, an editorial of November 7, 1941, hailed Moscow's dramatic defense against the Nazi siege and called upon Britain and France to take all necessary steps immediately to relieve the Russian front.[30]

In view of this consistent and uncritical support for Moscow, Sheng's present defense of his signing the "Tin Mines" agreement in 1940 carries little conviction. The pact underscored the degree to which the sequence of events since 1934 had transformed his regime into one which differed little from the outright satellite state of Outer Mongolia. Red army units remained in Sinkiang against the will of Chungking but not of Urumchi. Soviet geologists surveyed the province's resources for exploitation and export to Russia, without permission from the central government but without opposition from the provincial regime. Political agents from Moscow guided Sheng's propaganda line, while Soviet secret police ferreted out "conspirators" and assisted him in periodic purges. Whatever inner misgivings Sheng may have harbored as this process reached its peak in 1940-41, not until Soviet victory appeared doubtful did he move to establish Chinese-Nationalist authority in Sinkiang.

Notes

1. Interviews with Dr. Lo Chia-lun in Taipei, Taiwan, in 1954. Dr. Lo helped initiate negotiations for the Sino-Soviet nonaggression pact and was on familiar terms with Ambassador Bogomoloff. He is highly informed on Sinkiang affairs.

2. *Women ti ti kuo* (Our Enemy) (Taipei: Chung Yang Jih Pao, 1952), Vol. II, pp. 113 ff.

3. Lo interviews, *op. cit.* Anna Louise Strong flew from Alma-Ata to Chungking, via Kuldja, Urumchi, and Hami, in 1940. A Chinese pilot whom she met on the trip claimed he was trained by Russian instructors at Kuldja, and described in detail the quantities of aircraft and Russian pilots and technicians in China; interview with Miss Strong, January 30, 1958.

4. *Ibid.* In 1939 Japanese forces attacked along the Outer Mongolian border and in a major battle at Nomonhan were defeated by Soviet air and armored units.

5. F. F. Liu, *A Military History of Modern China, 1924-1949* (Princeton: Princeton University Press, 1956), p. 168.

6. Lo interviews, *op. cit.*

7. Edgar Snow, cited in A. K. Wu, *China and the Soviet Union, op. cit.*, p. 269.

8. Dr. Wellington Koo, in Wu, *op. cit.*, p. 270.

9. Interview with Dr. Sun Fo, December 19, 1957. See also Wu, *op. cit.*, pp. 257-58.

10. *Documents, op. cit.*, Vol. IX, dispatch of May 3, 1939. One "Sherif, attaché to Mahmud Sidjan," contacted Ma Pu-fang on December 13, 1937. This was probably Tewfik Sherif Pasha, mentioned earlier. Ma claimed that while he was sympathetic to Japan, he feared retaliation for having "captured a dozen Japanese secret agents in Ningsia province in 1936 who had been executed by order of the Central Government." Sherif received fresh orders from the Japanese consulate in Shanghai the following February, and again met Ma in May, 1938. This time Ma claimed to fear attack by Soviet airplanes should he move against Sinkiang as an ally of Japan.

11. *Ibid.*, Vol. IX, consul general in Bombay to Foreign Office, February 19, 1939.

12. *Ibid.*, Vol. IX, dispatch of November 12, 1940.

13. *Documents, op. cit.*, Vol. II, p. 550; intercepted telegram from the Wai-chiao Pu to the Chinese ambassador in Moscow, forwarded from Consul General Miura in Shanghai to Foreign Minister Arita, March 6, 1940.

14. Sun Fu-k'un, *Su lien lüeh to Sinkiang chi shih* (A Record of Soviet Plundering of Sinkiang) (Hong Kong, 1952), Vol. II, pp. 77 ff.

15. *Documents, op. cit.*, Vol. VIII, Minister Moriya in Kabul to Foreign Minister Ugaki, August 7, 1938, and to Arita, December 21, 1938.

16. *Ibid.*, Moriya to Ugaki, August 7, 1938, noting large quantities of Soviet silkworms distributed free of charge in Sinkiang. See also P. Fleming, *News from Tartary* (New York: Scribners, 1936); Fleming visited these areas as a correspondent from the London *Times*.

17. *Soviet Economic Aggression, op. cit.*, pp. 78 ff. Nationalist estimates placed annual output at 1,000 tons.

18. *Ibid.*, p. 116. This information came from Ambassador Panyush-kin in discussions over disposition of Soviet oil equipment with K. C. Wu and W. H. Wong.

19. A Nationalist survey in 1943 placed daily output of the wells at

30 to 40 tons with "possible production" of double this amount; T. K. Huang, *Report on Geological Investigation of Some Oil Fields in Sinkiang* (Nanking, 1947). For the Soviet figure, see *Soviet Economic Aggression, op. cit.*, p. 82.

20. The following information was made available by Dr. William Su Ting, who conducted geographical and geological surveys of the area in 1943.

21. A so-called "Treaty of Mutual Assistance," allegedly signed in Urumchi on January 1, 1936, is printed in Leonard Shapiro's *Soviet Treaty Series* (Washington, D. C.: Georgetown University Press, 1949), Vol. II, p. 154. References to such a treaty abound in the Japanese archives, although varying in timing and description of contents. No credible Chinese or Russian source has been found to substantiate these reports. A forged treaty apparently was circulated by Japanese agents at the time. The wording is singularly incautious, especially for this period. It includes a Soviet pledge "in case of some external attack upon the province to assist it politically, economically, and by armed force," as well as a reference to the province becoming "independent or the formation of a separate state." Sheng's pro-Soviet orientation seems never to have advanced to the point of putting in writing such clearly treasonable statements. Certainly in 1935 his position fell far short of that implied by such a pact.

22. Sheng Shih-ts'ai, *Liu ta cheng ti chiao ch'eng* (The Six Great Policies Study Manual) (Tihua: Sinkiang People's Anti-Imperialism Association, Jan. 1, 1942), Vol. I. This book was begun by Sheng, according to his introductory notes, in 1936, and revised in February, 1938, perhaps as a result of the Japanese attack on China. A second revision in November, 1939, followed the Nazi-Soviet pact. His third revision of March, 1941, may have resulted from the "Tin Mines Agreement" of November, 1940. These revisions apparently did not affect the reprinted materials issued earlier, but merely altered the design and conclusions of the book.

23. *Ibid.*, p. 10.
24. *Ibid.*, pp. 18-19.
25. *Ibid.*, pp. 28-29.
26. *Ibid.*, p. 48
27. *Ibid.*, p. 65.
28. *Ibid.*, p. 66.
29. *Ibid.*, p. 80.
30. For a convenient assembling of quotations from CCP writings, providing a precise parallel with those of Sheng both in timing and content, see *Hearings Before the Subcommittee to Investigate the Administration of the Internal Security Act and Other Internal Security Laws* (Washington, D. C.: Judiciary Committee, United States Senate, 82d Congress, 2d Session, 1952), Part 7A, Appendix II, Report by Brigadier General P. E. Peabody, Chief, Military Intelligence Service, War Department, pp. 2375-77; hereafter cited as *I.P.R. Hearings*. This report was assembled from classified dispatches by United States foreign service and military officers in China. It throws considerable light on political developments in Chinese communism.

5

Red Exodus: 1942–44

SINKIANG'S POLITICAL history frustrates the analyst who, in trying to reconstruct the course of events, must rely on the residue of memoirs, documents, and impressionistic accounts. To be sure, the main stream of action moves slowly through discernible channels, transporting the fragile ship of state with its assorted figures to varied destinations. Suddenly, however, the current quickens. The rush and roar of treacherous rapids surround the ship with a cloud of spray. Out of the ensuing confusion the vessel emerges, minus some of its passengers. None aboard can agree as to what precisely took place during the desperate, hidden struggle for survival.

So one can trace the factors responsible for the overthrow of Chin Shu-jen, for instance, but fail to fix with full certainty the complex maneuvers which resulted in Sheng's final winning of control in 1933. Both the interplay within Sinkiang and the intervention from Moscow and Nanking throw a curtain of confusion and contradiction around the evidence offered from various sources. Similarly, it is almost impossible to chart the detailed sequence of events which somersaulted Sheng from an apparently faithful servant of Stalin in January, 1942, to a "younger brother" of Chiang Kai-shek in July of the same year.

Certainly Sheng's followers in Sinkiang had no forewarning of his sudden switch of loyalty except, perhaps, for the suspension in April of the recognized organ for radical propaganda, the *Fan Ti Chan Hsien* (Anti-Imperialist Front). Prior to this, all utterances struck a consistent note, unmistakable in its inspiration. Thus, in November, 1939, Sheng called for "changing the imperialist war to one of internal revolt, thereby carrying out the proletarian revolution."[1] In 1940 he reinterpreted his "Six Great Policies" to provide a precise parallel with Mao Tse-tung's newly enunciated concept of "Hsin min chu chu yi," or "New Democracy."[2] The following year, Sheng proposed "that the Soviet government institute a Soviet regime in Sinkiang," although later claiming "I really did not mean it."[3] Finally, in his memoirs he quotes a long letter from Mao Tse-tung of February 4, 1942, expressing gratitude for recent gifts from Urumchi, and discussing the problem of meeting Sheng's requests for additional CCP advisers.[4] None of this betokened a casting off of subservience to Moscow.

His autobiography explains the cause of his switch of allegiance as disillusionment with Soviet handling of the 1940 treaty, and dismay at an alleged plot against his life which resulted in the murder of his brother in March, 1942. Other evidence, however, admittedly fragmentary, indicates quite different motivations behind the change-over.

A review of events in 1941 is suggestive. In March Foreign Minister Matsuoka met with Stalin and Molotov in Moscow. On April 13 Russia and Japan signed a nonaggression pact, with ominous forebodings for China. Were the two powers to arrive at agreed spheres of influence, as had St. Petersburg and Tokyo prior to World War I, it might seal the fate of both Urumchi and Chungking. These circumstances may have prompted Sheng to strengthen his credit with Stalin by suggesting a "Soviet regime in Sinkiang," as mentioned earlier.

Similarly, Chiang Kai-shek had cause to seek improvement of Sino-Soviet relations by compromising on Sinkiang. Japanese reports told of a high-level meeting on April 23, which appointed

Sun Fo head of a "Committee for the Adjustment of Sino-Soviet Relations."[5] Sun allegedly "approached the Soviet ambassador to China and proposed Soviet cooperation in mining development and highway construction. . . . It is believed that the Soviets will request establishment of spheres of economic influence in China's three western provinces."

In May the same sources reported "two representatives of Sheng Shih-ts'ai" had visited Chungking "to discuss . . . the proposal by the Soviet representative in Sinkiang."[6] This purportedly referred to a program of Sino-Soviet "co-operation" in military, economic, and political developments, with concessions for Russia paralleling those ceded in the 1940 "Tin Mines" agreement. Discussions between Ambassador Panyushkin and Chiang Kai-shek were rumored in this Japanese dispatch.

Available Chinese sources throw no light on these rumors. Sheng admits, however, that one of his brothers, Sheng Shih-yi, visited Chungking prior to Sheng's change-over in 1942.[7] He may have figured in the foregoing negotiations. Their successful conclusion would have relieved Sheng of the dilemma of continued commitment to Chungking on the official level, contradicted by consistent accession to Soviet pressure behind the scenes. For Chiang, such a deal would have countered the Stalin-Matsuoka agreement. Stalin, in turn, would have welcomed a legal recognition of the Soviet sphere of influence in Sinkiang.

Whatever negotiations among representatives of Moscow, Urumchi, and Chungking may have been contemplated or actually in progress, their prospects of success disappeared when Nazi armies crossed the Russian border on June 22, 1941. This development provided reassurance on at least one count: Russia was unlikely to make a deal with Japan at the expense of China. The need for concessions in Sinkiang disappeared.

The next question confronting Urumchi as well as Chung-king was: what impact would the Nazi attack have upon Soviet power? The answer was immediately forthcoming. As Soviet forces reeled under the incessant onslaught of air and armored might, Moscow's resources became strained to the limit. In October the Soviet embassy informed Chungking that all shipments of military aid to China would cease.[8]

This discouraging news was almost immediately offset by the Japanese attack on Pearl Harbor, guaranteeing full United States participation in the Pacific war. For Chiang Kai-shek, these events completely altered the picture as it had existed at the time of the Stalin-Matsuoka pact. Russia could no longer threaten China with serious co-operation with Japan. Nor could Moscow supply any of Chungking's needs, at least in the immediate future. At the same time, Soviet commitment on the German front reduced Red pressure on Sinkiang, while American commitment against Japan permitted an increase of Nationalist pressure, not only in Sinkiang but against the Chinese Communists as well. Such were the calculations of Nationalist strategists, anticipating United States assistance. They also could be confident of Japan's ultimate defeat by American forces, regardless of future Chinese participation in the war.[9]

While 1941 ended with these promising developments for Chiang Kai-shek, the future appeared less hopeful for Sheng Shih-ts'ai. If Soviet support were to be drastically reduced, his regime might be plagued with fresh revolts or with increased Nationalist pressure or with both. Under these circumstances, only a *détente* with Chungking offered a promising alternative. That such a move involved long and careful negotiation is evident from the sequence of events in 1942. In March General Chu Shao-liang secretly visited Urumchi as Chiang Kai-shek's emissary.[10] In April Sheng stopped publication of the radical journal of his "Anti-Imperialism Society." As further proof of his intent, Sheng executed another purge, in the same month, arresting key figures in "progressive" and Chinese Communist groups. Among those imprisoned was Mao Tse-min, brother of Mao Tse-tung.[11] Yenan felt the blow, as a later CCP account recalled, "In 1942, when war between the Soviet Union and Germany was in a critical stage, bandit Sheng Shih-ts'ai openly bared his anti-Soviet and anti-communist mien . . . to throw many Soviet personnel and Chinese Communist Party personnel in Sinkiang into jail, involving over three hundred innocent and progressive people. In spring of the same year, he again made mass arrests of over one hundred Chinese Communists in Sinkiang, including Chen T'an-chiu, Mao Tse-min, and Lin Chi-lu."[12]

Sheng tells of this purge, but explains it in a wholly different fashion and indicates only one set of arrests, not two. However, his account corroborates that of the CCP, which noted that, although arrests took place in the spring of 1942, intensive interrogation by Nationalist authorities did not occur for six months. No executions came until "autumn 1943." Sheng's autobiography recounts Soviet protests on behalf of those still imprisoned many months after their arrest. In addition, Sheng claimed that Tu Chung-yüan's "initial confession" placed Wang Ching-Wei as the head of the conspiracy. However, in the final version, Tu "confessed" that Chou En-lai had been the mastermind of the plot.[13] The changed allegations, both extracted under coercion, indicate that Sheng saw fit to alter his account of the purge at a later date. In this regard, it is of interest that the official version of Sheng Shih-ch'i's death, attributing it to Communist assassination, was not made public until December, 1942.

Thus, the purge signaled an initial willingness to collaborate with Chungking. However, it did not commit Sheng irrevocably, should negotiations collapse. By accusing the purged of conspiracy with the Japanese puppet, Wang Ching-Wei, and by not executing those arrested, he left the way open for retreat. This alternative proved unnecessary. In May in a second visit by General Chu, accompanied by the Minister of Economics, Wong Wen-hao, the discussions were quietly continued. Finally, an official delegation arrived with much fanfare on July 4, headed by Chu and Wong, and including the Minister of Propaganda, Liang Han-ts'ao, General Ho Ping-wu, and General Mao Pang-ch'u, field commander of the Chinese Air Force.

Moscow was not prepared to relinquish its prize in Sinkiang without a contest. The day before this notable mission from Chungking flew to the provincial capital, the former Soviet ambassador to Germany and vice-commissar of foreign affairs, Dekanozov, presented Sheng with a proposal from Foreign Commissar Molotov.[14] It outlined a formal agreement for joint operation of the Tushantze oil fields, then operating under oral understanding without participation by Sinkiang authorities or direct profit to the province.

This offer of practical benefit for further co-operation with Moscow was accompanied by an unusual tone of blandishment in Dekanozov's opening remarks, contrasting sharply with the atmosphere surrounding the 1940 negotiations, as reported by Sheng. Moscow's emissary noted "the worsening relations between Sinkiang and Soviet Russia and the unpleasant relations between Marshal Stalin and your honorable self," but dismissed this as merely "misunderstanding." Sheng's memoirs offer a credible account of the subsequent exchange, during which a combination of cajolery and threat failed to move him from a position undoubtedly bolstered by knowledge of the forthcoming delegation from Chungking.

Sheng's new orientation was evident in his counterproposal

to Molotov on July 17, suggesting that Nationalist authorities be included in the discussions. By this time, conferences between Sheng and the July 4 delegation had undoubtedly worked out the details of agreement between the two sides. Final cementing of the *détente* came in the flight of Madame Chiang Kai-shek to Urumchi on August 29, 1942, accompanied by the Special Commissioner for Foreign Affairs, Chaucer H. Wu. China's first lady conveyed a personal letter to Sheng from the Generalissimo, not only offering forgiveness for past deeds but accepting full responsibility for their consequences.[15] This promised Sheng, in his future relations with the Nationalist government, protection against unpleasant repercussions of the past decade.

It should be remembered that this reconstruction of events is certain only with respect to chronology. The motivations of participants are inferred from fragmentary evidence and are not confirmed by firsthand sources. Either discreet silence or official explanation characterizes most discussions of these negotiations. Nevertheless, the foregoing interpretation appears plausible in terms of what is known of the persons involved, and of Sheng Shih-ts'ai in particular.

One mystery may never be fully clarified. The account offered in Sheng's memoirs of his brother's death is difficult to square with Sheng Shih-ch'i's acceptability to Soviet circles at the time. He had recently returned to Sinkiang from military training in Moscow, and had been named commander of the motorized brigade in Urumchi. Had Moscow conspired in his assassination, Molotov's proposal to Sheng for joint management of the Tushantze oil fields would have been doomed from the start. Yet it was conveyed on the highest authority as a serious effort to halt the *rapprochement* with Chungking. The only alternative explanation is that Sheng Shih-ch'i protested acceptance of Chungking's terms, or perhaps resisted the anti-

Communist purge. Given his position of military power, swift execution may have been his punishment.[16]

Thus ended almost a decade of Soviet influence in Sinkiang. Faced with political defeat, with Sheng firmly under the control of Chungking, Moscow moved to salvage its economic gains through negotiations with the Wai-chiao Pu. Commencing August 20, 1942, these discussions on the disputed oil concession dragged on for almost a year. Finally, talks collapsed. Both sides agreed on a cash settlement for that portion of the equipment which the Russians could not withdraw. On February 21, 1944, the final transfer of title and authority to the central government took place as Soviet engineers turned over the capped wells and empty buildings.[17]

The Russian position in these negotiations is of interest, evidencing continued efforts to maintain a privileged position in Sinkiang despite increasing Nationalist intransigence. In addition, the discussions merit attention in view of a later Sino-Soviet pact on joint oil exploration and exploitation in Sinkiang, concluded between the People's Republic of China and the Soviet Union in 1950. The full provisions were not announced by Peking or Moscow, but the 1950 accord was to have been valid for thirty years. In October, 1954, an unprecedented Soviet delegation to China, headed by Khrushchev and Bulganin, prematurely terminated the agreements transferring to China all Soviet shares in the "joint stock companies." However, the original terms imposed in 1950 remained secret. The earlier Russian proposals of 1942-43, therefore, provide a suggestive precedent to the later concession.

The major stumbling block arose over the sharing of control, the Soviet draft offering a fifty-fifty division of investment, maintenance costs, and production benefits, while the Chinese held firm for a majority share of fifty-one per cent. Paralleling this disagreement over ownership and output was an impasse over management. Moscow first suggested that the company be under a general manager and a chief engineer, both Soviet citizens, with a Chinese assistant manager. Chungking countered with a board of directors with a Chinese majority and Chinese chairman, supervising a Chinese general manager with a Soviet assistant. As a compromise, the Soviet assistant could have veto power over signed decisions. Although Moscow's final proposal represented both sides equally on a board with a rotating chairmanship, dropping the demand for a Soviet chief accountant, it insisted on retaining the general managership. Negotiations came to a stalemate on this point.

More than prestige was at stake. Past Soviet practice in joint management, as in the Chinese Eastern Railway and the Irano-Soviet Fisheries Company of the midtwenties, offered little promise of significant Chinese participation in the proposed concession. While providing for nominal equality, these earlier ventures indicated that Soviet attention to key positions, such as managing director, chief accountant, and chief engineer, sufficed to ensure a primacy of Russian power in actual operations. Provisions for rotation remained a dead letter. Alternatively, as with the Chinese Eastern Railway, meetings of the board of directors were called irregularly, if at all, to forestall action by a Chinese controlled body.

Nor was this the only point of difficulty. Other Soviet demands during 1942-43 consistently pressed to limit Chinese participation and to exclude any third-party participation in the future exploitation of Sinkiang's oil. Despite the company's presence on Chinese soil, all guards were to be Soviet troops. The company would operate its own roads, radio station, telegraph and telephone lines. Russian personnel was to enjoy full freedom of movement across the border and within Sinkiang. All activities connected with the concession were to be free of duties, taxes, and other restrictions liable under Chinese law. No nationals from a third nation could be employed, nor could non-Soviet equipment be purchased for the concession. Finally, China could not buy out the Soviet share for twenty-five years, at which time no foreign funds could be used for Chinese redemption. If China lacked the means or the will to purchase the Soviet shares, the pact automatically continued in five-year intervals until the purchase-option was exercised.

These terms were harsh to the Chinese, particularly sensitive to "unequal treaties" and "foreign concessions" after two decades of agitation against such agreements. With extraterritorial privileges renounced by Western governments only on January 11, 1943, and in view of Soviet demands for "equality for all nations" and "anti-imperialism," it is no wonder that heated exchanges occurred as Chinese negotiators challenged their Soviet counterparts to live up to avowed elements of Soviet foreign policy.

Typical was the argument over division of ownership and applicability of Chinese law. After repeated reference to "the principle of equality" from Soviet Ambassador Panyushkin, K. C. Wu pointed out that this might be applicable if both parties were operating in a third nation. However, under the circumstances, it could only mean that all activity in China was subject to Chinese law, just as all activity in the Soviet Union would be subject to Soviet law. "But there is no such joint operation in the Soviet Union at the present time, so you have no precedent, no comparison whatsoever," countered Panyushkin. Wu replied that if the Russian's remarks were to be taken at face value, Chungking might very well nationalize the oil concession, seizing Soviet assets, just as the Bolsheviks had done earlier in Russia.[18]

Basic to Panyushkin's approach was his constant assertion that the concession had been operating prior to negotiations because of an oral agreement with Sheng. This argument implicitly called on the past Russian power position to justify his demands. From across the table, the Chinese position rested primarily on legal grounds, appealing to the principle of territorial sovereignty. That both sides gave priority to political over economic interests is apparent in their willingness to forego immediate oil deliveries, rather than concede primary points of control and management.

During these prolonged negotiations, Sheng pressed repeatedly for evacuation of all Soviet personnel. However, he no longer figured prominently in the scales of power, as evidenced by Moscow's bland ignoring of his three-month ultimatum to withdraw. Instead, attention focused on negotiations between the Nationalist representatives and their Russian counterparts. Ambassador Fu Ping-hsiung and Special Commissioner Chaucer Wu flew to Moscow in January, 1943, to discuss the Soviet evacuation. On March 17 Ambassador Panyushkin notified Chungking that all personnel and equipment attached to the aircraft factory and the Tushantze petroleum refinery would be withdrawn.[19] On April 10 Consul General Pushkin informed Sheng that, in addition, the geological staff would be evacuated.[20]

The sticking point appears to have been the problem of the Soviet troops guarding these installations, together with the "Red Eighth Regiment" at Hami. Acting on instructions from Chungking, Sheng warned the Soviet commander in March that unless his forces were withdrawn immediately, they faced transfer to the Japanese front.[21] Surface justification for this threat lay in the disguised nature of these units as regular Chinese Army troops. One month later, coincident with his note on the geological team, Pushkin reported Moscow's agreement to evacuate all Russian forces, including those at the aircraft plant.

Troop movements began in June, but almost immediately ran

into difficulty. On June 16 Ambassador Panyushkin protested to Chungking over "hostility" on the part of Sheng, and threatened suspension of all Soviet activity, including that of the trade agency, Sovsintorg.[22] In view of the past decade of activity, Panyushkin's request for assistance from Chiang Kai-shek in disciplining Sheng struck an ironic note.

Yet the difficulty mounted as Nationalist guards attempted to take over fortifications prior to the departure of Red units.[23] While Chungking proposed that Wu examine the situation firsthand before accepting Panyushkin's complaint, it informed the Soviet official that his report did not jibe with that received from Sheng.[24] On his part, Sheng cabled on June 25, 1943, "Part of the soldiers and officers and heavy equipment of the Soviet Eighth Regiment have stopped at the Tushantze Petroleum Refinery and the Tihua [Urumchi] Aircraft Manufacturing Factory, en route of evacuation from Hami. . . . It may be a conspiracy, or they may simply want to delay evacuation to await a certain opportunity."[25]

Sheng's report identified approximately one thousand Soviet troops still in the province, divided almost equally among the three points of the oil fields, the aircraft factory, and Hami. In addition, several dozen Russian airplanes and more than one hundred and forty Soviet engineers remained with the Hami garrison. Sheng's inability to force matters through discussions with Pushkin, clearly reflected in his telegram, may have prompted him to paint the picture in more pessimistic tones than was necessary. Certainly, relations between Soviet and Nationalist authorities remained critical throughout the summer, with mutual recriminations and accusations being exchanged over the speed with which Russian personnel were being withdrawn.

As will be seen in the next chapter, Chinese sources were by no means unanimously agreed that their goal should be a total and perhaps precipitous removal of all Soviet activity from

Sinkiang, including that of Sovsintorg. Chungking's readiness to assume complete responsibility for the province's economic and military security, however, was evident in intent, even if its ability to do so remained questionable. This impatience, coupled with Sheng's real or inspired fears, may have accounted in part for the friction attending the Russian troop exodus.

In addition, Moscow was loathe to abandon all means of leverage, pending cash settlement for that part of its equipment which could not be shipped to Russia. Delaying tactics on one side, countered by pressure to advance from the other side, placed local commanders under considerable tension and mutual animosity. This approached gun point in September, 1943, almost a full year after the initial conversations between Sheng and Pushkin concerning evacuation.[26] Only added pressure from Chungking, coupled with elaborate safeguards to minimize misunderstanding and to settle disputes on the spot, enabled evacuation to be completed without further incident.

Yet all was not quiet. The atmosphere of conspiracy and intrigue, long a feature of Sinkiang's political life, produced one last period of tension in the annals of Soviet-Sheng relations. Once more, a purge threatened the Urumchi administration, as Sheng imprisoned provincial department leaders and submitted them to interrogation under torture.[27] His autobiography claims this nipped in the bud a Soviet plot involving more than two hundred officials throughout the province. More critical sources, however, insist Sheng misread the signs of growing American interest in Sino-Soviet co-operation as indicating Washington sympathy for a Moscow-Yenan ascendancy in Asia. These accounts attribute Sheng's purge to a last-minute effort to win back Soviet support by ousting Nationalist authority from Sinkiang.

Objectively, there is much to render this analysis plausible.

Certainly the purge hit those installed in office since 1942 when loyalty to Chungking, rather than to Yenan or Moscow, determined appointment and privilege. The arrests came at a time of rising tension between Chinese Communist and Nationalist forces, marked by pitched battles and continual extension of Communist power, despite intensified efforts by Chungking to blockade and to isolate the Red areas. Internationally, Soviet comment became increasingly critical of the Kuomintang and of the Nationalist war effort, following a key article by the *Tass* correspondent in China in August, 1943. Finally, Sheng's purge coincided with warfare along the Sinkiang-Mongol border. Kazakh activity there involved Chinese and Mongol forces in hostilities, for which each side blamed the other.[28] Russian assistance, pledged to defend the Mongol position in April, appeared with these other developments to presage growing Communist pressure against Chungking.

From the vantage point of Urumchi, it may have seemed wise to hedge the 1942 calculation that Soviet power would wane in Central Asia. Not only was a Russian victory against Germany almost certain, but Soviet entry into the war against Japan appeared likely. In addition, Moscow now appeared to enjoy the friendly support of Washington. In November, 1943, the historic Teheran Conference of Roosevelt, Stalin, and Churchill ended in an ebullient glow of unity. All but the most sophisticated observers hailed it as a turning point in Allied relations, symbolizing future harmony not only in military operations against the Axis but in postwar political reconstruction of the world order.

Nor was the United States so distant from Sinkiang as in times past. In 1942 the defeated Republican presidential candidate Wendell Willkie visited the province en route from Moscow to Chungking.[29] The following year saw the first American consulate in Urumchi inaugurated.[30] Meanwhile, in China proper, growing criticism of Chiang Kai-shek's government from unofficial American sources paralleled increased attention and favorable publicity for Yenan.

Given this external situation, whatever may have been Sheng's expectations, his purge failed to win outside support. Moscow ignored Sheng while Chungking moved to head off any reversal of the process inaugurated by the 1942 switch. A sudden appointment to the Ministry of Forestry and Agriculture quietly removed Sheng from Urumchi, without violating the pledge of security given him previously by Chiang Kai-shek. All arrested persons were released and charges dropped. Sheng left the scene much as he had entered it, amidst revolt and disquiet. Turmoil within the province did not end with his departure, but the close of Sheng's reign sealed the fate of a Soviet sphere of influence as it had operated in Sinkiang for almost a dozen years.

Notes

1. Sheng Shih-ts'ai, *Six Great Policies, op. cit.*, p. 58; this section was written November 20, 1939.
2. *Ibid.*, Vol. IV, Chapter 1, written June 15, 1940, as quoted in Wei Jung-t'ien, *Sheng Shih-ts'ai ju ho t'ung chih Sinkiang* (How Sheng Shih-ts'ai Ruled Sinkiang) (Shanghai, 1947), pp. 7-11. Mao Tse-tung's *On New Democracy* was published on January 19, 1940. Although Wei has a different edition of *Six Great Policies* from that examined by the author, his extensive page references and parallel citations indicate its authenticity.
3. Sheng Shih-ts'ai to Chiang Kai-shek, July 7, 1942, in *Soviet Economic Aggression, op. cit.*, p. 68.
4. The author examined the original of this letter in Sheng's personal archives in Taipei, Taiwan, May, 1954; it appeared to be genuine.

5. *Documents, op. cit.*, Vol. III, p. 1487, consul general in Shanghai, report of April 26, 1941. In an interview with the author in 1957, Dr. Sun could not recall any such move.

6. *Ibid.*, Vol. IX, consul general in Shanghai to Foreign Minister Matsuoka, May 27, 1941.

7. Sheng refers to this trip without additional information in his letter to Chiang of July 7, 1942, *op. cit.*, describing it as "some time ago."

8. North, *Moscow and Chinese Communists, op. cit.*, p. 188.

9. *IPR Hearings, op. cit.*, pp. 2354-55.

10. Henry Wei, *China and Soviet Russia* (Princeton: D. Van Nostrand, Inc., 1956), p. 157, quoting a dispatch by Theodore White in *Time*, October 25, 1943. Corroboration of this and other information in Wei's account was given the author by an American, well informed on events of this period through eyewitness contacts.

11. Anna Louise Strong interviewed three of the 129 Chinese Communist survivors who were later returned to Yenan under an agreement between the Nationalist Government and the Chinese Communist authorities. Among these were Mrs. Mao Tse-min, who told how her husband had been tortured to death in prison and of her bearing a child while incarcerated. Miss Strong's informants described Mao Tse-min as in charge of financial policy and national economy, crediting him with stabilization of currency and other reforms. They put the figure of prisoners held by Sheng as 50,000. Interview with Miss Strong and information in her personal files, January 30, 1958.

12. *Sinkiang Jih Pao*, June 3, 1953.

13. Interview with Sheng Shih-ts'ai, August, 1955. Sheng claimed that Tu Chung-yüan later took poison "out of fear of the Chinese Communists."

14. *Soviet Economic Aggression, op. cit.*, pp. 78 ff. Reference to the Soviet proposal was made in a reply by Sheng to Molotov on July 17, 1942, but no details were given.

15. Sheng Shih-ts'ai to Chiang Kai-shek, November 24, 1946, in

Soviet Economic Aggression, op. cit., p. 73. Sheng reminded Chiang of the 1942 pledges communicated in writing. The official endorsement of this book by the Ministry of Foreign Affairs lends credence to Sheng's allegations.

16. One of the earliest accounts of this incident came from Chinese Communist sources as related in *Foreign Relations of the United States, 1942: China* (hereafter cited as *U. S. Foreign Relations*), memorandum by the Second Secretary of Embassy in China, John P. Davies, to Mr. Lauchlin Currie, Administrative Assistant to President Roosevelt, August 6, 1942, pp. 227-28. According to information apparently communicated to Davies from associates of Chou En-lai, then in Chungking, Sheng's offer to place Sinkiang under Soviet control came from his concern over "recent attempts of the Central Government to extend its influence in Sinkiang." Molotov reputedly turned down the offer on grounds of "good relations with the National Government." Sheng's anger resulted in the discharge of "four Chinese Communists acting as provincial departmental chiefs" and he "executed his younger brother who was a Soviet sympathizer." Moscow allegedly countered by turning over to Chunking copies of the letter from Sheng to Stalin and of Molotov's reply.

It is true that Sheng made this offer and that, after his switch, Soviet authorities gave copies of the correspondence to Chungking. Although the author was unable to see these documents, evidence in *Soviet Economic Aggression, op. cit.*, verifies these facts. It is unlikely, however, that the timing occurred as suggested above. Except for this error, probably made intentionally, the account follows a plausible line of analysis. The accusation of Sheng's having executed his brother comes from Nationalist as well as Communist sources, all unofficial and all without documentation.

Washington first learned of the affair from the United States naval attaché in Chungking, incorrectly identifying the executed as Sheng's brother, Sheng Shih-yi, who had taken part in the Chungking negotiations; see *U. S. Foreign Relations, op. cit.*, p. 202, memorandum by Captain Roscoe E. Schuirmann of the

Office of the Chief of Naval Operations, July 10, 1942. On August 30 he repeated this error, attributing the story to H. H. Kung, *ibid.*, p. 233. Since the attaché calls his informant "King" and identifies Kansu province as "Kensu," the mistake appears to be one of language, but led to incorrect inferences in his dispatches.

17. *Soviet Economic Aggression, op. cit.*, pp. 121 ff.

18. *Ibid.*, pp. 115 ff.

19. Minutes of conversation between the Vice-Minister of Foreign Affairs, K. C. Wu, and Ambassador Panyushkin, July 15, 1943; copy from *Wai-chiao Pu archives, op. cit.*

20. *Soviet Economic Aggression*, pp. 76 ff.

21. Sun Fu-k'un, *O ti ch'in hua shih* (A History of Russian Imperialism in China), p. 78. This account draws heavily on *Wai-chiao Pu archives* and includes photostatic copies of original documents. Sun's version of the Sheng-Pushkin conversations, however, was disputed by Sheng Shih-ts'ai in an interview with the author, August, 1955.

22. *Ibid.*; K. C. Wu also refers to this visit of Ambassador Panyushkin to Chiang Kai-shek of June 6, 1943, in his conversation of July 15, *op. cit.*

23. *Ibid.*, pp. 80 ff.

24. Wu-Panyushkin conversation, July 15, 1943, *op. cit.*

25. Copy of telegram from Sheng Shih-ts'ai to Ministry of Foreign Affairs, June 25, 1943; *Wai-chiao Pu archives, op. cit.*

26. Sun Fu-k'un, *op. cit.*, Panyushkin to Chiang, September 6, 1943.

27. The author interviewed survivors of these interrogations in Hong Kong and Taiwan during 1954-55. For detailed eyewitness accounts, see Chang Chih-chih, *Sheng Shih-ts'ai tsen yang t'ung chih Sinkiang* (How Sheng Shih-ts'ai Controlled Sinkiang) (Taipei, 1954).

28. This incident will be discussed in more detail in the following chapter, since it is not directly connected with the events of 1942-44 or the Sheng phase of Sinkiang affairs.

29. Willkie commented on the death of Sheng's brother: "The legends

which pass as news in Asia have it that Russians were accused of complicity in his murder. I could not learn what truth there was in the stories. Probably there was none," Willkie, *One World, op. cit.,* p. 86.

30. Chungking's interest in drawing United States influence into Sinkiang will be examined in more detail in the next chapter.

6

Postscript: 1944-49

IT WOULD BE misleading to end this study of Soviet strategy in Sinkiang with the departure of Sheng Shih-ts'ai. Moscow's interest in the province did not stop forthwith. Five more years of turmoil provided fresh opportunity for the Russians to "fish in troubled waters."

Not until the People's Liberation Army, from the new Communist government in Peking, "pacified" the province in 1949-50 did Chinese control extend throughout the proclaimed limits of territorial sovereignty in this area.

Two factors set this postwar period apart, however, from the main focus of our study. The end of Sheng's rule left Soviet policy without an ally in Urumchi. No longer could a Chinese provincial government screen a Russian sphere of influence. Instead, Soviet strategists had to turn to dissident nationality groups, whose anti-Chinese grievances cast them as willing partners in the drive to weaken Nationalist authority. This did not exclude use of the military, political, and economic means so successful during Sheng's regime. It meant, however, that they had to be employed in a more covert manner.

Secondly, the events following Sheng's leavetaking challenge analysis because of the nature of source materials. To be sure, this problem plagues the study of the earlier period. But for the postwar years there are neither firsthand memoirs nor third-hand intelligence reports to throw light from another angle upon the complicated picture. Conjectures, while tentative, at least can provide a critical review of existing evidence to serve as basis for more intensive research.

As noted before, informed observers were by no means of one mind as to the desirability of ending all Soviet activity in Sinkiang. Wong Wen-hao, Minister of Economics, returned from a month's investigation in July, 1942, to report inflation much less rampant in Sinkiang than in China proper, reflecting favorably on Soviet fiscal advice.[1] He noted that ninety per cent of provincial exports went to Russia, described Soviet investments as extensive, and praised the Tushantze oil-drilling equipment as of excellent quality.

After meeting with Wong, the American Ambassador to China, Clarence E. Gauss, cabled a prescient analysis to Washington, recognizing China's right to exclude Russian influence but warning, "What will be [the] reaction of inhabitants, majority of whom are not Chinese but Turks and distrustful of Chinese, if [is] question for future. They would not unaided be able to resist Chinese, but given Russian support they might become a formidable obstacle to Chinese plans. They do not seem to have suffered from Russian influence of recent years, and it is far from certain that Russians are in fact prepared to accept designed consequences of Sheng's transference of allegiance, although they may find it necessary and politic in present circumstances to refrain from open opposition."[2]

These estimates pointed up the two critical problems confronting Chungking: Sinkiang's economic orientation and its anti-Chinese population. Chiang Kai-shek's plans for "Northwest development," announced in late 1942, pledged large sums of money to finance transfer of some 10,000 officials, together with their families, to bolster Sinkiang's administrative, educational, and technical affairs.[3] Ostensibly benevolent, this subsidized migration appeared to some as an attempt to strengthen

Chinese control as against the previous role of Uighur, Kazakh, Kirghiz, and other groups in Sheng's regime.

Reinforcement of these suspicions came after establishment of Kuomintang headquarters in Urumchi, in January, 1943. Chinese soon replaced local officials in political and cultural positions of influence. An artificial exchange rate favored merchants from China proper, who shipped native produce out of the province at high profit. The influx of troops and civilians loaded new tax burdens upon the local populace, reminiscent of conditions which ultimately had toppled Chin Shu-jen. Cessation of Russian trade and withdrawal of Soviet advisers prompted a Chungking official to describe developments as a "considerable political success for the Central Government, [but] it will result in almost insolvable economic problems."[4] In November came reports that Special Commissioner of Foreign Affairs in Sinkiang, Chaucer Wu, had appealed in vain to the Soviet consul for reopening of commercial activity in the area.[5]

Russian recognition that potentially explosive economic and racial tensions might work to Moscow's advantage was revealed by a Soviet representative in Lanchow, in August, 1943. "Chinese policies [in Sinkiang], unless radically changed, will alienate rather than win the people. In any event, Sinkiang cannot avoid having closer economic ties with Russia than with China."[6] He dwelt at length on Moslem aspirations, opposed to alleged "Sinification" by Chungking, observing that this conflict could not be resolved satisfactorily except by greater recognition of Moslem participation in local government. His comments provided substance to Ambassador Gauss's warning that Soviet withdrawal might be merely a temporary expedient, to be reversed at the earliest opportunity. In fact, Soviet geologists and engineers frankly warned Chinese observers upon their departure, "We'll be back in two years!"[7]

Nationalist fears of this development appear to have prompted Chungking to seek United States involvement in Sinkiang. A high Wai-chiao Pu official first broached the possibility of American interest to Ambassador Gauss in September, 1942.[8] Gauss promptly pointed out the existing Soviet monopoly of oil exploitation rights, touching on an issue already critical in Sino-Soviet negotiations concerning the Tushantze fields. While these negotiations were in progress, Washington's representative to the Chinese Stabilization Board undertook an extensive survey of the province in the fall of 1942.[9] Although noting the extremely primitive transportation facilities, he placed output of crude oil at 150 tons per day, "with fair gasoline yield limited by equipment shortage."

This American report praised Sheng's "centralized administration under capable directors . . . evident inter-racial harmony . . . effective use of Soviet technicians and advisers in industry, agriculture, animal husbandry, and the professions." However, promising financial and capital investment developments were now "handicapped by stoppage of customary imports from Soviet [Union] of goods now needed in Soviet war effort."

Further indication of Chungking's interest in drawing Washington into the area came with a Chinese invitation to establish a United States consulate in Urumchi.[10] Remarking that none of his staff had ever suggested this to Nationalist officials, Gauss took it as a sign of Chungking's desire to offset Russian consular activity in Sinkiang. Already under confidential consideration in Washington, the proposal was promptly acted upon with O. Edmund Clubb, second secretary of the embassy in Chungking, detailed to Lanchow in February, 1943, thence to Urumchi on April 19, 1943.[11]

Yet American interest in Sinkiang did not signify willingness to invest capital or to extend credit for solution of the province's economic ills. It was precisely these problems of economic stability and development which, coupled with political mal-administration, provided tensions for exploitation by Russian strategists. Unrest soon led to open revolt in the winter of 1943-44. A Kazakh freebooter, named Usman, inflamed local antago-nism already aroused by Urumchi's efforts to establish adminis-trative controls over a group known for its fiercely independent nature. With his headquarters in the mountainous borderland between Outer Mongolia and Sinkiang, Usman's forces carried on running battles with Nationalist troops in December, 1943, and again in March, 1944.[12]

The affair took on international ramifications when Special Commissioner Wu cabled the Wai-chiao Pu on March 11 and 19 of Soviet aircraft and Mongolian troops acting in conjunction with the Kazakh rebels.[13] Although Wu reported mainly re-connaissance flights, sporadic strafing and intensive bombing on March 14 alarmed him sufficiently to prompt a request "for military representatives, airplanes, and reinforcements." It is difficult to confirm Wu's dispatches. Similarity of Russian and Outer Mongolian insignia may have misled observers. Soviet military commitment on the German front, and continued political need to maintain surface unity among the Allies, make unlikely Moscow's participation in a border fray. Nevertheless, Wu's local protests to Pushkin were matched by Chungking's strongly worded notes. Both were met by a Soviet "flat rejec-tion" of all charges, claiming them a "deliberate disruption" of relations.[14] While disturbances ceased, leaving Usman in con-trol of the disputed area, *Tass* announced from Moscow on April 3, 1944, "China has moved troops along the Outer Mongolian border. Soviet Russia, on the basis of its mutual assistance pact with Outer Mongolia, is obliged to render assistance."[15]

The incident, insignificant in its immediate consequences, highlighted the insecurity of Chinese rule in Sinkiang. The provincial garrison was clearly unable to pacify the vast area of mountain and desert, lacking good lines of communication and populated by hostile peoples of considerable warring ability. Furthermore, uncertainty of border demarcation opened the door to misunderstanding, if not to deliberate provocation, among Chinese, Russian, and Outer Mongolian patrols. A 1940 Soviet map presented the Mongolian-Sinkiang border much further west than did Russian maps of 1927, thereby giving Outer Mongolia an additional 83,000 square miles of land.[16]

Finally, a growing atmosphere of mutual suspicion and re-crimination marked relations between Chungking and Moscow, as World War II drew to a climax. Jockeying for power coincided with prospective Russian entry into the war against Japan. Old antagonisms combined with new tensions to produce an explosive mixture in Sinkiang. Given this volatile situation, it is difficult to assess accusations by both sides, much less fix responsibility for the clashes which followed. That animosity on both sides impeded peaceful settlement, however, is certain.

American attitudes provided an added dimension at this time, as Chungking tried to win support for its position in Sinkiang, with increasingly frequent exchanges with Washington concerning Soviet actions and intentions. After learning the Chinese position from Chiang Kai-shek, coupled with requests for advice, President Franklin Roosevelt replied on April 8, 1944, urging that "recent incidents be placed on ice" pending the end of the greater problem, World War II.[17]

Logical as was Washington's position, events soon proved its inapplicability. As spring passed into summer, Urumchi reported spreading discontent erupting into armed revolt, concentrated in the areas of Sinkiang adjacent to Soviet Russia.[18] Whether this unrest received Soviet support remains a moot question. Certainly there was indigenous unrest to be exploited by outside parties. Economic chaos worsened as inflation accompanied Nationalist currency changes and supplies of commodities shrank with the disappearance of Soviet trade. Political tension heightened as Sheng followed his purge and switch of 1942 with new arrests, anticipating his abortive attempt to swing back into the Soviet orbit in 1944. The ensuing breakdown of administration coincided with a complete abandonment of the rigid police controls by his successor, Wu Chung-hsin, who dismantled the elaborate apparatus of spies and informers which had served to check potential centers of rebellion and opposition to Urumchi. The outbreak of violence occurred principally in the Kazakh areas, where the traditional fighters on horseback spearheaded movements protesting political and economic conditions, unopposed by the former stringent police controls of Sheng's regime.

Thus, the situation resembled that recurring throughout Sinkiang's tumultuous history. When local tensions reached the breaking-point, outside parties used the opportunity to advance their own interests. Accumulating pressures, evident in the minor outbreaks of 1943-44, finally exploded into a major revolt on November 7, 1944. Referred to in Chinese accounts as the "Ining Affair" because of its center at Kuldja (Ining), this uprising followed a hiatus in Urumchi, with Sheng departing in August, and his successor, Wu Chung-hsin, not arriving until early October. Wu's regime offered no improvement over the last uncertain years of his predecessor. What may have originated as an anti-Sheng movement in the summer now fanned out into an anti-Chinese revolt, uniting Uighur, Kazakh, and Kirghiz against both the provincial and the central governments.

On November 8, 1944, the Special Commissioner for Foreign Affairs, Wu, cabled Chungking, "According to a telegram from Ili, on the morning of November 7, approximately 500 naturalized White Russians began a revolt in Ining with machine guns and grenades. They attacked provincial offices and the police offices. When our airplane flew to Ining for recon- naissance, machine guns in the Soviet consulate opened fire."[19] Wu's plea for reinforcements was met by two Nationalist regiments, but the 3,000 troops proved unable to quell the uprising, which spread throughout the area during the winter months.

Firm evidence on the relationship between the rebels and Soviet strategy is lacking. However, circumstantial proof of Russian direction and assistance merits consideration of Chinese charges. In contrast with previous incidents, local in character and of short duration, the Kuldja uprising was well co-ordinated and tenacious. Captured Chinese weapons stocked the rebel arsenal. Many of these guns originally had come from the Soviet Union, however, principally in deliveries to Sheng's forces. Their capture by the rebels enabled the use of ammuni- tion provided by Russian consulates inside the insurgents' area.[20]

Men as well as material support appear to have been pro- vided by the Soviet Union. Reserves for rebel forces were readily obtainable from ethnically akin groups across the border. The migratory nature of Kazakh herdsmen made it al- most impossible to identify them conclusively as legal citizens of either country. Participants in the revolt later testified that key leaders, as well as many followers, crossed from Russian territory during the winter of 1944-45.

Soviet sponsorship was further suggested in the co-ordination of rebel activity in the three districts housing Soviet consulates. That the insurgents would welcome such direction, both locally and from across the border, is understandable, given the paucity of command experience coupled with Sheng's purges of local leadership during the previous decade. Thus, their seeking out of Soviet aid followed a well-established precedent, notably observed by Sheng Shih-ts'ai. With the existing tensions between Moscow and Chungking, Russian acquiescence to rebel requests may have been delayed until the full promise of the uprising could be realized in late 1944, at which time Soviet aid became of critical importance.

While the Russian role in the early course of the rebellion must be inferred from evidence offered by biased sources, there is little doubt of Moscow's part in terminating the uprising prematurely. During the summer of 1945, legions of the self-proclaimed "Eastern Turkistan Republic"—which boasted its own flag, currency, and administration—pushed steadily toward Urumchi. In a major battle near Wusu in early September, they smashed the new Nationalist Second Army with combined air, cavalry, and infantry assaults, capturing a divisional commander and several thousand prisoners.[21]

At this critical juncture Soviet "good offices" mediated the dispute between rebel and Nationalist representatives through the agency of the Soviet consulate in Urumchi. This saved the capital from siege and possible capture. The fact of rebel acquiescence on the threshold of victory suggests Russian leverage, in line with the foregoing analysis of probable Soviet sponsorship from the start of the revolt.

Both the details of this mediation and the larger international context are relevant in assessing the weight of Soviet influence. Taking the local scene first, on September 7, the Wai-chiao Pu officially protested to Ambassador Panyushkin over the alleged presence of Soviet aircraft among rebel forces. On September 13 General Chang Chih-chung, commanding Nationalist forces, warned the Soviet consul in Urumchi that unless a cease-fire were effected immediately, China would make an international affair of the matter. The next day the Russian representative left the city, apparently contacting rebel headquarters. Within forty-eight hours Moscow informed Chungking of a request for "mediation" from the insurgents.

Nor did this end the role of the Soviet consulate in Urumchi. Throughout the subsequent months of negotiations, proceedings frequently stalled while the rebels demanded time to consider Chungking's proposals. Chinese observers interpreted these delays as necessitated by consultation between Soviet authorities in Urumchi and Moscow. Visible evidence of the Russian interest came at the climax of negotiations. After the Chinese side had signed the agreed terms, the Soviet consul whispered a last-minute objection to the rebel representative, who withdrew immediately without explanation. Only after another month did they finally agree to the conditions.[22]

The international context of these developments found Sinkiang occupying a minor place in the agenda of continuing discussions among American, Russian, and Chinese negotiators during the hectic months preceding the Sino-Soviet treaty, of August, 1945, and Russian entry into the war against Japan the same month. In April of that year, Ambassador Patrick Hurley conferred with Molotov in Moscow, mentioning the "Ining Affair" among other items, and interpreting Soviet policy in a way to which Molotov subscribed, "The Soviet Union is intensely interested in what is happening in Sinkiang and other places and will insist that the Chinese Government prevent discrimination against Soviet nationals."[23] This interpretation implicitly absolved Moscow of all responsibility for the revolt. Furthermore, it offered a pretext for future intervention under the guise of protecting "Soviet nationals," a group defying precise identification given the fluid state of the border peoples.

That Hurley's sanguine analysis was not shared by other American analysts is clear from a telegram of April 23, 1945, from George Kennan, chargé d'affaires in Moscow, to Averell Harriman in Washington, noting *inter alia,* "I am persuaded that in the future Soviet policy respecting China will continue what it has been in the recent past: a fluid resilient policy directed at the achievement of maximum power with minimum responsibility . . . the exertion of pressure in various areas in direct proportion to their strategic importance and their proximity to the Soviet frontier . . . domination of the provinces of China in Central Asia contiguous to the Soviet frontier."[24]

In May, Harry Hopkins, acting on a special request from newly inaugurated President Harry S. Truman, flew to Moscow. There, in a series of talks with Stalin, he tried to iron out differences of increasing severity plaguing Allied relations. Among them was China. Stalin "stated categorically that he had no territorial claims against China and mentioned specifically Manchuria and Sinkiang."[25] Chiang Kai-shek subsequently sought to nail down this assurance in writing through the forthcoming Sino-Soviet treaty, instructing his representative, T. V. Soong, "In the past years uprisings in Sinkiang have interrupted Sino-Soviet communications and prevented the maintenance of trade. We fervently hope that Soviet Russia can act in accordance with its previous pledge and assist in eliminating this uprising."[26] Chiang sounded a parallel warning with reference to the Usman imbroglio, "The Altai mountains belong basically to Sinkiang and should remain part of Sinkiang."

The Sino-Soviet agreements of August 14, 1945, contained both explicit assurances on Sinkiang and implicit guarantees covered in general provisions. An exchange of notes accompanying the treaty included a statement by Molotov, "As for the recent developments in Sinkiang, the Soviet Government confirms that, as stated in Article V of the Treaty of Friendship and Alliance, it has no intention of interfering in the internal affairs of China." Article V, in turn, pledged the signatories to "act according to the principles of mutual respect for their sovereignty and territorial integrity and of non-interference in the internal affairs of the other contracting party."

This was the international context providing the background for Soviet mediation in the fall of 1945. Stalin's willingness to compromise the apparent victory of the rebels came easily in view of the greater gains won at Yalta and in the Sino-Soviet pact, extending Russian influence in Manchuria, Sakhalin, and the Kuril Islands. These outweighed in strategic importance potential returns from further penetration in Sinkiang. Such penetration ran the risk of incurring American resistance, suggested in Washington's growing attention to the area and its inclusion in Soviet-American discussions. As an alternative, temporary conciliation with Chungking might provide an opportunity to stabilize already acquired gains, in Sinkiang as well as in the Northeast. The cease-fire provided a suitable counterpart to negotiations between Chiang Kai-shek and Mao Tse-tung in Chungking, which eased strained relations during September and early October. The atmosphere of seeming harmony was reflected in Ambassador Hurley's dispatch from Chungking prior to his departure of September 22, "The negotiators have agreed that they will collaborate for the establishment of a democratic government in China, for the reconstruction of China and the prevention of civil war."[27]

A practical incentive for Moscow to accept the rebel holdings as of September, 1945, lay in the fact that the "Eastern Turkistan Republic" comprised that portion of Sinkiang containing the richest mineral resources. In particular, the final attack of the insurgents carried them well beyond the Tushantze oil fields, thereby excluding this valuable area from Nationalist control. In addition to oil, the region's deposits of wolfram and tungsten, identified in considerable amounts by Soviet geological surveys taken during Sheng Shih-ts'ai's regime, make it difficult to believe a Russian statement to an American correspondent, "If we came in here, we would not get much."[28]

The final accord signed in Urumchi on June 6, 1946, offered ample opportunity for re-establishing a Soviet sphere of influence in the three strategic districts of Ili, Tacheng, and Altai.[29] Nationalist influence was completely excluded, sealing the area from outside inspection. Key provisions granted the rebels the right to elect all local officials and to maintain twelve thousand troops. Although half of this force was to be equipped by the central government, the commanding officer was to be locally appointed and no units could leave the insurgent area without local permission. In addition, the provincial government was to be reorganized with fifteen of the twenty-five commissioners to be chosen from Sinkiang residents, including six from the Ili-Tacheng-Altai districts. Specific posts alloted to the rebels' representatives included the vice-chairman of the provincial government and prominent positions in education, reconstruction, and welfare departments. Recognition of legitimate nationality grievances included provisions guaranteeing the use of Moslem ceremonies and texts, official adoption of the Uighur and Kazakh languages, and freedom of press, assembly, and speech. Chinese was not to be required until middle school. All police units were to be locally staffed and directed.

It seems clear that the uprising grew from spontaneous outbursts of local resentment against central authority into a Soviet-assisted revolt. It was not a homogeneous fusion of like-minded groups, but a hasty coalition joining diverse elements for a limited common goal. Within the rebel ranks, rivalry between Uighur and Kazakh was matched by tensions between nationality leaders and their Soviet advisers. Chinese observers sensed the latter friction during armistice negotiations, where rebel leaders evidenced greater willingness to arrive at terms than did their Russian advisers.

Given the extreme resentment against any outside rule manifested by some of the groups involved, as well as the opportunis-
tic nature of past actions by many native figures, it is no
surprise that defections and schisms soon appeared. Ali Khan
Türe, leader of the insurrection movement in the mountains,
disappeared in 1946, reportedly in opposition to Russian advisers.[30] Usman, still heading Kazakhs along the Mongolian-
Sinkiang border, split off in 1947, ostensibly in protest against
Soviet demands for extensive exploitation of the Altai gold
mines. His defection led to local fighting, once more involving
Chinese and Outer Mongolian units, in the so-called "Peitashan
Affair."

These schims posed an obstacle to Soviet control. They indicated that the "Eastern Turkistan Republic" was more than a
tool of Russian strategy, as charged by Nationalist circles.
Neither at the time of the revolt nor in later accounts were the
leaders identified as Communists. Although Chinese writers
singled out Akhmedjan Kasimov as one of several key figures
allegedly holding Russian citizenship, they discovered no connection between the rebels and the Chinese Communists. Later
Communist accounts about Sinkiang asserted, "No local Party
members of minority nationalities were found before liberation."[31] That the wellspring of the revolt was anti-Chinese
hostility rather than pro-Communist sympathy was revealed by
local writers after the collapse of Nationalist rule in 1949,
"When our people joined the armed struggle, overthrowing the
Kuomintang reactionary rule in Ili and other areas and ex-
terminating the Kuomintang armed forces, we considered the
entire Han race and the Kuomintang reactionary clique as one
... considering the entire Han race as our enemy."[32]

This anti-Chinese or "anti-Han" sentiment which provided
the main link between the rebels and their Russian patrons
stood Moscow in good stead, as Kuomintang circles differed on
the degree of compromise to show local groups in Sinkiang. As

long as the Nationalist government pursued an ambivalent, and at times hostile, policy toward non-Chinese, Soviet strategy could remain confident of finding ready supporters. This apparent identity of interests makes it particularly difficult to distinguish moves by the rebel leaders from those which may have been Soviet directed. The problem is further complicated by a striking instance of coincidence in timing of local developments in Sinkiang with international Russian strategy in 1947. Coincidence does not prove cause, but it compels consideration at this point.

It was 1947 which saw Communist and non-Communist groups in coalition governments of France and Italy drift apart, marked by increasingly hostile positions assumed by left-wing leaders. Finally, the Communists left both regimes in the late spring.[33] At the same time, the Greek civil war worsened. British inability to cope with the situation there prompted Washington to enunciate the Truman Doctrine, pledging military and economic assistance to both Greece and Turkey. In June came the outline of the celebrated "Marshall Plan" for European recovery, followed by an announcement of the Cominform, in September, 1947, amidst militant declarations by Soviet spokesmen, of the "two camp" division splitting the world. Regimes in Poland, Hungary, and in February, 1948, Czechoslovakia, moved sharply leftward, ousting non-Communists. The "cold war" began in earnest, in 1947, on the surface, at least, instigated by Communist activity. While local situations in each case provided surface justification for increased Communist hostility, the over-all pattern suggested a co-ordinated plan directed from Moscow.

So, too, in 1947, Sinkiang's political tensions burst asunder the coalition which had ruled in Urumchi since the armistice agreement of the previous year. Almost simultaneously, fighting exploded the truce which had prevailed along the Mongolian border for almost two years. As in Europe, these developments found ample cause in the local situation to preclude the necessity of explaining them in terms of Soviet strategy. With mounting problems created by the civil war in China proper, extremists among Nationalist circles advocated indiscriminate repression of legitimate complaints. Maladministration in Sinkiang, violations of the armistice terms, and coercion against local groups provided grounds for complaint.[34] Yet the timing of moves in almost precise parallel with steps taken elsewhere raises the possibility that agitation for action came from Soviet advisers, linking the Sinkiang scene with the world front of Russian policy.

Employing tactics similar to those used by French and Italian Communists prior to their break with moderate parties, Akhmedjan launched a bitter attack against General Chang Chih-chung's rule, in February, 1947.[35] Attributing increasing violence and unrest to Nationalist agitation against non-Chinese, he called for further revision of the provincial government. All executive powers were demanded for non-Chinese groups, except for matters concerning defense. He hastened to assure Nanking that "the expression 'Eastern Turkistan' does not mean that we advocate an independent Eastern Turkistan." However, his position paralleled the stand taken by Soviet spokesmen in 1924 on behalf of Outer Mongolian "autonomy," autonomy which proved identical with independence from China in all but legal title.[36]

General Chang, after touring the rebel areas, replied to Akhmedjan in May. Insisting that Sinkiang's immediate needs were more economic than political, he charged that intentional disruption of the peace stemmed from efforts to seize power, noting, "The violent disputes prevalent everywhere were created by the minority of people who attempted to rise to power through political intrigue. The majority of the masses do not wish these disputes, so much that even in the matter of elections to which they are entitled they show hardly any interest."[37] In view of Chang's high reputation for fairness and moderation among diverse political groups, his words commanded wide attention. Nevertheless trouble continued.

Masud Sabri, a wealthy Uighur in the KMT Central Executive Committee since 1935, succeeded Chang as provincial chairman in May. Although not Chinese, Sabri stood too close to Chungking for local groups, and protests anticipated his arrival. After his inauguration, a majority of the provincial assembly voiced opposition in a formal resolution.[38] Tension continued to mount amid mutual accusations of armistice violations. Provincial authorities discriminated against Moslems in appointments and police protection, while militant Nationalists provoked armed clashes with non-Chinese. On their part, the Kuldja insurgents maintained a steady drum-fire of demands and charges directed at Sabri's rule.[39]

Finally, in July, 1947, the coalition split wide open. Three successive withdrawals emptied the provincial assembly of members sympathetic to or affiliated with the Kuldja group. An exchange of letters between Akhmedjan and General Chang, acting in support of Sabri, found the protagonists irreconcilably apart on the question of political control. While Kuldja held out for removal of Sabri, Chang replied, "If you have no intentions against the peace, you will return to Urumchi and reopen negotiations with the government."[40] Protesting the inability of provincial and central government authorities and orders to penetrate the Ili area, Chang refused to capitulate to further demands. He warned, "The Sinkiang problem today is, psychologically, a question of supporting or renouncing the mother country."[41]

Coincident with these political developments, military action broke out along the disputed border between Sinkiang and Outer Mongolia in June. The "Peitashan Affair," as it is known in Chinese reports, resembled earlier such incidents in the lack of substantive evidence affixing responsibility and the confusion surrounding inadequately defined borders. As in 1944, Chinese accounts graphically described attacks by Outer Mongolian cavalry assisted by Soviet aircraft. This time, however, Usman claimed to be the attacked, rather than the attacker, for he had since broken with the insurgents and now represented National-ist interests in the area.

Soviet authorities insistently denied responsibility for the clash, asserting the territory lay within Mongolian sovereignty and charging Chinese troops with initiating the attack.[42] Inter-mittent fighting continued throughout June, ending with a Nationalist withdrawal from the area. Subsequent exchanges of notes between Nanking and Moscow failed to settle the conflicting claims for damages, and the situation remained tense in early 1948.

Disagreement among disinterested observers is so sharp as to suggest that both sides bore responsibility for the fray. As before, it is possible that Outer Mongolian aircraft were mis-takenly identified as Russian. At the same time, neither the Soviet Union nor Outer Mongolia appears to have sought peace-ful settlement of the dispute. Initial protests came from China, as did demands for compensation. In view of the political situa-tion elsewhere in Sinkiang, Russian handling of the "Peitashan Affair" seems to be part of a larger, consistent design to main-tain maximum pressure without, however, openly breaking with Nanking.

During 1948 the political deadlock kept Sinkiang divided. Although the rebels hauled down the green star-and-crescent flag and offered to abandon reference to the "Eastern Turkistan Republic," they insisted that Chang replace Sabri. Portraying their struggle as one of "liberation," with the familiar comparison to colonial peoples, an Ili editor commented, "Let us take a look at one of the British colonies, not necessarily a big one like India or South Africa, but a small one such as Ceylon."[43] Suggesting thereby the applicability of political independence while maintaining economic relations with China, he continued, "It is no longer possible to fool the oppressed and downtrodden people by empty words and pretty titles. Our present stand is that a people's liberty and rights must be left to the care of the people themselves."

These gestures of compromise were dismissed by knowledgeable Chinese as mere surface phenomena. Sensitive to the anti-Han origins of the revolt, one writer remarked in the reputable *Ta Kung Pao,* "Insofar as this means nothing more than foresaking a few popular slogans and changing their outward attitude, it definitely does not mean that they have any affection for the Chinese in Sinkiang. The most we can expect is that in the case of 'another revolution,' the Chinese, instead of being slaughtered at random, will in all probability be liquidated in a more orderly and civilized manner."[44]

While keeping a hand in the Ili area, Moscow did not cut the tie to Nanking. Even as Chinese Communist forces swept crumbling Nationalist defenses before them in 1949, Stalin continued to seek long-term commitments for economic privilege which would assure Russian interests against any change in Sinkiang or China proper. His chances were helped by continued willingness in Nationalist circles to negotiate, in the hope of driving a wedge between Russia and the Chinese Communists. As events turned out, this hope was not entirely without foundation.

General Chang Chih-chung, by now well versed in Soviet negotiating techniques, opened discussions in Sinkiang in January, 1949, concerning regulation of trade and economic activity. Not until May was the Sino-Soviet air line agreement renewed for five years, assuring the Russians virtual control over the Alma-Ata-Urumchi-Hami route. Previous experience had proved this would permit little Chinese participation, with no board meetings having been called for years at a time.[45]

Other Soviet proposals won no agreement, however. Among the concessions which Chang refused to grant was one similar to that forced on Sheng Shih-ts'ai in 1940, whereby Russia was to enjoy virtual control of Sinkiang's mineral resources for fifty years.[46] Paralleling the demands made to Sheng and Chungking during negotiations in 1942-43, general managers of the proposed companies were to be Soviet citizens. In addition, the Soviet Union was to enjoy full import-export freedom, although no reciprocal benefit was offered China. These terms proved too extreme. Negotiations collapsed, abandoned in the swift-moving action of civil war during the summer of 1949.

One last move marked Moscow's attempt to maintain advanced positions in Sinkiang at this time. As Chinese Communist forces marched into near-by Kansu province, the Soviet consul general in Urumchi approached Nationalist General T'ao Shih-yueh. According to a reliable source, the Russian proposed that T'ao declare Sinkiang independent, on the precedent of Outer Mongolia.[47] Following victory by the Reds, Sinkiang could be incorporated into a federal republic. "If you will do this, we will order the Chinese Communists not to continue their advance into Sinkiang." The only condition allegedly attached was removal of a regimental commander hostile to Soviet influence.

This account claims that T'ao, unwilling to capitulate and unable to evacuate, referred the proposal to high Nationalist circles in Canton for deliberation. Although some cabinet members felt acceptance of the Soviet offer might increase subsequent tensions between Russian and Chinese Communists, the majority decided in favor of a rear-guard action in retreat from Sinkiang. T'ao apparently refused to risk his men in this hazardous enterprise involving travel through difficult terrain, where food was in short supply. Those who wished to flee to Taiwan were given the opportunity. The remainder stayed with T'ao, surrendering peacefully to advancing Red units in the fall of 1949.

This information is difficult to corroborate, given the secretiveness of the negotiations. However, it appears consistent with the course of Soviet policy in Sinkiang since 1934. Stalin had kept Ma Chung-ying in reserve against Sheng Shih-ts'ai. Later, he had vetoed Sheng's admission into the CCP and limited Yenan's role in the province. During the Ili uprising, the Russians supported the rebels up to a point, then prevented their winning total victory by "mediating" with the Nationalists. This background of divide and rule, and of seeking insurance against future developments, makes credible the somewhat fantastic picture of Soviet representatives dickering with a Nationalist general facing defeat at the hands of advancing Chinese Communist armies in 1949. With the failure of this gambit, the last Soviet move in Sinkiang to ensure Russian, as opposed to Chinese, influence signaled an end to an era. From this point on, Soviet strategy would have to contend with the fact of Chinese control, exerted by a strong central government, no less sensitive than its predecessor to outside interference in its defined area of territorial sovereignty. In this sense, Chinese Communist ascendancy marked an end to the role of Sinkiang as a pawn of Asia.

Notes

1. *U.S. Foreign Relations, op. cit.*, pp. 229-30, Ambassador Gauss to Secretary of State Hull, August 19, 1942, reporting a communication from the Minister of Economics, Wong Wen-hao, to John Carter Vincent in the Chungking Embassy, based on Wong's visit to Urumchi from July 4 to early August.

2. *Ibid.*, p. 231.

3. *Ibid.*, p. 260, Gauss to Hull, December 11, 1942. The head of the Western European Department of the Chinese Foreign Office admitted in a conversation "that the problem of housing the new arrivals would be considerable."

4. *I.P.R. Hearings, op. cit.*, p. 2384; the official is not identified in this report. However, an informed Foreign Service officer identified Wong Wen-hao and Tsiang Ting-fu, the latter ex-ambassador to Russia and then Director of the Department of Political Affairs in the Executive Yuan, as representing "a more moderate or liberal point of view regarding Chinese Communists and Russia than is to be found generally among leading military and Kuomintang officials," *U.S. Foreign Relations, op. cit.*, p. 240, memorandum by counselor of embassy, John Carter Vincent, to ambassador in China, September 9, 1942.

5. *I.P.R. Hearings, op. cit.*, p. 2384.

6. *Ibid.*

7. Dr. William Su-Ting corroborated this information based on conversations with Soviet geologists at the tungsten mines. Similar comments were made to other persons interviewed in Hong Kong.

8. *U.S. Foreign Relations, op. cit.*, p. 243, memorandum by Gauss of conversation with the Chinese Political Vice-Minister for Foreign Affairs, Fu Ping-shiung, September 28, 1942.

9. *Ibid.*, pp. 617-18, Gauss to Hull, December 3, 1942, reporting a trip to Urumchi and environs by Solomon Adler, U.S. representative to the Chinese Stabilization Board.

10. *Ibid.*, p. 693, Gauss to Hull, October 31, 1942. The invitation was communicated orally by the Director of the American Department of the Chinese Foreign Office, "Inasmuch as the Northwest is becoming increasingly important on account of the prospective development of communication, perhaps the American Government may find it practicable to have a consular officer stationed at Tihua [Urumchi] for the duration of the war. If so, it would be agreeable to the Chinese Government."

11. *Ibid.*, p. 695, footnote 5; for earlier consideration of this move see *ibid.*, pp. 687-93, memorandum by Everett F. Drumright of the Division of Far Eastern Affairs, October 26, 1942.

12. *Our Enemy, op. cit.*, Vol. II, pp. 235-36.

13. Copies of telegrams of March 11 and March 19, 1944, from Chaucer Wu to the Ministry of Foreign Affairs; provided by the Ministry of Foreign Affairs, August, 1955. The aircraft reportedly had "a red star, and green and white symbols" and included "five P-5, six bombers, and one fighter." Wu cabled, "The Russian aircraft attack is obviously a plot to press Sheng to surrender, or he will be driven out by Russian-supported Kazakhs. The situation is very critical."

14. *Our Enemy, op. cit.*, quoting text of note delivered March 14, 1944.

15. *Ibid.*, p. 36; also cited in *The New York Times*, April 3, 1944.

16. *I.P.R. Hearings, op. cit.*, p. 2385; the maps were examined by an anonymous American observer in northwest China.

17. Feis, *The China Tangle, op. cit.*, p. 138.

18. The author interviewed Chinese observers resident in Sinkiang during 1943-44. Their accounts differed as to the degree of Soviet instigation attributed to the uprisings, but agreed on the growing unrest resulting from political and economic dislocation in Urumchi.

19. Copy of telegram from Special Commissioner Wu to Ministry of Foreign Affairs of November 8, 1944; from *Wai-chiao Pu archives, op. cit.*

20. This particular fact was established by Chinese sources after

the uprising. Reliable persons no longer affiliated with the Nationalist regime have testified to the validity of this evidence.

21. *Our Enemy, op. cit.*, pp. 254 ff. Eyewitness accounts corroborate this information. The following section is based largely on this publication.

22. Confidential interview with a member of the negotiating team, August, 1955.

23. Paraphrase of report by Ambassador Hurley to Secretary of State, April 17, 1954; as contained in statement of W. Averell Harriman in *Military Situation in the Far East, Hearings Before the Committee on Armed Services and the Committee on Foreign Relations, United States Senate, 82d Congress, 1st Session, to Conduct an Inquiry into the Military Situation in the Far East and the Facts Surrounding the Relief of Douglas MacArthur from his Assignments in that Area* (Washington, D.C.: Armed Services Committee, Senate, 1951), Part 5, p. 3335. Stalin remarked that only five per cent of Sinkiang's population was Chinese, and he blamed Chungking's unwillingness to respond to nationality demands for difficulties; Feis, *The China Tangle, op. cit.*, p. 318 n.

24. *U.S. Relations with China* (Washington, D.C.: Department of State, 1949), p. 97.

25. Robert E. Sherwood, *Roosevelt and Hopkins* (New York: Harper and Brothers, 1948), p. 903.

26. Chiang Kai-shek to T. V. Soong, undated cable quoted in Chiang Chun-chang, "Reflections on T. V. Soong's Moscow Discussion" (in Chinese), *Chung Kuo I Chou,* No. 100, March 24, 1952, pp. 14-16. This article was authoritatively written on the basis of official archives in Taiwan. Reference in the cable to a "previous pledge" by the Soviet Union with respect to Sinkiang is unclear.

27. *U.S. Relations with China*, p. 105.

28. Soviet Consul General Bikmurzhin in Kashgar to Frank Robertson in the summer of 1947; from an unpublished manuscript by Mr. Robertson.

29. The full text of the initial agreement of January 2, 1946, and the supplementary protocols of June 6, 1946, are given in Sun Fu-k'un, *Su lien lüeh tao Sinkiang chi shih, op. cit.,* Vol. II, pp. 10 ff. These two protocols may be what were widely reported as "two secret agreements," see David Dallin, *Soviet Russia and the Far East* (New Haven: Yale University Press, 1949), p. 366, n. 16, and Max Beloff, *Soviet Policy in the Far East, 1944-1951* (London: Oxford University Press, 1953), p. 98.

30. Notes in file of Henry R. Lieberman, based on a trip to Sinkiang as correspondent for *The New York Times* in 1948.

31. *Kuang Ming Jih Pao,* September 21, 1956.

32. *Sinkiang Pao An Hsin Wen,* November 18, 1949, reprinted in *Hsin Hüa Yueh Pao,* Vol. I, No. 4, pp. 883-85. This article dwelt on "Several Mistakes in Our Nationality Problem" and specifically attacked the attitudes cited as "narrow nationalism . . . our inability to distinguish friend from foe."

33. For a convenient summary of this period see Hugh Seton-Watson, *From Lenin to Malenkov* (New York: Praeger, 1953), pp. 291 ff.

34. Lattimore, *Pivot of Asia, op. cit.,* pp. 92-98, summarizes this period on the basis of contemporary sources including the principal newspaper of the autonomous region.

35. *Ibid.,* p. 94, quoting from *Sinkiang Gazeti,* Uighur edition, Urumchi, February 19, 1947.

36. The Commissar of Foreign Affairs, Chicherin, described the "autonomy" of Outer Mongolia, as "sufficiently wide to preclude any interference in the internal affairs of Mongolia on the part of China and to permit independence in its foreign policy," *Pravda,* March 6, 1925, p. 5.

37. Chang Chih-chung, speech of May 13, 1947, as quoted in *Ta Kung Pao,* Shanghai, August 25-30, 1947, translation in Lieberman files, *op. cit.*

38. Lattimore, *op. cit.,* p. 97.

39. *Ibid.,* pp. 97-98; most of these reports are drawn from the insurgent press.

40. General Chang Chih-chung to Akhmedjan, September, 1947, as quoted in Lattimore, *op. cit.*, p. 98, from a dispatch in *Time*, October 6, 1947.

41. Chang to Akhmedjan, December 10, 1947, quoted in *Ho Ping Jih Pao*, Shanghai, January 21, 1948, in Lieberman files, *op. cit.*

42. For a detailed account of the battles from the Nationalist viewpoint, including lengthy excerpts from diplomatic exchanges, see *Our Enemy, op. cit.*, Vol. II, pp. 246 ff.

43. *Chien Chin Pao*, Ili, undated but quoted in *Ta Kung Pao*, January 8, 1949, translation in Lieberman files, *op. cit.*

44. Lin Yen, "Recent Developments in Ining" (in Chinese), in *Ta Kung Pao*, January 8, 1949.

45. A summary of the Chang mission may be found in Lattimore, *op. cit.*, pp. 101-102; information on the earlier operation of the air line comes from the Lieberman file, *op. cit.*

46. *Soviet Economic Aggression, op. cit.*, pp. 142 ff.

47. Interview with a firsthand source in 1955.

7

In Retrospect

THE CONFUSION of events in Sinkiang from 1933 to 1949 screens the strategy underlying Soviet policy. Moscow did not move by fits and starts, however. It inherited certain responsibilities and behavior patterns from the policy of St. Petersburg. In addition, new policy features emerged from the aftermath of revolution. The resultant construct of ends and means, dimly perceptible through the haze of turmoil and intrigue in Sinkiang, bears sufficient consistency to permit evaluation of policy in terms of success or failure. In this way, the relevance of Sinkiang to other areas on the periphery of Russia may be analyzed so far as Soviet startegy is concerned.

Stated in the broadest terms, the twin goals of security and power motivated Soviet policy in Sinkiang, as elsewhere. Similar at first glance, these goals differ in characteristics. The first, security, is essentially defensive in nature, acting to protect Soviet interests at home against perceived threats from abroad. In Sinkiang, this meant halting Japanese encroachment, already successful in Manchuria and north China. Accomplishment of this defensive end involved offensive means, penetrating Chinese territory. Yet this does not obscure the fact that the goal of security faced an objective threat—Japan—magnified by the subjective emphasis of the Marxist-Leninist framework. Ample evidence in the Tokyo archives testifies to the desire, if not the ability, of Japanese imperialism to penetrate Inner Asia, seeking ultimate domination of Russian as well as of Chinese territory. Insofar as Soviet policy in Sinkiang checked this desire, it was a success.

The second goal, power, may be more explicitly defined as the extension of Soviet influence abroad for specific economic and political gain. Unlike the first goal, security, this was essentially offensive in nature, pressing into vulnerable areas on the Soviet periphery at the expense of neighboring regimes. Its presence as a motivating factor is demonstrated by the continuation of Soviet machinations in Sinkiang long after removal of the perceived Japanese threat. Chinese power was insufficient even to pacify the province, much less to challenge Soviet security. The exploitation of resources, the purging of those who would resist a Russian sphere of influence in China, and the arming of rebellious groups so as to exclude Chungking's authority, all supported a goal of extending Soviet power, not of maintaining Soviet security.

Moscow's policy proved less successful in pursuit of this second goal. The balance of power distributed among contending Russian, Chinese, and indigenous forces fluctuated greatly during this period. Soviet gains of 1934 to 1940 disappeared after the German attack weakened Russian pressure on the province. American entry into the Pacific war enabled Chinese counterpressure to increase. The return of Russian influence in 1944 was limited territorially by this increase in Chinese power, backed indirectly by the United States. Even this limited victory proved short-lived for Moscow, when Peking's new Communist legions won control of the entire province in 1949-50. To be sure, Sinkiang's Red rulers furthered the Soviet goal of security, assuring friendly forces along the extensive frontier. However, Mao Tse-tung was not disposed to tolerate unlimited Russian influence without definite benefits to China, and subsequently pressed for complete elimination of that influence from Sinkiang.

In appraising policy, the attendant battery of military, economic, ideological, and political means must be examined. Some proved more adaptable than others to the changing power relationships within Sinkiang. Some paralleled those employed by the czarist government, while others were made possible by the Bolshevik revolution. Whatever the means, none was limited in application to Sinkiang. Their impact merits attention insofar as similar situations elsewhere may suggest success or failure for parallel lines of action.

As in the nineteenth century, Russian troops entered Sinkiang during domestic insurrections in 1934 and 1937, suppressing revolts which the central government of China appeared incapable of handling. In both of these later instances, entry came at the invitation of duly appointed provincial authorities, albeit without approval from the central government. In neither case did Soviet military intervention lead to annexation of territory, as with czarist occupation of the Ili River Valley. Nevertheless, military action served Russian as well as Chinese interests. Used in conjunction with other means, armed force supported individuals and groups whose orientation promised to further Moscow's goals, and to suppress those who appeared to oppose these goals.

A counterpart to military support was economic assistance in the form of loans which served to tie the weak provincial economy to Soviet interests. While such loans bolstered Sinkiang's treasury, plagued by limited revenue and too distant for help from the central government, they also committed local produce in exports to Russia as payment. This furthered Moscow's economic grip, already strong through traditional trade ascendancy along the Russian border. Special pricing and a privileged position awarded by provincial regulations extended Soviet trade superiority throughout the province, leading to a position approaching monopolistic power. These economic tactics made the provincial government literally indebted to Moscow, while providing practical benefits for Russia in commercial and mining activity.

A third avenue of policy, ideological penetration, differed from military and economic means in that it was not present during czarist times. Like the first two courses of action, however, it, too, entered Sinkiang on the initiative of local authorities. For Sheng Shih-ts'ai, a crude compound of anti-imperialism and anti-capitalism, offered under the rubric of Marxism-Leninism, sufficed to equip him with ideological pretensions fitting his visions of political leadership. In addition, the Soviet Union's proclaimed nationality policy, however it might have varied in practice, suggested an immediate answer to the needs of Sinkiang's heterogeneous population. At the same time, it was not so extreme in its pledges as to embarrass Sheng's personal rule or to prevent his displaying nominal allegiance to the Republic of China. While a far cry from the highly articulated communism of Yenan or Moscow, Sheng's doctrine paralleled Russian propaganda sufficiently so as to provide a favorable atmosphere for extending Soviet influence in Sinkiang.

Finally, political means followed up ideological penetration to transform the province into something short of a full-fledged satellite, acting in response to Moscow's policies, but remaining legally within Chungking's jurisdiction. Ideological penetration entered Sinkiang principally through non-Soviet individuals who were influenced by events in Russia proper. In contrast, political controls were manipulated by Soviet agents acting within Sinkiang itself. Thus, in the former case, Sheng's espousal of Marxism required no action on the part of Moscow, although it was strengthened by material aid from Russia. However, it was Soviet advisers who directed indoctrination and education within the province, and who exercised police power and purge, so as to further Russian goals of policy. By enrolling Sheng in the Russian Communist Party, by surrounding him with Chinese Communists, and by limiting access to the area of all foreign influences, Moscow created a regime almost completely responsive to its dictates.

With the end of Sheng's subservience in 1942, Soviet strategy perforce shifted its target of attention, while still employing similar means toward identical ends. A combination of military and economic assistance, ideological influence, and political penetration fused the simmering revolts of 1944 into the phoenix-like "Eastern Turkistan Republic." Spawned from legitimate grievances, the rebel regime served Russian interests throughout its short life. An added tactic, absent during the Sheng period, was the employment of Soviet citizens both as leaders and as reserves for the revolt, facilitated by their ethnic ties to native groups in Sinkiang. First successful in Outer Mongolia in 1921, this strategem of using non-Russian subjects of the Soviet Union to further unrest in areas bordering the Soviet Union has found widespread application in Moscow's policy.

A contemporary parallel to this strategy of subversion in Sinkiang during 1944-49 occurred in December, 1945, with the creation of the "Autonomous Republic of Azerbaijan" in the Soviet-occupied section of Iran.[1] Simultaneously, the Kurds of northern Iran rebelled, demanding "autonomy." During World War II, Red troops, together with British and American forces, had moved into Iran to prevent German influence from controlling the country and to facilitate Lend-Lease shipments to the Russian front. Immediately after the war, local unrest in the northern section adjoining the Soviet Union sparked a revolt against Teheran, just as the Kuldja rebels had raised the flag against Chungking one year earlier.

The Azerbaijan affair differed from that in Sinkiang in that

Soviet troops were present, and they remained after March, 1946, in violation of the agreed time of withdrawal covering all occupation forces. Their presence blocked entry of Iranian units seeking to quell the revolt. This overt application of military means aroused strong American protests, both in diplomatic notes to Moscow and in public debates in the Security Council of the United Nations.[2] Subsequent withdrawal of the Red Army relieved international tensions, while Iranian authorities, with the collapse of the rebellion, quickly restored local order.

Several features of the Azerbaijan affair offer comparison with the Sinkiang revolt. Both uprisings occurred in areas adjacent to Russia, possessing oil reserves of interest to the war-ravaged Soviet Union. Both found a ready source of covert support from ethnically related groups residing across the Soviet border. Both began after the turning point of World War II had assured victory over Germany. Final settlement of the two disputes came separately, but within two weeks of one another. Initial armistice terms, signed by the Kuldja group on January 2, 1946, were not implemented until supplementary articles were agreed to on June 6. Only eight days later, a ten-point pact between the Azerbaijani rebels and Iranian leaders ended hostilities on June 14, 1946.

Only in their outcome did the two revolts differ substantially. The Kuldja insurgents won complete control of their territory, excluding all interference from central government authority. In contrast, the Azerbaijanis agreed to admit Iranian troops to the rebel area, thereby sealing whatever hope they may have had for genuine autonomy from the final pact.

The motivation behind Soviet withdrawal from northern Iran is difficult to establish because of the coincidence of events. In Moscow, Soviet negotiators won agreement from Iranian representatives to exclusive oil concessions in the insurgent area. This clearly was forthcoming only under duress. Red troop withdrawal may have been the *quid pro quo*.[3] This strategy failed, however, when, following Red evacuation, the Majlis in Teheran refused to ratify the treaty.

At the same time, United States pressure, both secret and public, challenged the continued presence of Russian troops in violation of wartime agreements. American accounts argue that it was this pressure, particularly that exerted through the United Nations, which ultimately forced Soviet withdrawal prior to Majlis action on the oil concessions. Whether one or both of these inducements, bribery on the one hand and threat on the other, prompted abandonment of the rebels, Soviet strategy suffered a definite setback in this instance.

The significant variable distinguishing the Azerbaijan failure from the Kuldja success lies in the means employed by Moscow. In Iran the open use of military force identified the rebellion as Soviet supported. It prompted American reaction which successfully attacked the symbol of foreign troops in an independent country so as to focus international attention on the incident. In contrast, the Kuldja affair relied mainly on carefully concealed military support, with primary emphasis given to ideological and political means. Here, the only opposition came from a weakened Chinese government, confronted with more immediate problems posed by Communist forces in Manchuria and North China, as well as by a collapsing economy. Publicly, at least, Washington ignored the affair.

Military means as such, then, would appear to enjoy limited success in Russian peripheral ventures. Indeed, their infrequent employment by Soviet strategists suggests that these limitations are recognized in Moscow. It is true that Red forces remained in Outer Mongolia from 1921 to 1925, establishing a satellite regime in the process. Yet the situation was exceptional. The remoteness of the area from world attention and its marginal interest for a China torn by civil war permitted use of military means with relative impunity.

Sinkiang offers surface similarities, as with the intervention of Russian troops in 1934 to strengthen a friendly regime against forces believed supported by Japan. With victory, however, came evacuation of Soviet units. The pattern varied slightly in 1937, when a small part of the Russian forces remained in the province. In this case, their presence soon received implicit, if not explicit, sanction from Chungking, as Sino-Soviet collaboration bolstered China against Japan. Nor did these troops resist when the Nationalists took over the province in 1942. Their size and their passivity makes it unlikely that Moscow relied upon the Red units as a cardinal means of ensuring the Soviet sphere of influence in Sinkiang.

This pattern indicates a secondary role for military means. Far more important is the major part played by ideological and political means, in Sinkiang as in other similar regions. Here the critical element is the voluntary alignment of persons and groups in areas bordering Russia with the outlook of Moscow, at least as verbally professed by Soviet propagandists. Owen Lattimore, in *Nationalism and Revolution in Mongolia*, describes the characteristics of a satellite, ". . . The regime in the satellite country does not merely accept, but actively wants the satellite relationship. . . . Its aim is to develop the satellite state under policies that will eventually make it homogeneous in social composition, economic characteristics, and political institutions with the state in whose orbit it moves. It regards the fulfillment of such policies as a desirable process of catching up."[4]

This analysis applies to Sinkiang, no less than to Mongolia. Sheng Shih-ts'ai's affiliation with Soviet policy was marked by his predilection for Marxism and by his genuine admiration for the Bolshevik experiment. Similarly, the Kuldja rebels found at least initial compatibility with Russian advisers, whose professed attitudes toward non-Russian peoples stood in sharp contrast to the dominant position assumed by Chungking's representatives. Had it not been for this seeking out of Soviet economic and military aid by groups predisposed to certain aspects of Bolshevik ideology, the subsequent use of political controls through both propaganda and police activity would not have been so successful for Soviet strategy.

Later descriptions of the Sheng Shih-ts'ai period, by non-Communist and Communist writers alike, throw favorable light upon his policies, while criticizing his ruthless means and his switch of loyalties. Thus, a refugee from the Ili area, formerly a titled leader of considerable wealth, remarked to the author, "It is true that those of our people who lived in Russia suffered from collectivization. It is also true that many of my subjects were killed by Sheng Shih-ts'ai and by the Chinese Communists after him. Yet is this entirely bad? I remember as a child how my father's household was the only one which could read. The rest of our people lived in darkness and ignorance. Then Soviet help and Sheng's rule enabled them to read. Now they can hope to improve their way of life. Can we deny our people progress for the sake of the few who die?" In spite of his loss of wealth and of status, this native leader in exile continued to admire much of the Soviet-Sheng regime.

These comments stand in contrast to his criticism of Soviet foreign policy, especially of its willingness to sacrifice temporary allies to Russian interests. The refugee recalled how a Soviet consular official had offered him a prominent position in the "Eastern Turkistan Republic." The native leader refused, not out of opposition to the goals of the rebels but through practical concern for his personal safety. As he later explained, "When the Russians pulled out and Sheng Shih-ts'ai swung over to the Nationalists, all those persons who were pro-Soviet or pro-Communists were killed or imprisoned. I had no assurance Russia might not once again reverse its policy. I could not afford to take the consequences." He correctly foresaw that Soviet sponsorship of the "Republic" would fail to protect its leaders from a subsequent purge by the Chinese Communists, taking over the area in 1950. The fate of the Azerbaijani rebels underscores this vulnerable aspect of Soviet strategy, which faces increased suspicion among target groups the more crassly it sacrifices their interests for Russian goals.

Nevertheless, even in exile this person recalled favorably the radical policies of Moscow and Urumchi, while criticizing harsh measures entailed in their implementation. Evaluation of Sheng Shih-ts'ai's policies, as distinct from those of his Soviet mentors, is admittedly difficult. So far as motivation is concerned, at least three different analyses appear in non-Communist writings on this period. At one extreme, bitter critics charged Sheng with opportunism and egotism, claiming he identified himself with Stalin's power merely to enhance his own prestige. They accused him of abandoning this line solely to escape retribution, with impending Soviet defeat in World War II. Finally, they explained his actions of 1944 as an ill-disguised attempt to move back into Stalin's graces.

More charitable accounts excused Sheng because he had saved Sinkiang from both domestic insurrection and Soviet annexation. While criticizing the level of Soviet control tolerated by his regime, they saw this as a case of bad judgment, rather than being motivated by either opportunism or traitorous conviction. By stressing Sheng's apparent safeguarding of Chinese sovereignty during a decade of turbulence, these writers attributed Machiavellian skill and foresight to his policies.

Finally, Sheng offers his own explanation of his actions. Its primary difference from official Nationalist accounts is in suggesting his ideological conviction of the progressive nature of Soviet policy. He portrays this conviction as weakening under the impact of Stalin's tactics, mainfested particularly by the 1940 "Tin Mines" concession. Sheng attributes his final break with Moscow to an alleged Soviet plot against the regime which resulted in the assassination of his brother in March, 1942.

Still another variant is that offered by Chinese Communist sources, uniformly describing Sheng's rule as one which began well but which ended badly. As one Peking analysis explained, "In 1932, armed uprising broke out all over the province and succeeded in winning a temporary victory. Under the mighty pressure of the people, Sheng Shih-ts'ai could not but stimulate progress and make a certain type of progressive change. From 1934 to 1940 social and cultural reconstruction effected some progress, but after 1940, the situation changed completely. Sheng Shih-ts'ai was basically a reactionary element, and at this time he openly went over to the Kuomintang reactionary clique."[5]

These four interpretations all suffer from political bias and personal distortion, and may be juxtaposed with those offered by contemporary observers of the Sinkiang scene. One such perspective comes from a former Nationalist official, long intimate with the province and present in Urumchi during the critical days of 1933. Now in exile, he holds no brief for either Russian or Chinese Communist policy, yet his activities of the time closely paralleled Sheng's strategy.

Arriving in Urumchi on a confidential mission from Nanking, he immediately conferred with Sheng, with whom he had been on good terms previously. Then he secretly met the Soviet consul, Apresoff, also a former acquaintance, proposing a scheme whereby Russian help against Ma Chung-ying could be paid for by Sinkiang exports. As he later recalled to the author his conversation with Apresoff, "Sinkiang is part of China, but it is too far away for the central government to help. While either Soviet Russia or Great Britain could take it at will, each refrains because of the other. Restoration of legitimate rule over the Ma rebels should serve Soviet interests, since it will keep Sinkiang part of China without any aggressive threat to Russia. Sinkiang can be developed economically, giving the Soviet Union raw materials and markets, since the people there need Soviet goods. Ma's victory would mean the exclusion of Soviet Russia to the advantage of Great Britain. Furthermore, a Moslem state in Sinkiang would force the Soviet Union to station troops from Turkey to Novosibirsk. In addition, you would lose Sinkiang's resources and markets."

Specifically, this Nationalist official then proposed, "Loan us three million rubles in exchange for native products of Sinkiang and we can use it to buy planes and ammunition. Russian aircraft can bomb the rebels while Sheng Shih-ts'ai fights out from the capital." Apresoff apparently confirmed this arrangement with Sheng. Immediate deliveries of Soviet aircraft and ammunition, coupled with fresh reserves of Russian troops, helped to lift Ma's siege of Urumchi.

This source recalls warning Sheng, "From now on you are Chinese and have a Chinese office. Watch out for the Soviet Union—you cannot rely on it. There must be a limit to the Soviet role. Its influence must not dominate Sinkiang." According to this person, Sheng might have abided by such advice except for his justified suspicions of hostility in Nanking and his consequent reliance upon Soviet support. Whether this last point is valid or not, it is interesting to note the parallel policy recommended by a person esteemed in Nationalist circles many years after Sheng took the fateful step of 1934.

A similar firsthand estimate, again from a Chinese acceptable both to Nanking and Urumchi at the time, notes, "Sheng did not always show wisdom in his decisions, but at least he faced his problems boldly and never took refuge in shallow optimism. He was a realist, and his approach to Russia was made only when careful examination of his position had convinced him that this was the only chance. While he knew that Soviet aid could be purchased only for a definite price—the virtual monopoly of Sinkiang trade—the alternative was to see the whole province given over to disorder. He may well have thought that a central government which can offer no aid to a hard-pressed frontier province cannot claim to dictate what policy shall be followed by the 'man on the spot.' Sheng was 'on the spot' both in the normal and in the American sense of that phrase, and he had to act quickly or perish."[6] Corroboration for this analysis comes from a British diplomat as well, visiting Sheng two years later, "Regarding the situation quite objectively, it is difficult to see what other line Nanking or Sheng could have adopted at the time. Both were the victims of capricious circumstance and the great distances separating Turkistan from China; while the Soviets, with all the resources and implements of modern warfare, were close at hand."[7]

These estimates concur in explaining the origins of Sheng's policies. They compel discounting later analyses which attempt to explain the entire period of his rule as a coherent entity, carried out with plan and consistency from start to finish. The inception of Sheng's reliance upon Soviet aid may be termed *Realpolitik,* Machiavellian, or opportunism, depending upon the connotation desired.

However, these contemporary estimates imply that he was riding a tiger from which, as the Chinese proverb puts it, one dismounts with difficulty. One must ask: did Sheng wish to dismount? His acceptance of Soviet good intentions would seem to follow from his early reading of Kautsky and Lenin, mani-fested in his first seeking membership in the Chinese Communist Party and his subsequent enrollment in the Russian party. Not only did Sheng's pronunciamentos of the time strike a consistent note, but his later writings in Taiwan, especially his autobiography, reveal sufficient residue of his Soviet orientation to give credence to his assertions of having had "a sincere belief in Marxism."

If this ideological appraisal is correct, Sheng's policy goals appear to have been threefold. First, he aimed, as did Soviet strategists, at security both for his personal rule and for the province as a whole. Perceiving different threats simultaneously from Tokyo and Nanking, all working through local opposition groups, he sought Soviet support as a necessary alternative to defeat. Secondly, he endeavored to enhance his personal power through economic and political gain, especially evident in his later years of rule. A driving ambition coupled with symptoms of paranoia here led him to extreme measures of cruelty and deceit, for which he is attacked by Nationalist and Communist alike.

Yet such critics often overlook his third goal, identifiable within his ideological framework. Sheng genuinely aspired to make Sinkiang a model province, which might ultimately serve as a symbol for spreading the Soviet system in China. This is not the place to examine in detail the material benefits accruing from Sheng's regime, much less to weigh them against the negative consequences of purge and autocracy. Suffice it to say that most firsthand accounts, whether friendly or hostile, agree as to the construction of schools, medical facilities, and roads, as well as to improved fiscal and enlightened cultural policies effected during his rule. To deny this third goal is to overlook a major aspect of his policy, one which stood well in comparison with subsequent Nationalist management of the province.

In terms of these criteria, Sheng Shih-ts'ai succeeded in at least two of his goals, security and power, and made signal strides toward the third, the welfare of Sinkiang. The concatenation of events in 1941 placed all three goals in jeopardy, however. Here he appears to have given first priority to personal security. His last two years in Urumchi provided an anticlimactic postscript, with the power and decision-making resting with Chungking.

Many of Sheng's means in support of policy find precedent in the regimes of Yang Tseng-hsin and Chin Shu-jen. The role of terror and reliance upon Russia did not begin with the events of April, 1933. Furthermore, his independence of the central government and his use of local military force place him in the line of traditional war lords, present throughout China during the first half of the twentieth century and especially evident in the remote provinces of the northwest. If any single aspect distinguishes Sheng from his predecessors, it is his systematic espousal of an ideology providing a framework for policy, borrowed predominantly from the Bolshevik revolution. In this sense, he is China's "Red war lord" par excellence.

Still a third party played a role, albeit a minor one, on the Sinkiang scene: the government of Chiang Kai-shek. Final evaluation of its policies must await the availability of more adequate source materials than those accessible for this study. In view of the attention given to Soviet strategy in Sinkiang, however, by postwar Nationalist writers, a preliminary examination of the fragmentary evidence related to central government policy is warranted.

Official analyses of policy generally require discounting, for the universal tendency of governments is to explain their actions in the most favorable light. This is particularly true, in the study under review because of a traditional, and perhaps

commendable, Chinese practice of discreetly skirting embar-
rassing situations which involve persons still active on the scene.
Thus, Sheng Shih-ts'ai's *coup d'état* of 1933 won official approval, despite the failure of Nanking's emissary, Huang
Mu-sung, to unseat him. Nor did later accounts of his rule
unveil the details surrounding his change-over in 1942. Even
more curious, not until defeat on the mainland and rupture of
relations with Moscow, did the Nationalist government issue
an authoritative White Paper on Soviet machinations in Sinkiang.

Undoubtedly, some concealment proved expedient in terms
of existing international forces. As long as Japan posed the
greater threat, Soviet depredations went ignored if they did
not come to public attention. Chinese officials steadfastly denied
Tokyo's inquiries and accusations concerning Russian influence
in Sinkiang. Similarly, Chiang Kai-shek seized the opportunity
in 1942 to extend his rule to Urumchi. However, he acted so
as to offer no open embarrassment to Russia, still a powerful
neighbor in Asia. Stalin might use that power to support Chungking or Yenan, thereby awarding victory in the postwar
struggle for China. Chiang therefore may have walked a careful
path in the hope of winning Soviet support, even if it required
weakening the line to Washington and sacrificing desired positions in the borderlands of Sinkiang, Mongolia, and Manchuria.

Firsthand evidence bearing on this period is fragmentary,
but a cursory review of negotiations in 1944-45 suggests plausi-
bility for this analysis. In discussions with Vice-President
Henry Wallace in 1944, for instance, Chiang Kai-shek displayed
marked vacillation toward Russia, ranging from strong accusations of bad faith to optimistic proposals for coming to terms
with Moscow.[8] Similarly, Chiang's instructions to T. V. Soong
during negotiations leading to the Sino-Soviet pact of 1945
showed willingness to go beyond American interpretations of

the Yalta provisions, both with regard to concessions in Manchuria and to granting Outer Mongolia complete independence.[9] This compromising position, protested by Washington's representatives at the time, appears to have sprung from an attempt to persuade Stalin to refrain from supporting the Chinese Communists and to render full assistance to the central government.

Stalin's assurances, coupled with Soviet mediation in Sinkiang, may have spurred hopes in this direction. Chinese negotiators accompanying General Chang Chih-chung in the prolonged armistice talks in Urumchi steered clear of American representatives in order to avoid arousing Soviet suspicions.[10] Finally, they accepted terms which foreclosed any possibility of asserting Chinese authority in the rebel districts, yet they made no public protest against Soviet connivance in the revolt. In contrast with Iran, China did not appeal to the United Nations nor did Washington force the issue with Moscow.

A parallel situation in Manchuria may offer a clue as to the pattern of policy. In late 1945 Russian occupation forces refused to facilitate Nationalist entry into the area, while offering no barrier to Chinese Communist guerrillas fanning out from bases in North China. Negotiations with the Red Army commander, Malinovsky, proved futile. Despite clear evidence of Soviet obstructionism, Chungking's representative, Chiang Ching-kuo, elder son of the Generalissimo, opposed informing American correspondents of Russian bad faith and of Soviet looting in Manchuria.[11] Purportedly, he sought, in agreement with high Nationalist circles, to avoid ruffling Soviet sensitivities, in the hope of arriving at an ultimate agreement.

As a final effort to reach direct settlement with Stalin, Chiang Ching-kuo made a dramatic but abortive flight to Moscow in December. Unaccompanied by any Chinese officials, his trip remained secret for some time. Later accounts describe it in a contradictory fashion. Chiang Kai-shek's memoirs, *Soviet Rus-sia in China,* asserts that during two weeks of conferences, Stalin tried in vain to win an exclusive sphere of influence in Manchuria and to woo China to "an independent policy, lean-ing neither to one side nor to the other."[12] A different version, given the author by an informed Nationalist official, asserts that Ching-kuo's trip represented a last-minute effort to head off anticipated support for Yenan, by offering extensive con-cessions in Manchuria and loosening of the tie with Washington. According to this source, Stalin rebuffed the move, preferring to remain free for any future eventuality.

Whatever the details, the over-all pattern of policy suggests that, contrary to Nationalist assertions, this period was not one of unremitting struggle against Soviet encroachments. Instead, it was a time of pragmatic search for a compromise solution which might restrain Soviet backing of the rival Chinese Communists. In such a situation, Sinkiang was expendable, as was Outer Mongolia. The Urumchi truce talks of 1945-46 appear compatible with Chungking's strategy, tacitly granting a Russian sphere in the rebel areas, in return for which Moscow might implement its pledge in the Sino-Soviet treaty not to intervene in the domestic situation of China. Failure of the policy by 1947 opened the door to recriminations from both sides, to border clashes along the Outer Mongolian frontier, and to subsequent Chinese denunciation of Soviet strategy in Sinkiang.

Seen in this light, Chungking may have regarded Sheng's policies as expedient during the thirties. With his defection from the Soviet side in 1942, some attempt was made to substi-tute American for Russian influence, at least in economic activity within Sinkiang. After the war Chinese policy appears to have vacillated between Washington and Moscow, as alterna-tive sources of support. In the meantime, repression of non-

Chinese groups in Sinkiang, coupled with inadequate economic measures, dissipated the victory over Russian influence of 1942. At no time after Sheng's departure was the province securely under Chinese control. In this light, Chungking's policies would appear to have failed completely, although subsequent examination of more complete records may mitigate this interim judgment.

In surveying the Sinkiang scene, one is struck by the repeated setbacks delivered to aspirations of Uighur, Kazakh, Kirghiz, and other native groups for control of their own fate. This study has not attempted to encompass their struggle, focusing instead on the contest of power among Russian and Chinese strategists. Yet the record would be incomplete without at least mention of the impact of that contest upon the peoples inhabiting Sinkiang's desert and mountain vastness.

Sheng Shih-ts'ai provided an impetus for self-expression and autonomous development of the indigenous peoples, unprecedented in the province's history. Although his purges systematically frustrated ambitions of rising native leaders, his educational and cultural policies started a trend which could not be reversed for long. Nationalist appointment of Turki and Kazakh officials in titular positions of prominence, in 1946, signaled recognition of this new pressure from below. The seeming stability of the Kuldja regime augured well for eventual self-rule by native cadres, gaining administrative experience in the three rebel districts. Finally, the close association of this movement with Soviet sponsorship betokened favorable treatment in the event of Chinese Communist ascendancy.

Yet history willed otherwise. From the moment of Red victory in China, trouble beset the rebel group. A mysterious airplane crash, on August 27, 1949, unreported by Peking for several months, wiped out much of the Kuldja leadership, ostensibly en route to the first plenary session of the Chinese People's Political Consultative Conference. Akhmedjan, Isakh Beg, and other key figures met their death, leaving only Saifudin to represent the Uighur-Kazakh coalition.

The second blow fell with dissolution of the armed forces in the insurgent area, following the taking over of Sinkiang by the People's Liberation Army. Precedent for this move had been resisted bitterly and successfully by the rebels during negotiations with Nationalist delegates five years previously. Now it was explained as ensuring that "this Nationalities Army be without any suspicious attitudes or mistaken understandings and that it have the closest unity with the People's Liberation Army."[13] More ominous was the attendant warning, served in the form of a self-criticism of the revolt by Saifudin, "In our liberated districts we have still not been able to liberate the people from the oppression of feudalism. That is to say, the Ining uprising which struck down the Kuomintang bandits in western Sinkiang only opened the way to ridding the Sinkiang people of the feudal oppression, enslavement, and killing."

The year 1951 saw these words implemented in a sweeping purge which liquidated key officials in the three districts, including most of the original revolutionary leaders who had not perished in the airplane crash of 1949.[14] Not until these three events had virtually eliminated the founders of the Kuldja regime, did Peking finally restore a semblance of autonomy with establishment of the "Ining Kazakh Chou" on November 24, 1954. Less than a year later, Sinkiang was formally inaugurated as the Sinkiang Uighur Autonomous Area.

Thus, during the first years of Chinese Communist rule, indigenous elements in Sinkiang found no respite from the traditional tensions which had plagued the province for so long. In particular, Kazakh resistance to Peking's "pacification" led to widespread fighting and wholesale exodus of Kazakh refugees into India, Afghanistan, and westward into Turkey. Peking's injunctions against "British and American imperialists, lurking agents of the Kuomintang reactionaries, and pan-Islamists and pan-Turkistanists" fell on deaf ears, as clashes continued between the PLA and local rebels. Following an intensive pacification and re-education campaign during 1953, in the guise of "friendship delegations," Peking laconically admitted, "It was only after all this that the entire Kazakh people returned to the fold of the Fatherland."[15]

Even the close of the First Five Year Plan found "local nationalism an outstanding and serious problem" in Sinkiang, according to Saifudin, Peking's Party spokesman for the area.[16] He accused "advocates of local nationalism" with having "placed the interests of their own nationalities in the first place . . . creating a lot of fuss about the so-called 'nationality' question." Saifudin warned that "anyone who advocated 'national self-determination' or the establishment of a 'republic' was either ideologically confused or a reactionary with personal ambitions, plotting to split up the fatherland. It was extremely wrong for anyone to suggest that 'Sinkiang' should be renamed the 'Republic of Uighurstan' or the 'Uighur Autonomous Region of East Turkistan.' "

Particularly sensitive to the rallying cry of rebel nationalities in the past, Saifudin expanded on this point. "The name 'East Turkistan' was actually used for a very short time during the revolution of the three districts, but the name of Sinkiang was still used outside of these three districts. It is inappropriate to use 'East Turkistan'—a term used only for a short time and in a small portion of the land. . . . If the term 'Uighurstan' implies the meaning of the 'Uighur Republic,' we are strongly against it. We are equally against it if the term is used to mean that the land belongs to the Uighur nationality only and that it is an independent region and not a part of the Chinese territory."

Thus, Peking had not solved its problems by designating the area the Sinkiang Uighur Autonomous Region in 1955. On the contrary, resentment of Peking's authority may have been enhanced by misinterpretation of the degree of autonomy to be enjoyed. Thus, Saifudin criticized "serious wrong tendencies of opposing and expelling people of the Han nationality." Those local residents who had co-operated with central government authorities were attacked by their fellow Uighur or Kazakh citizens "as the 'running dogs of the Han nationality.' " Saifudin also cited "the erroneous stand against the study of the Han language." Admitting that less than half the members of the CCP committees above the *hsien* level belonged to non-Chinese groups, he countered that "the so-called 'nationalisation of the CCP committees' is an erroneous stand . . . [which] assails the responsible Han comrades in CCP organs, undermines the unity and unification of the party, and discredits the Marxist-Leninist principles of party construction."

In sum, the successors of Sheng Shih-ts'ai were not entirely free of the dilemma he encountered. Complete suppression of non-Chinese aspirations heightened tension. Accession to demands for self-rule, however, weakened control over the area. Yet the story of Sinkiang under Communist rule is another study in itself. So, too, is the account of Moscow-Peking relations as they impinge upon this area, once China's back door but now lying athwart a principal avenue of exchange between Asia's two most powerful allies.[17] With the unification of China under Red rule, a new era began for Sinkiang. No longer could Soviet policy move on the four wheels of military, economic, ideological, and political penetration to the exclusion of Chinese authority. Russian influence was not thereby automatically excluded. Stalin's success in establishing joint Sino-

Soviet stock companies in 1950, exploiting Sinkiang's oil and nonferrous metals, as well as operating civil air lines, testified to his unwillingness to forego all interest in the area. But liquidation of these companies, established for thirty years, came only four years later with the historic mission of Khrushchev and Bulganin to Peking in 1954. All Soviet shares reverted to Chinese ownership. The only element of Russian control remaining lay in the repayment of the Soviet investment through future deliveries of Sinkiang's exports.

In retrospect, the period following Sheng Shih-ts'ai's defection in 1942 appears one of continually declining Soviet power in Sinkiang. Temporary resurgence through the Kuldja revolt or the Peitashan incident forestalled, but did not prevent, the eventual establishment of Chinese authority throughout this province. Whatever might be the future course of relations between Moscow and Peking, it seems certain that no opportunity will permit Soviet strategy a return to the tactics employed in Sinkiang from 1933 to 1949.

Notes

1. For a summary of Soviet strategy in Iran, see George Lenczowski, *Russia and the West in Iran, 1918-1949,* (Ithaca: Cornell University Press, 1949), pp. 284 ff; also George Kirk, *The Middle East 1945-1950* (London: Oxford University Press, 1954), pp. 56-78.

2. *Ibid.*; see also Harry S. Truman, *Memoirs* (New York: Doubleday, 1955-56), Vol. II, pp. 94-95; and James Byrnes, *Speaking Frankly* (New York: Harper & Brothers, 1947) pp. 116 ff.

3. Ye L. Shteynberg, *Sovetsko-Iranskiye otnosheniya i proiski Anglo-Amerikanskogo imperializma v Irane* (Soviet-Iranian Relations and Efforts of Anglo-American Imperialism in Iran) (Moscow, 1947), pp. 14-15, suggests the Soviet withdrawal

resulted from agreements reached in Moscow in April, coincident with the oil concessions; for quotation and analysis see "The Borderlands of Soviet Central Asia: Persia," *Central Asian Review*, Vol. IV, No. 3, 1956, pp. 323-24.

4. Owen Lattimore, *Nationalism and Revolution in Mongolia* (New York: Oxford University Press, 1955), p. 42.

5. *Hsin Hua Yüeh Pao*, Vol. I, No. 2, pp. 361-62, reprinted from *Chieh Fang Jih Pao*, October 4, 1949.

6. Wu, *Turkestan Tumult, op. cit.*, pp. 232-33. Wu took part in negotiations between Sheng Shih-ts'ai and Ma Chung-ying, as an unofficial emissary from Nanking in 1933.

7. Eric Teichmann, *Journey to Turkestan* (London: Hodder and Stoughton, 1937), p. 105.

8. Feis, *The China Tangle, op. cit.*, p. 150; see also *U.S. Relations with China, op. cit.*, pp. 549-59.

9. Chang Chun-chang, "Reflections," *op. cit.* In Chiang's first instructions he appeared far more implacable with respect to Soviet demands, especially concerning Outer Mongolia, than in his second cable wherein he stated, "The Chinese Government wants to use the greatest sacrifice and sincerity in searching for a basic solution to Sino-Soviet relations. It wants to avoid all further confusion and unpleasantness and to obtain harmony between the two countries . . . deeply hopes that Soviet Russia will understand the great sacrifices and sincerity of the Chinese Government." These instructions suggest that Chiang rather than Soong was responsible for concessions at this time, against which Harriman protested in vain.

10. Interview with a participant in 1955.

11. *Ibid.*; the person is different from the source in note 10.

12. Chiang Kai-shek, *Soviet Russia in China* (New York: Farrar, Straus and Cudahy, 1957), p. 147. Chiang Ching-kuo saw Stalin, unaccompanied by any Chinese; interview with Chiang Ching-kuo, November, 1954. The elder son of the Generalissimo needed no interpreter, having spent twelve years in Russia as a youth and having married a Russian girl before returning to

China. See the author's article, "Mystery Man of Formosa," *Saturday Evening Post,* March 12, 1955. An editing error in that article incorrectly asserted, "Ching-kuo remained silent when he listened to a counterproposal which might have complicated the Gimo's relations with American as well as with his own followers," *ibid.,* p. 118. Ching-kuo refused to discuss the details of this trip.

13. *Hsin Hua Yüeh Pao,* Vol. II, No. 4, pp. 765-68.

14. *The New York Times,* December 23, 1951; this dispatch quotes official Chinese Communist broadcasts.

15. *New China News Agency,* Lanchow, May 6, 1954.

16. Radio Peking, December 25, 1957, report of Saifudin, secretary of the Sinkiang Uighur Autonomous Region CCP Committee, delivered before this group on December 16, 1957.

17. For an analysis of this problem during the first five years of the Moscow-Peking axis see the author's article, "Nationality Tensions in Sinkiang," *Far Eastern Survey,* Vol. XXV, No. 1, January, 1956; also Oleh S. Fedyshyn, "Soviet Retreat in Sinkiang? Sino-Soviet Rivalry and Co-operation, 1950-1955," *The American Slavic and East European Review,* Vol. XVI, No. 2, April, 1957.

RED FAILURE IN SINKIANG

by

GENERAL SHENG SHIH-TS'AI

Edited by Allen S. Whiting

PART TWO

1

Beloved Sinkiang

SINKIANG IS a vast land of exceptional beauty. I wish I were an artist or a playwright so that, for the benefit of the world's millions and future generations, I could paint hundreds of murals and write hundreds of plays depicting the beauty and greatness of that province. But such talents are beyond me, and I must rest content with drawing upon my pleasant memories of the past with which to sketch the faintest outline of a land which holds the rich heritage of Inner Asia in the endless tracts of mountain, desert, and ruins of civilizations long since dead.

Sinkiang receives short shrift in the Chinese annals, wherein thousands of years of tumultuous history are compressed in the *Tzu Yuan* (Book of Chinese Words and Terminology) as follows:

> Sinkiang is situated in the northwestern part of China. It was the land known as Hsi Yü (Western Region) during the great Han and T'ang Dynasties. In the early period of the Ch'ing Dynasty, the area north of the Tien Shan range was occupied by the Jungars while the area south of it was ruled by the Moslems. During the reign of Emperor Ch'ien Lung, the Jungars and the Moslems were conquered and Chinese military garrisons were established at Ili. Those military garrisons were placed under the charge of a commander, a deputy

commander and an adjutant general. The Moslems in Shensi and Kansu provinces rebelled and subsequently occupied Sinkiang during the reign of Emperor T'ung Chih. In the fourth year of the reign of Emperor Kuang Hsü, the rebellion was suppressed and Sinkiang became a Chinese province.

But a bareboned historical sketch tells little of Sinkiang's pivotal position as a contact point between the civilizations of Russia and China. Nor can it suggest the physical features of Sinkiang which have determined the path of such diverse adventurers as Marco Polo and the plundering Khans, of Indian merchants and British explorers. In truth, with the exception of its southeastern border which adjoins Kansu and Tibet, this sprawling land mass, representing one sixth the total area of China, is completely exposed to foreign influence and infiltration. Nowhere separated from its neighbors by clearly and unambiguously demarcated borders, it is bounded by India on the southwest, Soviet Russia on the west and northwest, and Outer Mongolia on the northeast. Such frontiers make Sinkiang the crossroads of civilizations and cultures, as well as the avenue of intrigue and invasion. Geographically remote from the capitals of Moscow, Tokyo, London, and Washington, it nevertheless has suffered direct interference in its nomadic, oasis life from agents of conflicting Russian, Japanese, British, and American interests. Yet all the while it remains officially Chinese soil.

On three sides the area is enclosed by mighty mountain masses, broken by infrequent gaps where persevering travelers and traders brave the ferocious winds and hazardous paths to enter this strange land of another era. The snow-clad Tien Shan (Celestial Mountains) extends across the province from west to east, dividing it into two parts. North of the mountains lies the Dzungaria Basin, which extends upward to the foot-hills of the Altai range, bordering Outer Mongolia. South of the Tien Shan is the Tarim Basin, terminated by the Kunlun range along India and Tibet.

Although both sections of Sinkiang are basically desert, spotted with oases and varied only by stretches of broad steppe, the climate is not identical in north and south. The mildness of southern Sinkiang is in marked contrast with the late spring and long winter of the northern part. While the pastoral life of the south finds colorfully dressed girls dancing native steps with their rugged boy friends on a carpet of swaying blossoms, the north huddles beneath an ever-deepening blanket of snow as a howling wind piles high the drifts. The crowning summit of the Celestial Mountains, rising to heights of more than 20,000 feet, boasts a cap of snow throughout the year.

The Tarimu *Han-hai* (*han-hai* means "dry sea," or desert) is the largest desert in the world, extending almost 900 miles from east to west and 350 miles north to south and covering more than 100,000 square miles. The endless expanse of sand dunes, rising and falling in gales like shifting waves, is often called the "tide of the dry sea." When a whirlwind swoops down with its sudden fury, tall swirling columns of sands sweep over the surface with tremendous speed, resembling numerous yellow pagodas rising from the desert. Histories of the Han Dynasty tell us that thousands of warriors of the fifty-five kingdoms which then held sway in Sinkiang perished not by the sword but by the sand. The sands which smothered these oasis cities and nomad states two hundred years before the birth of Christ defeat the efforts of those who believe man can conquer nature, and then mock his defeat by preserving intact the ruins of temples and dwellings for later challengers to ponder.

Hsüan Tsang, the famed Chinese scholar of the T'ang

Dynasty who crossed the Sinkiang desert on his way to India, wrote in his diary:

> The sand drifted as the wind blew, blurring the trails and making one lose his way across the wild desert. Travelers often collected human skeletons and animal bones along the way to erect signboards or roadmarks for the benefit of other travelers. Oases were scarce. The simoon made both men and the beasts of burden sick. It whistled a peculiar sound similar to the singing and shrieks of human beings. This phenomenon, combined with the great loneliness that oppressed one's mind, accounted for the death of many travelers from fear and exhaustion.

More concise but not less descriptive is the observation of the twentieth-century Swedish explorer, Sven Hedin, in *The Silk Road,* "The limitless expanse of yellow sand looked like a roaring sea suddenly frozen into a solid mass."

Sinkiang's natural marvels are not all destructive, however. It boasts resources whose full extent has never been fully surveyed, although there are vast deposits of coal, gold, tungsten, oil, tin, silver, copper, lead, and salt. Uranium is thought to exist in such vast amounts as to make Sinkiang a prime source of supply for Soviet Russia as well as China. Nor is its agricultural wealth to be ignored, with an abundance of fruits, some of which are known the world over for their luscious flavor and gigantic size. Turfan grapes and Hami melons stand out, but a close step behind come apples, pears, pomegranates, and other succulent products. In addition to these subsurface and above-surface items, Sinkiang exports cotton, silk, and furs. Small wonder that its fertile lands, concentrated in their productivity among the vast stretches of steppe and desert, hold a deep-seated appeal for those who know Sinkiang through its soil and who have lived for generations off the melting snows, the wide meadows, and the current trade that comes from caravans and merchants exchanging the products of the remote industrial world for the age-old riches of this fantastic realm.

Remote as is this region in space and time from the turmoil of the twentieth century, it has not been spared the tumultuous tempests which have raged over our globe with such ferocity. Standing at the northwest corner of our country's frontier, Sinkiang is traditionally regarded as the back door of China. With Japan's blockade of China's seacoast during the Sino-Japanese war, the province became the most important life line to the outside world. The truck and the airplane conquered the mighty stretches of desert and mountain to bring valuable supplies from the Soviet Union, later supplanted by deadly bombs aimed at Chinese Moslem rebel troops. Such famous American friends as former Vice-President Henry Wallace, the late Republican presidential candidate Wendell Willkie, and scores of others took the overland route through my capital into China. Indeed, so sudden was the transformation, we felt that Sinkiang had suddenly become the front door of China. With its vast fertile land and rich resources, with its deep evergreen forests and meadows in the south and snow-capped lofty mountains in the north, with its great deserts and oases, with its strategic importance as both the front and back door of China, Sinkiang had been able to live in peace and happiness before its occupation by the Chinese Communists in 1950. In those days it was a lovely and proud province. Then tragedy befell our land, as the Red flag flew over the Celestial Mountains and class struggles ripped the people asunder. The fall of Sinkiang was echoed throughout the land by the laughter and the clink of glasses raised in toast at Communist headquarters, while outside the bitter cries of the people living under Red oppression rent the air. But some day the laughter may turn to mourning, while the bitter cries may turn to cheers.

2

Coup d'État

IT IS IMPOSSIBLE to grasp the full impact of the past twenty years upon the peaceful, nomadic life of Sinkiang without recalling the many troubles which plagued the province in previous decades. Before the uprising of April, 1933, Sinkiang was a land of stagnation, backwardness, and violence. Because of the ignorance and selfishness of the Chinese governors Yang Tseng-hsin and Chin Shu-jen, the financial and economic situation was so pitiful that the province was sarcastically called "the land of beggars who begged with gold rice-bowls." This referred to the abundance of rich mineral resources which lay untapped beneath our land, while starvation and misery crawled over its surface. Maladministration and incompetency further depressed the economy with a burdensome bureaucracy that was both corrupt and inefficient.

No less serious than the economic problem was the nationality issue. The peoples of Sinkiang are made up of fourteen different nationalities: (1) Chinese, (2) Uighur, (3) Mongol, (4) Kazakh, (5) Moslem (Tungan), (6) Sibo, (7) Solon, (8) Manchu, (9) Kirghiz, (10) White Russian, (11) Taranchi, (12) Tadjik, (13) Tartar, and (14) Uzbek. Indeed, so many races live in the province that it has been called "a living ethnological museum." Because of the failure of Yang and Chin to carry out a program of racial equality, the tribes suspected and hated one another. Religious freedom was violated; differing beliefs divided the population along hostile lines.

This issue was one which repeatedly erupted in violent uprising, sometimes directed by the ruling authorities against recalcitrant tribes, sometimes by frustrated minorities seeking vengeance against their oppressors. Misgovernment and exploitation by the Chin Shu-jen administration finally provoked the Uighur rebellion of 1932-33, headed by Khodja Niaz, and the Moslem revolt, headed by Ma Chung-ying. Weak defenses and poor generalship, stemming from the incompetence of the provincial authorities, permitted Ma to sweep across the vast desert from his mountain stronghold in Kansu province. When Khodja Niaz joined hands with the famed Moslem rebel, the entire province flamed in revolt. Although the rebellion was suppressed and Ma retreated to Kansu with heavy wounds inflicted during the fighting, the provincial structure had been greatly weakened and the seeds of the April, 1933, coup nourished in the hotbed of dissension and intrigue.

In addition to this internal threat, external dangers beset the province. Knowing that Sinkiang offered an important gateway between China and the outside world, foreign imperialists, fascists, and Communists all focused their covetous eyes on the province. They knew that racial tensions, cultural backwardness, and political and military weaknesses made Sinkiang an easy target for imperialistic attack. By 1932 Japanese war lords plotted with Ma Chung-ying, instigating his invasion with the aim of creating a Moslem state in Central Asia which would lock China's back door to outside help. Meanwhile, British imperialists incited the Uighurs to launch the "Eastern Turkistan Republic" movement, with Khodja Niaz as "president" and Sarpiti as "premier." Their hope was to make southern Sinkiang a sphere of exclusive British influence, profitable for extension of trade from India. Last but not least, Soviet Russia began to fish in troubled waters. Moscow's consulates throughout the province served as bases for Russian underground agents plotting against the local government with the ultimate object of creating a puppet regime that would pledge its allegiance to Moscow.

A signal difference set apart the Soviet imperialism from that of Japan or of Great Britain. Whereas the last two forces could offer nothing to their local puppets but arms and money, Russia's moral and ideological force among the population as a whole gave it a definite advantage. Although Sinkiang seemed mired in a slough of social stagnation, it had long since felt the repercussions of the Russian revolution. Geographical proximity to Soviet republics on three sides permitted infiltration of ideas and interests which simultaneously served frustrated nationalities in Sinkiang hoping to emulate the success of their formerly backward oppressed brethren across the borders, and the plotters in the Kremlin who wished to make Sinkiang a faithful satellite.

In this sense, the ferment in Sinkiang remained ripe for exploitation by all three imperialist powers, and it seemed inevitable the people would have to ally with one in order to defeat the other two. The question was: which ally could provide the greatest help for Sinkiang itself? Hope was slim that the central government could meet the pressing needs. The chaotic history of the Peking and Nanking regimes since the revolution of 1911, the Japanese seizure of Manchuria in 1931, and the continuing wars between Nationalist and Communist as well as among various Nationalist war-lord factions augured ill for Sinkiang's future. At the same time the four million people in the province, particularly the sober, hardheaded "Progressives" of the younger generation, began to realize the impossibility of living in a perpetual state of strife, poverty, foreign encroachment, and domestic corruption.

Small wonder that the impulse toward revolution arose spontaneously. Little by little, a growing band of persons became acutely conscious of the need for a new revolutionary administration which could replace the decadent old regime. When the revolutionary mood of the people reached fever pitch, the Soviet Union exploited the delicate situation to accelerate the outbreak. The coup d'état of April 12, 1933, resulted, ousting Chin Shu-jen and turning a momentous page in the history of Sinkiang.

On the night of April 12, while I was sleeping in my camp at Uraba, as commander of local forces against marauding troops of Ma Chung-ying, I dreamed that I had returned to *Hung Miao Tai* (Red Temple) in the southwest section of Tihua (Urumchi). Entering the temple gate, I saw Governor Chin Shu-jen standing before the entrance with his back toward the idol. He wore a yellow garment, a yellow hat, and a pair of yellow shoes made of woven grass. Beside him stood two other persons, also in yellow garments and hats. Although I honored him with a proper military salute, he did not return it but merely beckoned me to walk into the hall of the temple. As soon as I had done so he suddenly turned, closed the main gate, and departed with the two other persons. Left alone in the temple, I awoke from the dream in fear and wonderment.

At breakfast the following morning I recounted my dream to several officers under my command and asked whether they thought it an omen of good fortune. They all smiled but said nothing. Calling one to my side later, I asked him, "It seems curious I should be shut up in the temple by Governor Chin. Is this a premonition I will be made a prisoner?" He, too, merely shook his head without reply. A moment later we heard the drone of an airplane high overhead. It was a passenger flight from Tihua; on board was Li Hsiao-t'ien, a leader in the coup. Jumping out of the plane a few seconds after it touched the ground, he greeted me with a smile: "A revolution took place yesterday afternoon at the capital! The *kuei-hua* army (White Russian mercenary troops) mutinied and attacked the Governor's headquarters. Governor Chin and his wife jumped over the wall of their house and fled."

With this good news, Li urged me to return to Tihua within a few days. In the meantime, representatives of the various nationalities organized a caretaker regime to administer affairs of the province pending establishment of a new government. Liu Wen-lung, former education commissioner of the provincial government, was elected provisional provincial chairman, while General Cheng Jun-ch'eng, brigade commander of the Northeast National Salvation Army in Manchuria, was named provisional chairman of the Sinkiang Military Affairs Commission. General Cheng, however, refused to accept the post. On April 14 I returned from the front and upon my arrival in Tihua was invited to attend the next meeting of the caretaker committee. It was resolved at this session to abolish the Sinkiang Military Affairs Commission and to re-establish the Border Defense Commission. The group unanimously elected me to be provisional commander of the border defense organization.

But the coup had not yet run its full course. Once again, with external and internal attacks, Sinkiang faced chaos. On the outside Japanese fascists, taking advantage of the April uprising, again incited Ma Chung-ying and Yu Hua-t'ing to attack the capital. Yu Hua-t'ing was actually a Japanese agent; his real name was Tadashi Onishi. After occupying the strategic points of Hami, Kitai (Kuch'engtse), and towns east of Tihua, Ma's forces seemed ready to link up with Khodja Niaz in an attack upon the capital itself. Meanwhile, British activities among the Uighurs in southern Sinkiang added still another threat to our security.

Internally, the victors of the uprising planned one more stroke for power. This time I was their target. Ch'en Chung, Chang Hsin, T'ao Ming-yüeh, and Li Hsiao-t'ien had successfully staged the coup under Russia's instigation. They did not yet have full control of the government and the army because Stalin regarded the provisional provincial regime as only a transitory administration, similar to that of Kerensky after the Russian revolution of March, 1917. Therefore, when I was in Kitai after Ma's defeat at Tsenichuantze by the troops under my command, the Ch'en-T'ao-Li clique hatched a plot against me. According to their plot, a riot was to be staged at Tihua for the suppression of which I was to be called back to the capital. On the way back my assassination was to take place.

Always on the alert for danger from any direction, I returned to Tihua under a cloak of secrecy. Through careful questioning of reliable friends, I learned the details of the plot. Once the evidence was in my hands, justice was swiftly meted out to the ringleaders, Ch'en, T'ao, and Li. They were sentenced to death and shot. All others connected with the assassination attempt were pardoned, in order to demonstrate my leniency and to rebuild unity in the shattered province. Only then could peace reign in the capital.

Thus ended the first chapter in the new history of Sinkiang, in the course of events which were to remove forever the backward, stagnant, oppressed society that had existed for centuries. In its place was to grow a progressive, united, prosperous province of four million souls, divided by nationality but united in peaceful brotherhood. The Ch'en-T'ao-Li plot was not to be the last directed from within at the ruling power. Ever mindful of the fate that befell former governors Yang Tseng-hsin, who was murdered, and Chin Shu-jen, who barely escaped with his life, I had to cope with repeated threats to my family as well as to myself.

Furthermore, although I had defeated the internal attack, Sinkiang remained the prey of Japanese and British imperialists, not to mention the growing threat of the Soviet Union against whom we were truly defenseless. I resolved that one day we must become strong enough to oust all intervention. In the meantime, with a weak cavalry and less than 10,000 infantry, it would be impossible for the new provincial government to extirpate the alien forces which daily plunged deeper into the heart of Sinkiang. The central government of Nanking was then concentrating its efforts in suppressing the Communist rebellion in southeastern China while maintaining an uneasy policy of talk-but-retreat before the Japanese penetration of north China. No help could come from this quarter. Under such circumstances, the only alternative to ensure Sinkiang's security was to play one alien force against another. If successful, this tactic would destroy the alien forces from the East and the South by the alien force from the West. I therefore moved to the calculated risk of bringing in Soviet help to solve Sinkiang's growing crisis.

3

Soviet Russia and the New Sinkiang

MINE WAS NOT the first regime to seek Soviet assistance. Governor Chin Shu-jen had negotiated for Russian arms and munitions in exchange for which he had granted trading rights to Soviet representatives. My plan went further, however, in that it sought to link a positive policy of friendship for Soviet Russia with substantial amounts of military, economic, and technical assistance. To make clear the policy of the new Sinkiang, I sent Ch'en Te-li, and Yao Hsiung to Moscow during 1933 to strengthen friendly relations and, at the same time, to press for early delivery of the arms previously promised to Governor Chin.

Recognizing the new provincial government as substantively different from its predecessors and resting content with a friendly but uncontrolled regime for the moment, Stalin began a change of tactics. Instead of trying to oust me through a further coup, he appointed Garegin Apresoff, his close associate and a man well versed in Central Asian affairs, to be the new Soviet consul general in Tihua. Apresoff accompanied Ch'en Te-li and Yao Hsiung on their return from Moscow in December while I was still in Tapan City, midway between Tihua and Turfan, directing operations against the continuing revolt of Ma Chung-ying.

After his initial courtesy call, Apresoff made a special visit

to my headquarters to stress the fact that Russia regarded our
relations as something different from the standard setup of
the past. Before leaving Moscow, he had been summoned to
the Kremlin for a personal conference with Stalin. According
to Apresoff, the Soviet leader had stated explicitly, "When you
see Commissioner Sheng in Sinkiang, tell him that it is the
Soviet policy to extend aid and assistance to him for suppression
of all internal disturbances."

Such an offer was indeed staggering in its implications, for
we were still faced with dangerous revolts on all sides, aided
and abetted by rapacious imperialistic powers. But Stalin
recognized that it was to the Soviet interest as well as to the
interest of Sinkiang that these imperialists be defeated, for
what was the back door of China was also the back door of
Soviet Russia.

Furthermore, he knew that a new order was being built in
Sinkiang which could provide strength and unity, where only
chaos had prevailed, provided it could gain respite from foreign
intrigue and invasion. This new order was founded on two
related programs promulgated by my regime, the so-called
"Eight Points" and "Six Great Policies." To understand their
significance is to grasp the basic direction of my government
for the subsequent decade.

What the old regime left behind was a province torn by
internal strife and external disturbances. The people were
suffering from poverty, fear, and hatred. Educational and economic programs were neglected. In the face of this crisis, the
first task of the new provincial government after the April
coup was to win support among the people so as to rally unity
against those who would overthrow the regime. Restoration
of peace demanded a cessation of nationality tensions among
the fourteen races of Sinkiang. Religious freedom must assure
safety of worship. Corruption could no longer plunder the

provincial wealth, bandits must be exterminated, and the food problem solved. With these things in mind, the provincial government promulgated the "Eight Points for Sinkiang." These were: (1) equality between races, (2) religious freedom, (3) immediate rural relief, (4) financial reforms, (5) administrative reforms, (6) extension of education, (7) realization of self-government, and (8) judicial reforms.

Although such pledges went to the core of the domestic problems, they failed to tackle the over-all internal and external dangers threatening Sinkiang. For this reason we sought to develop a program which would protect the territorial integrity of Sinkiang, cope with the various aspects of the Soviet "border policy," and accelerate the building of a new Sinkiang. Thus, the "Six Great Policies" were announced: (1) anti-imperialism, (2) kinship to Soviet Russia, (3) racial or national equality, (4) clean government, (5) peace, and (6) reconstruction.

These six points were skillfully worded so as to meet all our objectives without sacrificing any of our principles. They have been much misunderstood in some quarters, but viewed as an integral whole they reveal our basic strategy. Anti-imperialism caused the people to fight imperialistic and fascist aggression with a growing consciousness of nationalism. Kinship to Soviet Russia simultaneously lessened the people's fear and hatred of our mighty neighbor and served to win aid and assistance from Moscow. Racial or national equality demonstrated to the fourteen tribes that Sinkiang belonged to themselves as well as to China and that not only Russia could evolve a nationality policy of equality. Clean government instilled standards of efficiency and honesty among public officials at all levels of the provincial administration, going hand-in-hand with the racial equality principle to remove exploitation of one group by another. Without the restoration of peace, of course, none of the reconstruction program could be carried out. On the other hand, only by carrying out the reconstruction program could the province hope to be strong enough to maintain peace.

Such a program was ambitious, admittedly, but it was not impossible. The translation of word into deed resulted in subsequent three-year reconstruction programs which improved the standard of living, raised the cultural level of the various tribes, and placed the provincial government on the road to efficiency and democracy. By carrying out the eight points and the six policies, Sinkiang changed as from night to day. Peace, prosperity, unity, and happiness took the place of turmoil, terror, starvation, and enmity. The repeated plots of counter-revolutionary forces and alien aggressors were smashed. Democracy brought new voices to direct Sinkiang's government, typified by such meetings as the congress of Mongol-Kazakh-Kirghiz tribes, the provincial congress of women of all nationalities, the congress of representatives of the Mongol groups, and others, all of which gave their opinion and guidance to the various three-year projects.

Such was the new Sinkiang to which Stalin decided to grant assistance. That his efforts were justified was to be shown by the resolute manner in which alien forces were destroyed, plots of conspirators suppressed, and important Sino-Soviet routes of communication during the later years of war were safeguarded. That his efforts were insufficient to assure him control of Sinkiang as a permanent possession became evident in the subsequent moves made, first to dominate me, and later to kill me, which Stalin's agents undertook in Sinkiang. Herein lay our most difficult policy of all: kinship to Soviet Russia, while maintaining the territorial integrity of Sinkiang as a province of China.

In order to comprehend the significance of subsequent Soviet moves in Sinkiang, it is necessary to analyze the basic aims of the "border policy" of Soviet Russia. The strategy and tactics of this policy became clear to me only in retrospect, only after I had suffered ten years of struggle with the Kremlin leaders and after my bitter experience of what their aid was to accomplish for them. That policy is still operative, despite the death of its architect, Stalin. Its consequences will be felt everywhere that Asian peoples fall for the siren song of the Soviet leaders, in the Middle East and Southeast Asia no less than in my native land.

Essentially the "border policy'" falls into three stages. During the first period, the aim of Soviet diplomacy is to win the friendship of regimes existing on the periphery of Russia. This means supporting them in "anti-imperialist" moves designed to exclude rival influence of other world powers. The reverse side of this coin is a "pro-Soviet" orientation. In the second stage, the external pressure of Soviet diplomacy working in conjunction with the internal pressure of Soviet subversion, whether through open Communist movements or through covert "united front" tactics, seeks to impose an Iron Curtain around these neighboring countries. In fact, this marks their transformation into Soviet satellites. Finally, incorporation of these bordering areas into the Soviet Union would make them *de facto* and *de jure* Russian territory. Where local resistance is weak, as with Tanna Tuva, the policy has moved through all three stages. Where local resistance or foreign pressure is stronger, as with Outer Mongolia and Eastern Europe, the policy has perforce remained content with the first two stages.

In Sinkiang, Stalin knew that the first stage had been successful with the consummation of the Russian-endorsed coup and the promulgation of the "Eight Points" and "Six Policies." His problem was to move into the second stage as smoothly as possible without arousing the combined antagonism of Britain, the United States, and China. Once this was accomplished, it would be only a matter of time before Sinkiang would be directly absorbed into the Soviet Union.

That such absorption was always in the minds of the Russians is clear from their emphasis upon the unity of the fourteen nationalities of Sinkiang with their fellow tribesmen in the various Soviet Republics. Soviet advisers in my province repeatedly declared that "The peoples along the Sino-Soviet frontier are all brethren. The racially related populations will one day be united as citizens of the same nation. This cleavage at present is like a watermelon cut into two halves which sooner or later will again combine as a single entity."

Such words revealed the true purpose of Soviet aid and advice. It mattered little that the "watermelon"—Sinkiang—originally belonged entirely to China. It was only because of the czarist occupation of part of Sinkiang in the nineteenth century that the "watermelon" was cut into two halves! Stalin might better have compared it with a snake which, having swallowed half of a fish, is determined to gorge itself upon the rest of the unfortunate victim.

Another factor, however, made Sinkiang, together with its Chinese counterparts of Mongolia and Manchuria, unique in the over-all "border policy" of Soviet Russia. This concerns the place of China in the world revolution. As the first socialist country as well as "the fatherland of the world proletariat," the Soviet Union considered its obligation was to render aid to Communists in all other countries in their revolts against "feudal" or "capitalist" oppressors. According to Moscow's interpretation, China ranked high in the priority list of revolution because it was in the throes of turmoil and faced a more immediate crisis than did other Asian countries. Furthermore, as a neighbor of Russia it was in an advantageous position to receive socialist succor. Since Sinkiang is the bridge between the two countries, seizure of that province was of strategic significance in sovietizing all of China.

Herein lies a clue as to a fundamental source of tension between the Russian and Chinese Communists. While they continually emphasize the "inevitable contradictions of the capitalist world," their own sphere is threatened with rupture because of inherent contradictions of aims. It is in my own experiences as the target of plots and counterplots directed from Moscow and Yenan that this basic clash of policy receives full proof. Before recounting such instances, however, we must look at the over-all structure of the Communist conspiracy as organized through its headquarters in Moscow.

The co-ordinating center for all Communist parties was the Communist International, better known as the Comintern. Conflicts of interest between the All-Union Communist Party (CPSU) and those of other countries were hammered out in stormy debate during the early period under Lenin. When Georgi Dimitrov became secretary general of the Comintern's executive committee, he tended at first to treat the representatives of other countries with due respect, and listened to their views as the reflection of national aspirations of their different homelands. Gradually, however, the CPSU became so dogmatic in its hierarchy that the opinions of other representatives were often ignored. As Stalin increased his overt role, the democratic aspects of Comintern membership became more and more of a fiction. Finally, conflicts of interest became inevitably determined exclusively according to the interests of the Russians. This aroused a strong undercurrent of opposition to the authoritarian role of the All-Union Communist Party, opposition which in some instances allied with the Trotskyites and in other instances sought strength from fascist quarters. As we shall see later, this Trotskyite-fascist opposition was to make its weight felt in Sinkiang.

In order to make the Communist parties of various countries bow to the will of the Soviet Union, the All-Union Communist

Party declared that since the USSR was the first socialist state and the fatherland of the international proletariat, its interests came before all others. Specifically, this meant that should any clash arise between the Russian and the Chinese Communists over Sinkiang, Soviet dictation would settle the issue.

But inherent in the "border policy" is conflict between the Russians and all national Communists on the periphery of the Soviet Union. While the Soviet Union's objective was to incorporate Sinkiang into the territory of the USSR or to make it a satellite like Outer Mongolia, the aim of the Chinese Communists was to keep it under China's sovereignty and to make it a base of socialist industrialization. Of the various objectives of the "border policy," only the last one mentioned, sovietization of Sinkiang as a prerequisite for the sovietization of China, was in accord with the aims of Yenan.

This clash between two sections of the "international proletariat" who continually swore "unshakable unity" remained submerged in the prolific resolutions and manifestos coming from the Comintern. Even someone as involved in the relations of the two groups as myself found it difficult to grasp the essential nature of this relationship. Yet its inherent tensions explain many of the contradictory and confusing elements in the struggle for Sinkiang. In particular, it is revealed in the peculiar resolution of my application for membership in the Chinese Communist Party. But that is a story for discussion at another point. Here I must complete the background of the nature of the struggle among various groups in Sinkiang, so that the detailed account may appear in clear perspective.

Another consequence of Soviet policy has been mentioned above but must be more fully explained, namely, the Trotskyite opposition. After Lenin's death, a triumvirate of Joseph Stalin, Nikolai Bukharin, and Leon Trotsky won control of the party, government, and army in the Soviet Union. They differed radically from one another on views of the state, on world revolution, and on interpretation of Marxist doctrine. Sharpest was the split between Trotsky and Stalin. Trotsky pointed out the impossibility of building socialism successfully and completely in one country while hostile capitalist powers surrounded it. Stalin held the view that an independent socialist society, or "socialism in one country" was not only possible but necessary.

The conflict was an ideological one, but it soon developed into a factional struggle for power between Trotskyites and Stalinists. The situation became acute as more and more power became concentrated in the hands of Stalin who, by his aggressiveness and able maneuvering in the party, attempted to discredit and eliminate both Trotsky and Bukharin as political opponents.

It was clear that Trotsky and Bukharin could not tolerate Stalin's iron hand. In prestige, position, ability, and experience, as well as in the field of learning, both men were more than a match for Stalin. In fact, they were unrivaled in the study and interpretation of the Marxist doctrine. Trotsky, alone, by his eloquence and ability to instigate mass enthusiasm, had thrown Stalin into the shade on more than one occasion. Under such circumstances, politics in the Soviet Union revolved around the tripartite struggle for power for many years, including the time when a new Sinkiang remained dependent upon Russia for so much help.

Because of the intimate connection between Russia and Communist parties throughout the world, the struggle spilled over the Kremlin walls and seeped into debating halls and underground cells around the globe. Finally, Stalin's tactics won out; his theories were endorsed by both the All-Union Communist Party and the Comintern. Trotsky, purged and discredited, first went into exile and then swung to counterattack by organizing underground movements designed to overthrow the Stalin regime. Assisted by opposition Bukharinists, these movements won support not only in Russia but in China, India, Spain, and other leading centers of revolutionary activity.

Although such plots were nipped in the bud because of poor co-ordination, the existence of opposition groups posed a constant menace to the Stalin regime. Attempts on his life as well as successful assassinations of such leading figures as Kirov and Gorky proved the need for ruthless vigilance. The confessions of Karl Radek, the purge of leading Trotskyites, and, finally, the death of Bukharin and the murder of Trotsky himself in Mexico demonstrated Stalin's effective action against opposition. It might be noted in passing that the death of these persons did not wipe out all Trotskyite activity. Activities aimed at weakening and destroying the Stalin regime continued right down to his own death in 1953. For instance, in the first weeks of the German attack on Russia during World War II, the Trotskyites instigated hundreds of thousands of the Red Army to lay down arms and to go over to the side of the Nazis. Hitler's personal ignorance of the Trotskyite influence and his merciless massacre of Russian war prisoners caused him to meet the same fate as did Napoleon. The Trotskyite influence also accounted for Tito's defection from the Stalinist camp. While many factors lay behind the rupture between the two leaders, it is undeniable that the most important one was the influence of the Trotskyites in the Communist Information Bureau (Cominform) who painstakingly plotted to create cleavages within the Soviet world and to isolate the Stalin regime.

Although the Trotskyites met defeat in the Soviet Union, they never abandoned their efforts. Meanwhile, the German and Japanese fascist war lords, recognizing potential allies among such influential groups, pledged support to the Trotskyite plot. Such support was more than welcome to the struggling opposition, which knew it had little chance of victory without foreign assistance. For Sinkiang, this alliance promised fruitful rewards, inasmuch as its pivotal position allowed the Trotsky-ites to link up with the German-Japanese drive and to outflank the Soviet Union, penetrating its weakest areas. The final step would be a joint assault by the Axis and the anti-Stalinists to establish a new regime in Moscow.

Although the Sinkiang authorities never allowed the Trotsky-ite-Nazi-Japanese fascist plot to overthrow the government, constant efforts were made toward this end, first through political intrigues and mass riots, and then through terrorism and assassination. Had these plots succeeded, the Trotskyites could have attacked Russia from that province during World War II in a move paralleling the German invasion from Europe. They would then have reorganized the vast Soviet armies who surrendered without opposition to the Nazis, rallied Trotsky's followers and the enemies of Stalin in the Soviet Union, and overthrown the Stalin regime by force. Had this come about, the history of the last war would have been written somewhat differently! One item of proof of this plot is the fact that Marshal Kutzumich of the Alma-Ata Military Zone and Marshal Bleucher (Galens) of the Far Eastern Red Army at Chita both fell before Stalin's purge in the late thirties as condemned Trotskyites. Sinkiang formed an important part of their scheme, and we shall see how close they came to killing me and to opening China's back door to the world-wide fascist-imperialist plot.

So complex a network of intrigue can best be understood if we summarize the main factors responsible for the riots and disturbances which threatened Sinkiang during the ten years of my administration:

(1) Sinkiang's rich resources of tungsten, gold, oil, and coal, together with its possibilities for exploitation of livestock production, made it the object of foreign attention by covetous aggressors.

(2) The province, with only a meager army of 10,000 troops, was too weak to defend itself and could expect little military aid from the remote central government at Nanking, bogged down in anti-Communist and anti-Japanese movements.

(3) Sinkiang's socioeconomic backwardness and its racial problems made it an easy prey for both foreign aggressors and Chinese traitors who wished to incite riots and create cleavages among the local population.

(4) Moslems, comprising the overwhelming majority of the population, were easily moved by appeals from imperialists and fascists for creation of "an Islamic state" or "an Eastern Turkistan Republic."

(5) After winning Outer Mongolia, Soviet Russia turned to Sinkiang as an object of expansion, since sovietization of Sinkiang was a prerequisite to sovietization of the world. In order to win the world, the Soviet Union and the Chinese Communists must first win Asia. In order to win Asia, they first had to win China, which was considered to be the weakest link in the whole chain of the continent. To win China, however, they aimed first at winning the nation's weakest province, Sinkiang.

(6) Before India's independence, Great Britain hoped to make southern Sinkiang a sphere of influence, which would safeguard India against Russian or Japanese penetration.

(7) Japan hoped to cut China off from the rest of the world by an effective land and sea blockade. Thus, the Japanese instigated Moslem uprisings and plotted in Sinkiang to sever the vital overland route between China and her possible allies.

(8) The strategic importance of Sinkiang fitted neatly into the political schemes of the Trotskyites who received succor from the German and Japanese imperialists.

Thus, for ten years I was faced with constant threats to my life and to my people. Yet, despite the combined forces of aggression and subversion, Sinkiang was able not only to survive but to progress. That this was possible was due to the loyal support of the four million inhabitants who saw in the "Eight Points" and "Six Policies" the hope of a new Sinkiang. It is the great paradox of history that the very success of these programs was made possible by the assistance of Soviet Russia who, at the same time, was plotting to seize the province. To understand how such duplicity was possible, as well as to trace the way in which the forces outlined above carried into effect their various plots, we must now turn to the tactics by which the imperialists, Trotskyites, Soviet and Chinese Communist sought to overthrow the Sinkiang government and make it a victim of their aggressive designs.

4

Trotskyites in Turkistan

NOT LONG AFTER I was made responsible for Sinkiang's welfare,
I soon realized that my countrymen and I were the target of a
far-reaching conspiracy extending from Tokyo to Berlin, linked
by the international Trotskyite movement. In their never-end-
ing quest for power and their desperate search for means to
overthrow Stalin, the Trotskyites joined with the German and
Japanese fascists in a plot to seize Sinkiang as a base for
operations against the Soviet Union.

Just as the Communist parties in all countries are the
"younger brothers" of the All-Union Communist Party, so the
Trotskyites of all countries bowed to the wishes of the Russian
Trotskyites. In carrying out their activities in Sinkiang, the
Chinese Trotskyites took orders from their Russian counterparts, and some of the Chinese oppositionists had actually been
sent into Sinkiang on orders from groups in the Russian underground.

With the expulsion of Trotsky from Soviet Russia and the
subsequent purge of his followers by Stalin, it seemed this cause
had suffered a crushing blow. However, Trotskyite remnants,
potentially strong at home and abroad thanks to a growing
discontent with Stalin's agricultural policies and the failure of
the Red revolution to spread, continued to plot against the
Soviet elite. Obsessed with acquiring political and military bases

either inside or outside Russia, the Trotskyites infiltrated at all levels.

Versed in clandestine activity, from many years of struggle with Stalin's secret police, the Trotskyites developed numerous conspiratorial tactics. According to the confessions of Karl Radek, for instance, they planned to instigate the German Communists to assassinate Stalin. Similarly, they planned to bribe Molotov's chauffeur to overturn his automobile, thereby killing Stalin's close friend. Finally, they connived with Stalin's personal doctor in efforts to poison the Soviet premier, and actually succeeded in having lethal drugs administered to the famed writer, Maxim Gorky.

Disguised as members of the All-Union Communist Party or as Chinese Communists, the Trotskyites in Sinkiang tried to create discord between my people and Soviet Russia and to undermine the prestige of Stalin. A typical tactic was to talk against Trotsky and discredit his ideas but to attack anyone who took exception to Trotskyism in practice. They pretended to give wholehearted support to Soviet Russia and to worship Stalin but actually spared no effort in crushing Russian elements and Stalin's followers at every turn. They seemed to give every support to the policy of kinship to sovietism but left no stone unturned to create dissension between Sinkiang and Soviet Russia. They emphasized that whatever Stalin had said and done should be taken as truth, but they objected to "idol worship" and asserted that revolutionary theories changed in accordance with the revolutionary development. In short, the Trotskyites waged an unceasing campaign of dissimulation and intrigue in Sinkiang.

The mastermind behind the Trotskyite plot was none other than the Soviet consul general in Tihua, Garegin Apresoff. Under the guise of a loyal member of the All-Union Communist

Party, Apresoff gradually worked his conspiratorial colleagues into influential positions throughout the Soviet adviser corps as well as in the various governmental bureaus of the capital. With the *rapprochement* evident between Russia and China in the spring of 1937 and the formidable opposition this would raise for Japan's anticipated conquest of Asia, the Fascist-Trotskyite plotters sprang into action. Their goal was nothing less than assassination of Sinkiang's political and military leaders, overthrow of the provincial government, and armed uprising throughout the Soviet Union.

The uprising was planned for April 12, 1937, the commemoration day of the famous April Uprising four years earlier. According to the plot, a riot was to be staged in Tihua on that day, followed by a rebellion of the Kazakh nomads in the Altai region. At the same time Divisional Commanders Ma Mu-ti and Ma Hu-shan were to trigger a mutiny in southern Sinkiang. According to the confession made by one of the conspirators, after seizing power the Trotskyites planned to lay low for a while, continuing my basic policies of anti-imperialism and pro-Russianism on the one hand and the six great policies on the other. Should Stalin's suspicions not be aroused and this coup be explained as an "anti-Fascist uprising" they would then have purged the entire province, filling all posts with loyal Trotskyites. At the same time German and Japanese advisers would be alerted to fly into Sinkiang at the proper time, ousting all Stalinist Soviet military personnel, and turning the province into a base in the vulnerable rear of both Russia and China.

Fortunately, the assassins hired to murder me were apprehended and arrested. In the course of their trial the whole plot was exposed and nipped in the bud. The ringleaders were rounded up, while the less important Trotskyites were subsequently caught and tried. With the threat to northern Sinkiang quelled, the provincial government decided to crush the rebels of the Altai region by force of arms. Meanwhile, the main power of the provincial army moved southward to Karashar against the mutiny of Ma Mu-ti and Ma Hu-shan. Thanks to the heroism of the officers and troops, the hearty support of the people in southern Sinkiang, and the man-power and material assistance from the Soviet Union, the mutineers were defeated. Thus ended this international plot: Sinkiang remained unified.

The extent of the Trotskyite network is proved by the fact that 435 persons were convicted of conspiracy. Of these only 33 were sentenced to death, following the wise policy of leniency to all who were mere followers as distinguished from ringleaders or foreign spies. Important military and political figures of the various nationalities in Sinkiang took part in the plot, including such high-ranking persons as the two former subordinates of Ma Chung-ying, Divisional Commanders Ma Mu-ti (Uighur) and Ma Hu-shan (Moslem). Other military conspirators included Chief Fan Liang (Chinese), of the Judge Advocate General's Department in the Border Defense Commission, and Major-General Polinoff (White Russian). On the political side, the more important persons included Khodja Niaz (Uighur), Vice-Chairman of the Sinkiang Provincial Government; Chang Hsin (Chinese), Education Commissioner; Ma Chao-wu (Moslem), Civil Affairs Commissioner; Yu Wen-ping (Uighur), Reconstruction Affairs Commissioner; Pa Yen (Kazakh), Deputy Commissioner of Reconstruction Affairs; Huang Han-chang (Chinese), Secretary-General of the Sinkiang Provincial Government; Ch'en Te-li (Chinese), Administrator of the Ili Region; Burhan (alias Pao Erh-han, a Tartar and at present Chairman of the Sinkiang Uighur Autonomous Region under the Communists), General Manager of the Sinkiang Local Products Company; and Kuang Lu, former Chinese consul general in Russia. Prince Silik of a Mongolian league was also one of the supporters of the plot.

In addition, conspirators came in from both Russia and China proper in preparation for the uprising, communicating through the Soviet mission under the direction of Apresoff who enjoyed diplomatic immunity. Among the Russian Trotskyites, were Stakolytkov, Wan Hsien-t'ing, Liu Hsien-chen, Ch'eng Yi-chun, Wang Shou-chen, Yu Cheng-fa, Luan Pao-ting, Wang Pao-chien, and Chang Yi-wu. Chinese Trotskyites who came from outside Sinkiang included Sung Fu-yao (alias Sung Nientzu), Ho Yu-chu (alias Ho Keng-kuang), Cheng Tung-p'ai, Hsü Lien (alias Hsü Po-ta), Kuo Hsi-liang, Tu Ho-nien, Chang Ya-shao, Yang Po-tsing, Chou Chung-hui, Fu Hsi-jo, Pien Hsieh-tsing, Chung Ching-t'i, Wang Nai-chung (alias Wang Li-shih), Wang Yen-lin, Tsui Chi-ming, and Kang P'ing-ling.

It can readily be seen that unraveling such a plot required the utmost care and detection, so high had the infiltrators reached within my government. To take a typical case, Chang Hsin had plotted as early as 1933 to assassinate me, together with the other three plotters apprehended at that time, Ch'en Chung, T'ao Ming-yueh, and Li Hsiao-t'ien. By simulating hatred of these men however, he had maintained the government's confidence and was esteemed as a person of merit throughout the original April Uprising.

Again in 1937, he participated in plotting an abortive coup. Once more he concealed his malicious intent by displaying his "loyalty" to the government on every possible occasion. In his opening address at the celebration meeting, he reaffirmed his pledge of support to the Sinkiang government and its leaders, declaring that he would "fight mercilessly against all who betray the Revolution!" Fortunately I did not fall victim to his tactics because I had always been on the alert against precisely such treachery. His part was later revealed in confessions by captured conspirators.

Less easy to deal with were the insidious whisper campaign and rumor spreading initiated by Trotskyites located throughout the Soviet consulates in Tihua, Karashar, Ili, Tacheng, and Altai. Just prior to the attempted uprising, Sinkiang was swept with stories emanating from these sources to the effect that all the officials appointed by former governors Yang Tseng-hsin and Chin Shu-jen would soon be arrested on various false charges so that the vacancies left could be filled by my personal friends and relatives. This touched off a wave of unrest among officials in all levels of administration. Many of those appointed by former governors submitted their resignations in order to protect themselves against later retaliation as charged by the Trotskyite-inspired rumors. Some of these misguided officials actually participated in the plot, probably out of resentment against an action which had never been planned in the first place.

Another rumor started by oppositional elements charged that officials of the previous regime would be called "corrupt" and their property confiscated unless they voluntarily contributed large sums of money to my administration. Similarly Trotsky-ites tried to foment dissension among our many diverse nationalities by claiming that my policy of kinship to sovietism was antireligious, and therefore the religious tribes in particular should join hands to overthrow my rule and the six policies. These rumors were purposely spread to sow suspicion and to bring about mass hysteria so as to facilitate the activities of the Trotskyite elements of subversion. Unfortunately, as the above list indicates, many representatives of the various national groups were tricked into plotting against me through this tactic.

As we shall see shortly, these tactics were by no means

confined to the Fascist and Trotskyite plotters. They were duplicated and improved upon by Soviet and Chinese Communist conspirators. But the Sinkiang government learned in 1937 how to deal with its enemies. Such experience was to serve it well in the next years of crisis.

5

Communists: Comrades or Conspirators?

As THE FASCIST-TROTSKYITE PLOT showed, I would have to find outside support if I were to defend Sinkiang against foreign intrigue. With war clouds gathering ever more ominously over Nanking, I could expect little help from the central government. My Marxist beliefs and my familiarity with the nationality program of the Soviet Union inclined me toward Moscow as an avenue of assistance. Nevertheless I could not rest at night for the gnawing suspicion in my mind that neither the Russians nor the Chinese Communists could be fully trusted to help Sinkiang unselfishly.

On the positive side of the ledger, it was clear by 1937 that Russia was willing to provide China with arms, munitions, and even man power in defense against the Japanese invaders. Within China itself the Communists had a more forward-looking program in terms of China's needs than did many groups within the Kuomintang. Because of Sinkiang's location it was logical to rely on the strong neighbor across the border for material support and military assistance. Already in 1933, and in 1937, Moscow had proved it was ready to meet my needs for pacifying the many turbulent elements within the province.

Against this, however, stood cause for concern. When the Chinese Communists were forced into the southern part of China after the disastrous Canton revolution in 1929, the central government opened up a series of extermination campaigns and ringed the Red area with armed blockhouses. As Chiang Kai-shek's troops won repeated successes in their "anti-bandit" campaigns, it became evident that flight was the only alternative to annihilation for Mao Tse-tung and his followers.

Accordingly, the Chinese Communists abandoned their celebrated capital of Juichin in Kiangsi province and began the so-called "Long March" to escape Nationalist armies. After thousands of miles of wandering and suffering, continually fighting rear-guard actions and plundering the countryside as they went, the Reds settled in Shensi province, with their base at Yenan.

This was as close as they could get to an overland route to the Soviet Union, who it was hoped would render them significant military and economic aid. But the supply lines through Outer Mongolia were long and arduous, and the Japanese had penetrated Mongol groups throughout this area by promise for a pan-Mongol union and cleverly placed bribes. If the CCP were to link up with Moscow, it would have been more expedient to work through Sinkiang. Evidently Mao's followers did not know that Moscow was already supplying me with money, men, and munitions and that Sinkiang provided a safe refuge, for instead they continued their journey to the northwest at additional cost of lives and equipment.

Sinkiang did not offer an unmixed blessing for the Reds, however. On the one hand, seizure of the province could give them a defensive-offensive base with proximity to the Russians. It might serve as an area for industrial programs and progressive nationality policies, combining the rich raw materials and the diverse population in a model Soviet province within China. With the lack of famine because of Sinkiang's well-developed irrigation system, the region could support the extra guerrilla forces necessary for raiding Nationalist-held territory. Finally, it could serve as a springboard for Chinese Communist penetration of Moslem groups in Central and Southeast Asia.

Against these attractions, however, Sinkiang posed a threat to Mao Tse-tung and his followers. While the Reds had tried for more than ten years to win support for their policies in central and southern China, my six great policies had already unified the many nationalities of Sinkiang. The brutal Communist land reform policy practiced in Kiangsi had to be abandoned in favor of more moderate measures. At the end of the Long March the Reds knew that they were incapable of winning China by themselves. Only by abandoning the name and army designations of the Red troops and joining with the Kuomintang against Japan could they win the support of the Chinese people. Had Japan not struck China at this very time, forcing a national emergency which brought surface unity within the country and between China and Russia as well, Mao Tse-tung might well have been summoned to Moscow or purged from the party, as had all his predecessors, so total appeared the failure of his policies.

Against this dark picture, Sinkiang shone like a rosy beacon, summoning hope to all the genuinely progressive and liberal reform groups in China. It had routed the fascist-imperialist plotters. It had unified the many races. It had begun programs of socialist construction and socialist welfare, together with assistance from the Soviet Union. Small wonder that Yenan looked with mixed feelings upon my rule, recognizing the advantages of my friendly co-operation and yet fearing the success of my rival power and prestige.

Stalin and Mao decided on a policy of winning my support in order to lull my suspicions and thereby to lay the groundwork for eventual overthrow of my regime. At the same time, each of them plotted against the other, since there can never be full agreement between any Russian and Chinese over who will control China's borderlands. From the past centuries of history these have been areas of conflict between the two peoples. Even while they were singing the comradely strains of "The International," the Russian and Chinese Communists looked at each other with shining eyes, but suspicious hearts.

Since I had proved that the six great policies were the best answer to the needs of the Chinese people, Sinkiang had become the focus of attention of many Communists from Yenan. This was particularly convenient, because Tihua lay on the route to Moscow and provided a convenient stopping-off place for those who made the journey from Moscow to Yenan and return. Naturally, I was interested in what these travelers had to say, and finally I decided to test the sincerity of Yenan by expressing my willingness to join the Chinese Communist Party.

This was not so radical a decision as might appear, for after the Japanese attack on July 7, 1937, all China united under Chiang Kai-shek in defense of the homeland. As in 1924-27, the Chinese Communists joined with the Nationalists in a common front, burying their long-standing feud and agreeing to merge forces against the enemy. My membership in the Chinese Communist Party under these circumstances would in no way be disloyal to the nation's leader, Generalissimo Chiang, for the Communists themselves were pledged to his support.

It was during 1937 that Ch'en Shao-yü and K'ang Sheng, both high-ranking Communists then on their way back to Yenan after several years in Russia, stopped by to see me in Tihua. Ch'en made clear their interest in me by remarking, "When I bade Stalin farewell, he asked me to speak personally to Sheng *Tupan* (Commissioner Sheng)." I interpreted this favorably and awaited a propitious moment just prior to their departure for raising the question of my joining the CCP.

"Your joining the Chinese Communist Party would be a

matter of pride for all of us," Ch'en replied. He added that as soon as he reached Yenan he and K'ang Sheng would take the matter up with "Comrade Mao." I knew that this interlude reflected favorably upon my prospects, since once Yenan was aware that I stood high in Stalin's eyes, my membership would be eagerly sought after.

I was justified in my feeling, for not long afterward another prominent member of the CCP, Jen Pi-shih, flew to Sinkiang on his way to Moscow. I knew that Jen was a member of the Politburo and wondered whether he would reveal any of the thinking at this top level of the CCP apparatus. Much to my pleasure and surprise, he greeted me warmly and as soon as we were alone in my office, declared, "Chairman Mao has put the matter before the Chinese Communist Politburo. All Politburo members, including Chairman Mao, Chu Teh, Chou En-lai, Ch'en Shao-yü, K'ang Sheng, Ch'en Yün, and myself welcome your joining the Party and look upon this with a feeling of pride and honor."

At last I felt assured of the comradeship and sincerity of the CCP leaders, and a feeling of warm confidence arose at Jen's words. This was indeed recognition of the success of the six great policies and acknowledgment of Sinkiang's progressive place in the Chinese revolution. But my pleasure faded quickly, as Jen cautioned against immediate consummation of my membership. "Owing to the many years of close relations between Sinkiang and the Soviet Union," he added, "and because of the importance of your position, we will have to report this matter to the Comintern and to Stalin before we initiate procedures for your joining the party."

I listened to him with mixed feelings. On the one hand, I knew that Stalin would have no objection to me personally, and that any formality of this sort was merely a temporary delay in proceedings. On the other hand, I wondered anew what precisely was the relationship between Moscow and Yenan? Were they plotting together to keep me from having access to the secret meetings of the CCP? Or was Yenan so subservient to Moscow that so simple a question as my Party membership had to be cleared with the Kremlin even though the entire Politburo of the CCP had already expressed its enthusiastic agreement?

I awaited the return of Jen Pi-shih anxiously. This question of my relations with Yenan and Moscow was of no small importance for the future of Sinkiang. My suspicions were not quieted by Jen's message after his trip to Russia. "The Comintern and Stalin realize that you have acquired all the qualifications for party membership," he said, "but they believe you should refrain temporarily from joining the Chinese Communist Party. The delicate role Sinkiang now occupies in the international scene and the importance of your own political position in China combine to make your present membership undesirable. Of course you must recognize that this is a decision in the interests of all concerned and in no way reflects unfavorably upon you or the progressive policies which you have followed in Sinkiang."

His honeyed words aroused no suspicions on my face, and I replied diplomatically, but in my heart I was filled with wonderment. Clearly there was more to this than met the eye. Perhaps there was disagreement between Mao and Stalin, or perhaps Jen was testing my willingness to obey Party orders. I resolved that there was only one way to settle things. I would go to Moscow and see Stalin personally.

Looking back on it now, I am not a little surprised at the ease with which I arrived at a decision to take my personal and provincial problems before a man who was not only leader of a great power but the acknowledged head of the greatest international revolutionary movement in history. Yet at the time the decision did not seem so momentous or hazardous. It was clear that Sinkiang occupied a pivotal position in both Soviet and Chinese Communist strategy. It was the life line of supply to China, fighting Russia's battles as well as her own against Japan. It was also the line of communication for Yenan and the most auspicious place for the new socialist society to emerge. As promulgator of the kinship to Soviet policy and of the reforms in Sinkiang, I was of key importance to both Stalin and Mao. If there were any dispute as to my future relationship with these two men, it seemed only natural that I should iron out the problem with Stalin himself.

Before I left for Moscow, I was to have one last reminder of the conspiratorial network which seems to enmesh all "comradely" activities within the Communist movement. One of the emissaries from Yenan who had been working in my provincial administration, Fang Lin, approached me upon learning that I was to visit the Kremlin. "In case you meet Stalin or Molotov, or other Soviet dignitaries," he said, "and in case they ask you about the work of the Chinese Communist Party workers in Sinkiang, please tell them that I and the others are doing fine here." I replied that I certainly would say something good about the work they had all been doing, since I was genuinely pleased at the help and co-operation they had given me, particularly in propaganda and education. Fang showed distinct pleasure at my reply and withdrew with a smile.

The episode was not ended, however, for, on the eve of my departure, Fang called on me again and said, "In case you meet Stalin, Molotov, or other Soviet dignitaries in Moscow and in case they ask you about the work of the Chinese Communist Party workers in Sinkiang, please do not make a great show of politeness to us. You can criticize us if you like." Astonished at his words, I replied, "I suppose you are saying this out of politeness because your words are in direct contradiction of what you told me last time." To this Fang remonstrated, "No, I am not saying this out of politeness. I am frank with you. The Party welcomes criticism because the judgments and criticisms of others will help us to improve ourselves. Besides, this really is not contradictory to what I said last time but only an addition to it."

"Well, Mr. Fang," I retorted, "we have been on intimate terms with each other and I think it is highly unnecessary for us to talk in the usual 'party line' way. Several days ago you asked me to say something good about you and your fellow workers in the presence of Stalin or Molotov. Today you tell me not to make a show of politeness in Moscow and to criticize you if I like. I ask you: is this contradictory or not?" Fang Lin made no answer but simply bowed briefly and left.

I was to have cause to recollect these two rather enigmatic conversations at a later date, when Fang Lin proved that the line between comradeship and conspiratorial activity is a thin one among the Communists. At the time, however, I simply chalked it up to the timidity of lower level Chinese Communists before the Kremlin and their anxiety about the possible implications of criticism. I determined that I would speak frankly to Stalin about the entire problem of Sinkiang, its need for Russian assistance, its future role in the Chinese revolution, and finally about my own desire for membership in the Chinese Communist Party. Only in this manner could I truly determine the sincerity of Soviet friendship and plan the future path of Sinkiang in terms of a new China.

6

Conference in the Kremlin

ALTHOUGH RUSSIA and China were partners in a sense, fighting Japan with Chinese man power and Russian fire power delivered in the form of aircraft, artillery, trucks, and advisers, I took no chances of my trip leaking to Nationalist authorities. The surface unity between the Communists and the Nationalists belied continuing underlying tensions. While Yenan pledged allegiance to the Generalissimo and I was theoretically free to affiliate with either of China's two major parties, there was no doubt that the marriage was one of convenience and neither partner expected it to last indefinitely.

Therefore, I concealed my preparations from my associates, and as the time approached for the long journey to Moscow I made known certain illnesses which had, in fact, been troubling me for some time. My predicament was a difficult one, for while I was acting in the genuine interests of new China and endeavoring to safeguard Sinkiang against all forms of foreign control, misinterpretations of my mission might cast me in the eyes of many as a traitor. I feared that, if I informed the authorities of my intent, malicious persons would conspire to besmirch my motives. The only alternative was secrecy and the hope that at some later time I would be able to tell my story fully and frankly.

August, 1938, marked one turning point in the turbulent history of Sinkiang, for that month found me, accompanied by my family, en route to Moscow with a mission of considerable importance. Not only was the delicate question of maintaining Sinkiang as a Chinese territory complicated by the growing numbers of Soviet advisers and amounts of Soviet aid, but the role Sinkiang was to play in the war against imperialism was of concern to me. Would it be possible to bargain with Stalin so as to win Russian support, while avoiding the satellite status of Outer Mongolia? Or would Stalin play a cunning game of limited help in order to keep Sinkiang dependent on his whim?

As the train wound its slow, tortuous journey through Central Asia, these thoughts and doubts kept returning to my mind. One of the problems of dealing with the Russians was the atmosphere of conspiracy and intrigue which permeated everywhere. The fantastic story of General Ma Chung-ying, the young Moslem hero-warrior, was a case in point. I regarded Ma as a hero because his almost legendary career had won my esteem for its bravery and determination, even though we were bitter enemies for many years. His deeds were told many times over around campfires in Central Asia, and his fate at the hands of the Russians cut short a valiant life.

I knew of Ma as early as 1928 when he was but seventeen, yet his ambitious, reckless personality rallied thousands of men of Moslem faith to fight against the oppression of local war lords in Kansu province. Ma's boldness inspired fanatical devotion in his men, and, when the provincial authorities recognized the determination of the rebels, they appeased them by naming Ma the commander of the 36th Division, based at Kanchow, Liangchow, and Suchow.

About this time the Trotskyites in China, co-operating with the Japanese imperialists, decided to work upon Ma's susceptible ego and to transform him into a cat's-paw for winning control of the millions of Moslems in Central Asia. In August, 1930,

Tokyo sent Tadashi Onishi as a clandestine emissary to Ma, masked under the name of Yu Hua-t'ing. He incited Ma to seize Sinkiang and to establish a Moslem state there, promising that Japan would supply the necessary arms and money.

It was indeed a tragedy that Ma fought against the interests of the people of Sinkiang, for had he been on the progressive side he would have been an invaluable warrior. As it was, he joined with Chang Ya-shao, Yang Po-tsing, and Tsai Hsüeh-chun, all Chinese Trotskyites, in three futile invasions of the province. The first and second attempts were defeated by the provincial forces, and, in the third instance, Soviet troops and planes tipped the balance of power against Ma.

At this point, the life of Ma took a strange turn. Faced with death or capture at the hands of the pursuing provincial forces, he first moved toward India where he hoped to gain refuge. Alert to the possibilities of British intrigue in Sinkiang through Ma as a mediary, the Soviets moved quickly to contact the fleeing general in southern Sinkiang. To the amazement of the world, the same Ma Chung-ying who had been defeated disastrously, by Russian arms supplied to the provincial government, only a short time later entered the Soviet Union in a vehicle provided by Moscow!

The explanation for this apparent turnabout in Soviet tactics became evident much later. At the time it was thought that Stalin was keeping Ma as a check upon my own power and that at some future date the Russians would overthrow my regime with Ma as a powerful, popular figurehead. Actually this was the line spread by Trotskyites, who wanted to estrange Sinkiang from the Soviet Union and particularly to weaken my relations with Stalin.

It was foresight on Stalin's part, however, which caused him to offer Ma refuge with the prospect of returning to his Moslem people. By this move, Stalin not only denied British imperialism a valuable agent in Central Asia but also gained a promising ally against Japan, who was intriguing among the Moslems in northwestern China. Since Stalin knew that eventually Japan would seek to spread her control westward from Manchuria, he recognized in Ma a prize asset.

Had history worked out according to this plan, all might have been different for Ma Chung-ying. But as I noted earlier, the pervasive spirit of conspiracy casts uncertainty upon the future of all in the Soviet Union. Ma's tragic experience cautioned me against any undue optimism as I journeyed to Moscow, for his was a lesson in the problem of dealing with a Stalin who was surrounded by plotters, schemers, and foreign agents.

According to some of the Chinese Communists who had been living in Russia during the years immediately after Ma's departure from Sinkiang, the young General was initially treated very favorably and was quite receptive to his new environment. Accompanied by his confidants and secretaries, he brought with him a vast store of wealth, mostly in gold, and a handsome herd of camels. In a fine hostel some forty miles away from Moscow, Ma studied Russian two hours a day, went to the theater regularly, and appeared in good health and spirits.

Whenever Ma needed money, he simply asked his Russian hosts to sell part of his gold. Frequently, he gave them precious jewels as gifts and generous bonus presents at holidays, so that news of his wealth became generally known. Gradually, the circle of Russian attendants widened, and demands became ever more frequent for loans from Ma. His generosity resulted in more than five hundred ounces of gold being loaned to those around him. Gradually, Ma became more suspicious of the ability of some borrowers to spend the money wisely or to repay it even in part, and his personal secretaries advised him to forego further handouts. Naturally this aroused tension between Ma's group and the Russians, tension which pointed up the basic question: was General Ma a guest or a prisoner of the Soviet Union?

One day the Russian attendants heard that Stalin was about to grant General Ma an audience, prior to sending him back to China. Fearing that he would ask Stalin to punish them for their incessant demands for money, they plotted to kill him. First, they poisoned his food and drink with drugs injurious to the heart and lungs. When the young general, always hale and hearty, began to spit blood and to exhale with difficulty, his secretaries assumed he had an attack of tuberculosis. Ma, however, became suspicious and ordered one of his most trusted staff officers to take charge of the cooking. He recovered from the attack but ceased his studies of Russian, refused to go out in public, and took no further interest in his study of Marxism-Leninism.

Thwarted in their initial scheme, the Russian attendants then submitted a confidential report to Stalin, shrewdly designed to discredit the general in the eyes of the Kremlin. After noting Ma's "dejection" because of his "attack of tuberculosis," the report went on to quote alleged criticism by Ma of Marxist-Leninist ideology and to emphasize Ma's religious practices. His indifference to Russian entertainment, his refusal to study the language, and his insult to the government by stationing one of his own men to supervise the cooking were cited as evidence of Ma's "hostile attitude." In the tense atmosphere of the mid-thirties, with purge and persecution whipping through the Soviet Union, this report seemed certain to doom Ma Chung-ying.

Stalin refused to accept the report, however. He could not believe that Ma would change his attitude overnight, and therefore assigned new attendants to the hostel for further examination of the facts. Since the new attendants were from the secret police, the NKVD, and therefore comrades of those previously indebted to Ma, it was a foregone conclusion that a second report would only verify the facts of the first. Stalin finally had no choice but to cancel his plan to receive Ma and to forego, at least for the time being, the proposed return to China.

About this time I learned in Sinkiang of Stalin's plans to unite the Moslem peoples of Central Asia, prior to sovietizing this area and building it as a buffer against Japanese imperialism. Originally Ma was to be the leader of this movement, and thus his period of language study and political indoctrination was highly important to the Kremlin. Apresoff, the Soviet consul general in Tihua, once approached me on this matter, acting on instructions from Stalin. Apresoff asked for my opinion on the advisability of Ma's returning to Sinkiang, preliminary to uniting the Moslems of Chinghai and Kansu provinces against Japanese imperialism.

I told Apresoff that, while I admired Ma and would welcome him as a subordinate to me, it was unthinkable that he should interfere with the provincial authorities in Kansu and Chinghai. Were Ma to use Sinkiang as a base of operations against Chinese rule in northwest China this would embarrass my relations with those groups and particularly with the Ma family of Kansu. My refusal, coupled with the intrigue against Ma, canceled the plan at that time.

The next move by the Russian attendants was to petition Stalin to deport Ma and his secretaries on grounds that they "made reactionary remarks." By this time, Stalin was aware of growing trouble but was too preoccupied with important domestic economic problems and foreign policy to pursue the matter further. He approved the petition for deportation. With this *prima facie* evidence of Kremlin support, the NKVD executed Ma Chung-ying, together with his entire staff. After destroying one of China's most promising young generals and seizing all of his wealth, the intriguers informed Stalin that Ma had been conspiring with the Trotskyites against the Soviet Union. That Stalin believed this story was to become evident to me in my conferences in the Kremlin.

I knew all but the final details of Ma's tragic tale and wondered en route to Moscow whether plotters around Stalin had poisoned his mind against me, as they had against Ma Chung-ying. Was this why my membership in the CCP had been postponed? Even my fellow passengers in the train seemed insecure and frightened, unwilling to converse with one another or to share the comradeship that comes from long and arduous travel together. Hardly a month passed in 1937 and 1938 that news of some new execution or trial did not tell of high-ranking Soviet officials convicted of conspiring with foreign powers against the socialist state. Small wonder that my eager anticipation of seeing Stalin personally was tempered by anxious doubts as to the fate of myself and my family, alone and without diplomatic protection in this land racked with unrest, rumor, and fear.

As we stepped off the train in Moscow's cavernous central station, a "welcoming party" of Soviet officials whisked us into waiting limousines and hurried us through the dark streets to a hostel outside the city. My fears seemed unfounded. Surely, if we were to be imprisoned, there would have been much less ceremony and reception in connection with our arrival. True to the declared reason for my trip, ill health, the next day found me receiving careful medical attention at the Moscow Hospital, where every courtesy was extended. Despite my several trips to this public institution and the brief but proper reception at the station, my visit escaped general notice and even the Chinese ambassador to Russia apparently did not learn of my pilgrimage to the Kremlin.

Within twenty-four hours of my arrival, I received an invitation to that spired collection of ancient buildings which housed the highest echelons of the Soviet government. According to the message, both Molotov and Voroshilov would be happy to grant me an audience. Much to my surprise, Stalin was also present. In fact, his might well have been the only name on the invitation, so completely did he dominate the conversation compared with his two colleagues. Never did they differ with him; seldom did either of them offer a point in advance of Stalin.

Interestingly enough, Litvinoff, then Commissar of Foreign Affairs, took no part in this or the subsequent conferences I had in the Kremlin. I recognized that my negotiations were not to be considered official, especially since I was acting without the knowledge of the recognized government of China. It was only proper, then, for the talks to be held with Stalin acting purely as Party spokesman and to maintain the fiction of separating the formal conduct of policy by the government of the U.S.S.R. from the informal affairs of the Communist Party of the Soviet Union. In this, as in other matters, the Russians have maintained a peculiar devotion to legal niceties. It forced other countries to employ legal channels of protest when the Russian "legal" authorities actually lacked control over the most serious aspects of Soviet policy, namely the subversive arm of the Communist International.

Stalin opened our interview by asking about the war situation in China. In particular, he expressed interest in the various revolts in Sinkiang which had occurred almost simultaneously with the Japanese invasion of the China coast and below the Great Wall. After listening closely to my account, he agreed that the local Sinkiang uprisings in 1937 had been Trotskyite machinations, aided and abetted by Nazi-Japanese militarist plotting to establish an advance base for assault against Soviet Russia. Voroshilov pursued the military details, especially those concerning transportation and communication, highlighting thereby Russian concern over the possible use of Sinkiang as an avenue of invasion to the soft underbelly of the Soviet Union.

Molotov then quizzed me on matters political, economic, as well as cultural. His incisive mind and probing questions commanded respect for his careful, if plodding, methods. Although I was somewhat fatigued by this trio of inquisitors, I welcomed the interval following tea at which time I was encouraged to raise matters of personal concern. Being curious about the fate of the former Soviet Consul General, Apresoff, I casually inquired after his health. It was of particular interest, since one of my companions on the long trip from Tihua had been Apresoff's successor, a mild-mannered Russian by the name of Maney. Stalin brusquely replied that Apresoff had "gone the way" of Ma Chung-ying. In other words, Apresoff had been killed in the purge. Stalin then asked whether Maney had made any mistakes in Sinkiang. Although I replied in the negative, it seemed certain that Maney's trip had also been made under the pretext of "ill health." Unlike myself, in his case the cure might be execution!

In this, as in subsequent meetings, Stalin remained friendly and considerate, remembering the proper pleasantries before and after the business at hand. At no time, however, did he indulge in rambling discourse or intimate confidences. He was clearly a man of many responsibilities and one determined to carry them out in a businesslike way. Before each interview Stalin had apparently received a complete and detailed briefing on the situation in Sinkiang, for on every occasion he showed a complete grasp of the problems I raised and was ready with suggestions and solutions for the various questions at hand.

Our next conference gave me more opportunity to outline plans for developing Sinkiang, culturally and economically, toward the goal of a model socialist state. While my plans suggested an autonomous status for the province, at no time did I raise, nor did Stalin discuss, the possibility of Sinkiang becoming an independent republic, much less attaching it to the Soviet Union. Rather the goal was in terms of carrying the ideals of socialism and progressive reforms ahead in Central Asia so that they might penetrate the important areas of the Middle East and Southeast Asia.

In particular, I urged that Stalin speed deliveries of industrial equipment, which had been ordered previously but had never arrived, and I pointed out how this might build our Three Year Plan successfully. "If Sinkiang, the most under-developed province of China, could be improved with the assistance of Soviet advisers, experts, and technicians, together with Russian-made capital equipment, this would not only affect developments in China's northwest provinces. It would also carry considerable impact in India, thereby allowing 450 million Chinese and 300 million Indians to better understand communism. It would strengthen their friendship with the Soviet Union. It would prove that the Russians, and their leader, Stalin, are faithfully carrying out Lenin's will to help the underdeveloped peoples of Asia."

Speaking about Stalin's special interest, nationalities, I added, "Once a new Sinkiang comes into being with all nationalities enjoying a happy and prosperous life, it will prove that communism is the savior of mankind. All religious groups, including Moslems and Buddhists, might then see that by developing our economy in this fashion their fanciful paradise in heaven can come into reality on earth. These religious people comprising eighty percent of Sinkiang's population, will then support the six great policies and will strive to make a new Sinkiang serve in the forefront of battle against Japan."

I realized that my words had come in the rush of excitement

and enthusiasm for my native country, but Stalin smiled sympathetically and said, "You are quite right." Molotov and Voroshilov nodded agreement. After a few puffs on his pipe, Stalin turned to Molotov and somewhat abruptly remarked, "Rush the delivery of capital equipment to Sinkiang." In response to my request for weapons and munitions, which had also been ordered previously, he suggested that Voroshilov and I take the matter up at a separate conference.

Since everything seemed to be proceeding smoothly and Stalin was obviously in a favorable mood, I decided to broach the delicate and more personal problem of my future relations with Yenan. "I am a devoted disciple of Marxism-Leninism," I told Stalin, "and in 1937 I applied for membership in the Chinese Communist Party through Ch'en Shao-yü, K'ang Sheng, and Teng Fa. The Politburo of the CCP, including Mao Tse-tung, Chu Teh, Chou En-lai, Ch'en Shao-yü, K'ang Sheng, Teng Fa, Ch'en Yün, and Jen Pi-shih unanimously approved my application but deferred final action until consultation with the Third International." I then recounted Jen Pi-shih's explanation of why my membership should be deferred further, and concluded, "I should like to know what your decision is about my joining the CCP because I wish to receive party training and indoctrination immediately."

Stalin's reply was swift and unequivocal: "You may join the party now. I shall talk with you again about this before your return to Sinkiang."

I felt that a great weight was off my chest, that we had arrived at a frank and full understanding both of Sinkiang's problems and of my own prospects. It was with considerable ease and assurance, therefore, that I followed Stalin's lead and turned to a discussion of international events and of Sinkiang's relationship to the world struggle. As in the first meeting, Stalin wished to know more about the conspiracies engineered by Great Britain, Japan, and other imperialistic and fascist nations in Sinkiang. I summarized Ma Chung-ying's abortive efforts to create a Moslem state in Sinkiang and the collapse of the so-called "Turkistan Republic" in the south, a movement backed by Britain operating from India. "At the present," I assured him, "there is no major conspiracy active except for some scattered groups in southern Sinkiang who occasionally are lured into becoming British agents."

Molotov and Voroshilov seconded these observations about fascist aggressive intrigue but, as usual, it was Stalin who seized upon the smaller details and placed them in the context of an over-all statement of strategy and tactics. With respect to the immediate international situation and the long-range prospects of the Chinese civil war, he warned, "In addition to preventing those in southern Sinkiang from becoming British agents, it is equally important to guard against the infiltration of fascist and imperialist Trotskyite spies. China, during its war with Japan, must maintain a superficial peace with Great Britain. It is the fascist countries, such as Germany, Italy, and Japan, which are desperately pursuing aggressive policies while the imperialists such as Britain, France, and the United States pursue milder colonial policies. Comparatively speaking, it is easier to deal with imperialists than fascists. It is likely that China and other peace-loving countries will eventually stand side by side with Great Britain, France, and the United States to fight against Germany, Italy, and Japan. Ever since the October revolution, human history has moved into an epoch of colonial revolution and proletariat revolution. But because the capitalist imperialist and fascist countries remain strong, the Communists must have a period of 'peaceful coexistence' with at least some of the enemy."

I asked what he meant by the term "peaceful coexistence." Stalin sat thoughtfully for a moment, and then replied, " 'Peaceful coexistence' is an important strategy in the process of proletariat revolution and world revolution led by the Communist International. Until we are sure the Communist world can destroy the imperialist countries, communism and capitalism must 'coexist peacefully.' But the final victory absolutely belongs to communism, for imperialism is nothing but capitalism in decay."

Turning to the situation in China, Stalin concluded his lengthy discourse, "During the war against Japan, Sinkiang's position is vital. Its present mission is to serve as the innermost base of resistance. Its future mission is to guard the international communication line for attack. The present war situation is unfavorable to China, but Japan will not be able to conquer China alone. If China can get help from allied countries, Japanese forces will be ousted. A considerable period of 'peaceful coexistence' between the Chinese Communists and Nationalists will follow their victory over Japan. In order to win the war against Japan, to deal with both the Chinese Communists and Nationalists during their period of 'coexistence,' Sinkiang should maintain close contact with both Chiang Kai-shek and Mao Tse-tung. During the war and after the victory, the Nationalists will be materially superior to the Communists but victory of the Chinese Communists is ultimately almost a certainty."

I left Stalin's chamber's with a new understanding of how this short, unprepossessing looking man was able to rise to direct the world's strongest international revolutionary movement. I could not be unimpressed by his ability to relate the present to the future, the particular to the general. He had put into a few words thoughts with which I had been grappling for many months, sharply defining the precarious position of Sinkiang, balanced delicately between Yenan and Nanking, between imperialist and Communist.

By comparison, my discussion with Voroshilov was terse

and unimaginative. With Stalin, no record of the talk was taken, at least not to my knowledge. Voroshilov, however, meeting me in the Red Army headquarters, had a stenographer present to transcribe our conversation. I had the feeling that no word was unintentional, and the record would be examined by Stalin.

Voroshilov met all my demands, agreeing that material ordered by the former governor, Chin Shu-jen, would be delivered within two months. I scanned his list of items and found all the missing equipment for which we had been waiting eagerly more than five years. Apparently Stalin had resolved whatever doubts may have been in his mind about the wisdom of aiding my government and was now prepared to push the program to the hilt.

Just before I left Voroshilov's office, he inquired about the Soviet military consultants and instructors in Sinkiang, saying, "Please tell me whether they have committed any mistakes." As with Stalin's inquiry about the new consul general, I felt this was less a move to please me than a means of getting more information on subordinate officials. Apparently even a Chinese informant could hand over a Russian citizen to the secret police!

As can be imagined, the mental strain of these conferences began to tell on me, especially since I had not really been in good health and the long trip had proved most arduous. The next day was doubly welcome, then, for it brought the only true social occasion of the entire visit. At Stalin's behest, my family joined me at the Molotov *dacha,* in the pleasant countryside far from the gray Moscow environs. In addition to the three leaders with whom I had been negotiating, Mikoyan, Commissar of Foreign Trade, and another prominent official took part.

It was a relaxing atmosphere, and Stalin made the most of it, joking and drinking toasts to all about. A different personality emerged from that customarily seen in public and official conferences. To our pleasant surprise Svetliana, his daughter, joined the party and proved quite affectionate with her father, as he playfully combed her lovely hair. We later learned that she visited him regularly once a week, on leave from a near-by boarding school.

Although we Chinese are known for our generous toasts and the flow of wine at meals, the famous Russian capacity for drinking put us to shame as the dinner progressed. At one point Stalin came to where my wife and I were sitting and feted us in a manner rivaling our celebrated Chinese hospitality. Avoiding all official topics, he appeared to relax and enjoy the escape from his burden of responsibility, here in the bosom of the Molotov home. But it would be misleading to think the evening one of unlimited hilarity and fun, for following supper we adjourned to another room where we saw a sober and moving film, entitled, "If War Should Come Tomorrow." Nor was our departure as care-free and casual as the party warranted. Accompanying Stalin back to Moscow in his car, I was amazed at the frantic speed with which the car raced down the deserted road, free of all traffic controls and obviously driven so as to lessen the possibility of assassination.

These happy moments set the tone for the days of casual sight-seeing and strolling, which I was then able to do with my family in Moscow, secure in the knowledge that Stalin was acting to meet the needs of my province as well as of myself. On the eve of my departure from the Soviet capital, however, one final event took place which threw all that had preceded into a new perspective.

As we were packing for the trip home, a party official called at our hostel with personal instructions from Stalin. According to this message, I was to be given special consideration on the personal advice of the Georgian dictator, and admitted to the All-Union Communist Party immediately. In other words, although I was Chinese, I was to become a member of the Russian Communist Party! The envoy added that I would become subordinate to the Politburo in Moscow upon signature of an affidavit, but that at some later date I would be "permitted" to join the Chinese Communist Party.

Once again it seemed that I was being pushed around like a pawn on a chessboard, yet the bearing of this official, as well as the tone of the message, left no alternative but to sign the affidavit. Were I to hesitate or question Stalin's decision, I and Sinkiang might lose all hope of Soviet support. The Russian leader was already suspicious enough, and with good reason, of persons plotting to disrupt his plans and overthrow his power. In view of the generous commitments which Voroshilov and others had made to me, it seemed to be asking little to join the Russian Communist Party, especially since I had a promise of later transfer to the CCP.

Stilling my renewed doubts, I agreed. Shortly thereafter, a second official came with my certificate of membership, No. 1859118, together with a copy of the party regulations. Still a third messenger came in the early morning hours when our packing was finished and we were awaiting the official limousine, this one bearing gifts and accompanied by seven packing cases of presents from the Kremlin. Compared with the few souvenirs I had brought from Tihua, these seemed to be an overwhelming token of friendship.

Small wonder that we left the city in an aura of cheer and optimism. I had seen Stalin not once, but three times. I had been dealt with by the most important men in the Kremlin as though I were head of China, instead of being merely governor of a province, and a rather underdeveloped province at that. We had broken the log jam that had delayed delivery of weapons and munitions for six long years. We had established a firm economic basis for the Three Year Plan that would transform Sinkiang from a struggling nomadic wilderness into a base for China's future industrialization. Most important, Stalin had personally expressed concern over Sinkiang's importance and confidence in my direction of Sinkiang's future. Surely these auspicious signs were more significant than any mechanical details concerning my party membership!

In fact I thought of a clever reason justifying Stalin's tactic at the time: deception. By enrolling me in the Russian Communist Party, I could flatly and honestly deny to questioners any connection with the Chinese Communists in Yenan. So far as my Marxist convictions were concerned, I had never attempted to conceal them, and all who knew me were familiar with my ideas. My independent thinking was tolerated by Nanking, for the simple reason that Nanking lacked the power to remove me. This was true of many so-called war lords who ruled their provinces as virtual satrapies, granting only token allegiance to the central government during this period.

But indeed I was naive to attribute this motivation to Stalin. His deception was far more cleverly designed than I imagined, and it was directed not only against the central government but against a number of parties simultaneously. Only later did I realize that, by enrolling me in the Soviet apparatus, Stalin gained an instrument of blackmail, for while my Marxist views were tolerated grudgingly by the Nationalist leaders, being subject to discipline from the Kremlin would lead to outright denunciation as a traitor. As the circumstances show, this was the furthest thought from my mind but the surface features were admittedly unattractive to outsiders.

Secondly, Stalin attempted to keep me subordinate to Moscow, thereby preserving Sinkiang as an exclusively Russian sphere, to the disadvantage of Yenan. Not until I recognized his tactic of divide and rule was this maneuver clear to me. Yet looking back upon my Soviet party membership I can see its place in the over-all Stalinist pattern of splitting China from her allies, of splitting Chinese from Chinese, and finally of splitting Communist from Communist. Such was his masterful cunning which kept rival power centers from forming which might threaten his own power!

Within a year of my trip to Moscow, Stalin was to sign the Nazi-Soviet pact, reversing with a stroke of the pen the worldwide anti-fascist struggle. Within two years, I was to feel the full force of a Moscow ultimatum, virtually dictating my turning over all vestiges of independent control in Sinkiang to Soviet authorities. Within three years, Stalin personally was to plot against my life. So swiftly does the fate of man change and disaster strike at the moment of greatest glory.

7

The Red Noose Tightens

ALTHOUGH YENAN and Moscow clashed in their ultimate objectives for Sinkiang, each desiring to wrest it from control by the other, both agreed on the immediate goal: sovietization by all possible means. Insofar as this meant a progressive attitude toward the nationality question, a transformation of Sinkiang's feudal economy, and arousing the political consciousness of the masses, there was no conflict with my six great policies. However, I was too popular and too powerful an independent figure for the Reds to tolerate my existence, and every year saw increasing infiltration of Sinkiang by plotters designing my death and the destruction of my administration.

Clear as the strategy and tactics of the Communists appear in retrospect, it must be recognized that my awareness of their plotting came slowly. It was difficult to remain suspicious of those who helped to detect the fascist-imperialist spies, who aided the reconstruction of Sinkiang's economy, who developed our fighting power through assistance and advice. Only gradually did the accumulation of evidence by my own police agents present the true picture of conspiracy directed from Moscow and Yenan.

One of the most insidious means of poisoning the minds of Sinkiang youth against me and my administration was the clever use of propaganda. This softened up the loyal Sinkiang patriots in preparation for assassination and riots which would enmesh their confused minds in action against the government. Communist theoreticians from Russia and Yenan worked openly as my advisers, but secretly spread rumors maligning my administration.

The methods they adopted varied according to the political training and the educational level of specific groups. To the intellectuals, especially the faculty and students of colleges and the instructors and cadets of military academies, the theories of Marxism-Leninism were propagated in a manner to reflect unfavorably on my six great policies. Special attention was given students related to persons high in the government so that these misguided youths could serve a double purpose. On the one hand, they could propagate doctrines at home which might win new converts to the conspiracy. On the other hand, they could ferret out staunch Sinkiang patriots as targets for assassination when the conspiracy erupted in violence. Those students who vacillated were threatened or cajoled into a neutral stand, so that they would not inform the government of these subversive activities. Thus did the Reds corrupt the ancient doctrine of right relationships and, in particular, undermine the concept of family loyalty in their efforts to win power.

One of the incidents which aroused my suspicions along these lines took place with a close friend who had been a native of my village and a schoolmate many years before, Tu Chung-yüan. Because of our intimate relationship, he was sent into Sinkiang by Chou En-lai, ostensibly as a tourist but actually in order to write articles extolling the achievements of my government. This was in the honeymoon period of my relations with Yenan, and I was naturally quite pleased to renew an old acquaintance under such auspicious circumstances.

When Tu returned to China proper after his tour, he published a pamphlet entitled "Sheng Shih-ts'ai and the New Sinkiang," written in such a way as to win friendship and confidence for Tu throughout my province. While the statistical data and the facts he included were all accurate, he carefully refrained from a single word of criticism, although I would have been the first to admit shortcomings in my own regime.

Following the pamphlet's appearance, Tu visited Tihua again. Now his business was more serious, for, as he explained to me, "I am here again because I am interested in Sinkiang's affairs. Is there any way I can be of service to the province?" Prompting from me failed to elicit any preference on his part. "Whatever you decide will be fine with me," he said, "I have no opinion as to my job whatsoever."

I was quite happy to have this opportunity to make use of Tu, since I lacked experienced engineers and industrial planners, and so a few days later I asked him to serve as Commissioner of Reconstruction Affairs. "You are a graduate of the High School of Technology in Japan," I said, "and since your return from that country you have served in various capacities in industry. I think that as Reconstruction Commissioner you could give us a great deal of help in developing a new Sinkiang."

Tu remained silent for a moment, obviously not enthused by my proposal. Then he explained that his interests had shifted and, as a journalist, he had felt his talents lay more in communication through cultural and educational work. Although I was a little disappointed at his declining my first offer, I was willing to co-operate with an old colleague and responded by offering him either Commissioner of Education or Chancellor of Sinkiang College. I added, "Both jobs suit your interest, and it is up to you to make the choice."

"I am really not interested in desk work or going to meetings," Tu replied. "I prefer to take up the Chancellor's post."

This conversation piqued my curiosity, for Tu seemed as

unlike a college chancellor as anyone I had known. Why had he taken so apparently an insignificant and meaningless a job after traveling hundreds of miles from Chungking to offer his services? I resolved to pursue the conversation further and meanwhile to place a close check upon his activities as well as those of his subordinates in the college.

Some time later we were discussing the prospects of world revolution and in particular the spreading influence of Marxism. Tu commented that a close friend of his, Kao Tsung-ming, had started from the Three People's Principles of Dr. Sun Yat-sen but since had moved steadily leftward. Under the influence of Tsou Tao-feng, publisher of the magazine "Life Weekly," and Hu Yü-chih, editor of the same journal, Kao had embraced Marxism and finally had joined the CCP. Before Kao accepted Marxism, according to Tu, he had told his son that the epitaph on Kao's tombstone should read: "Here lies a man who led a meaningless life." After joining the CCP, however, he instructed his son to change the epitaph to read: "Here lies a man whose life was not all an empty dream."

I then asked Tu if he too believed in Marxism and had he joined the Chinese Communist Party likewise. Tu replied that while he was a follower of Communist ideology he had not yet joined the party. When I asked if Kao had ever advised him to do so, Tu replied in the negative.

As so often, I recognized this as a bout in shadow talking, not as a full and intimate exchange between friends. Tu could feel free in admitting his Marxist faith, because he knew that Sinkiang was following a pro-Soviet policy. His denial of party membership seemed suspicious, however, because Kao and Tu had been so close as to make highly improbable one joining the party without the other following suit. I wondered if Tu were acting on party instructions in concealing his membership.

If this were so, had he accepted the chancellor job also because of orders from Chou En-lai?

Not long afterward a flow of Tu's friends were introduced by him to me and all enthusiastically volunteered their services. These included Shen Yen-ping (alias Mao Tun), Chang Chung-shih, Sa Kung-liao, Liu Kuei-ping, and Hsin Kuo-wen. All were Chinese Communist agents disguised as cultural workers. While I knew of their clandestine party membership, I could not object too strenuously because our province was desperately in need of intellectual stimulus and ideological development. All I could do was place observers close to these persons to ascertain what means they took to carry out their objectives.

When the Tihua police department arrested Liu Kuei-ping and Hsin Kuo-wen on charges of "tempting the students," I knew the first test had come. It was too early for a showdown, however, and Tu Chung-yüan asked for a leave of absence. Shen Yen-ping, Sa Kung-liao, and Chang Chung-shih left Sinkiang, one after another, on pretexts of family problems, parental death, and the like. This was a welcome solution at the time because I had little to go on. Had they stayed longer, legal action against them might only have aroused the indignation of the unsuspecting Chinese cultural circles who had not yet realized the ulterior motives of these Communist agents.

Nothing better illustrates the dilemma I faced in simultaneously attempting to advance Sinkiang as a progressive province and to combat the Communist conspiracy, than a case study of a student in Sinkiang College. According to his story, given to my investigators in the summer of 1940, he was approached in late 1939 by a fellow student, Chou Ming-wu, in the dormitory. In the course of the usual ideological discussion current among students at the college, Chou remarked, "Sinkiang is still in a state of feudalism and obviously the six great policies based on the material forces of a feudalistic society are not supported by the progressive masses of the proletariat. These policies are only of a transitory character, useful only during the period of feudalism. Personal leadership, not party leadership, characterizes the present political pattern of Sinkiang. Furthermore, the leader is apt to make mistakes because he is surrounded by a group of people representing the past. Only by adopting a system of collective leadership can all the political mistakes be avoided. China today is making a choice between the Communists and the Kuomintang. There is no third course for her. Therefore, the six great policies which are independent of both these opposing forces have no ideological basis whatsoever."

The student thought Chou was merely sounding off in typical student fashion. His failure to contest Chou's remarks, however, evidently marked him as a possible convert, for six months later Chou once again approached the informant. This time he moved more boldly, warning, "The government has started the mass arrests of youths in this province. If the situation remains unchanged, a reign of terror will follow. In the age of revolution of the proletariat, Marxism is the only doctrine that can serve correctly as our guiding principle. Since it can be applied to all parts of the world, all other theories, such as the six great policies, ignore actual conditions. Although the government adopts the policy of kinship to sovietism, communism and Communists are not tolerated in this province. This certainly is the greatest political mistake the government has committed."

Chou's comments were directed at my first cautious moves against what I sensed to be a conspiracy against my regime, but his listener knew only the surface evidence of increasing vigilance on the part of the provincial authorities. Therefore, Chou played upon this student's idealism and ignorance, portraying my regime as counter-revolutionary and outlining plans for forming a new revolutionary center, directed by a member of the All-Union Communist Party, Ch'en P'ei-sheng.

This center, under the guise of a "research study group," resembled the typical Communist underground organization in every way. As explained to the student by Chou, "Before you join the research body on my recommendation, you must do some preparatory work. First, you must try to stimulate the interest of your schoolmates in research and study. Then you must examine the character of each student. Before the end of the semester you must give me a name list of the best students eligible for membership in the organization." According to the information given to my investigators, the "research group" was to train the youth prior to formation of a full-fledged Marxist political group in Sinkiang which was to act as the spearhead for a "proletarian revolution." Obviously, this was nothing more than a means of turning the loyalties of the new intellectual class against my government to the advantage of Moscow and Yenan.

My investigators alerted me to the growing tension in the province during the summer and fall of 1940, and I determined to keep the Soviet advisers as far from the centers of political and military power as possible. It seemed incredible that such close associates as Tu Chung-yüan and so important a mission as the Soviet assistance group should conspire against me. But the evidence appeared ominous in its portent; I could not rest my fears a single night.

Early in September, trouble broke out in the Altai region, especially in the districts of Kokotohai and Tsingho. At first my commanders advised a strong show of force which would quell the uprising immediately and at the same time demonstrate Tihua's ability to enforce authority. I suspected the worst, however, and put down the revolt with a minimum of troops, while leaving my main force concentrated around the capital.

My fears proved justified. Among the agents rounded up in the revolt were several who confessed to taking part in a vast underground conspiracy. According to their account these uprisings were merely decoys to lure away my loyal troops so that a major coup could take place in Tihua. The plan called for the fatal blow to be struck at the memorial meeting of the anniversary celebration for the Mukden Incident, September 18, 1940. Latoff, chief Soviet Military adviser, was to mount the rostrum at my side bearing two flags, one white and one red. At the wave of the red flag, trained assassins were to operate in groups of three, each assigned to a single military or political leader. With these key persons out of the way, Latoff would wave the white flag, touching off a riot that would spread through the province and would overthrow my administration.

That such a plot reached into every sector of the provincial government was proved by the network as revealed by one of the agents interrogated by my police. His roster included Ouyanjak, Soviet consul general in Tihua, and Latoff, chief Soviet military adviser; Tu Chung-yüan, Chancellor of Sinkiang College; Chang Hung-hsin, Finance Commissioner; Li Pei-k'o, General Manager of Sinkiang Pharmacy; Wang Chao-ch'ing, Regimental Commander of Tihua Garrison Forces; Yao Hsiung, Garrison Commander and Administrator of the Ili Region; Ch'en P'ei-sheng, Director of Border Affairs; Tsui Jun-chang, battalion commander; Yang Te-hsiang, Garrison Commander of the Altai Region; Chiang Tso-chou, Principal of the Sinkiang Provincial Middle School; Liu Kuei-ping and Hsin Kuo-wen, friends of Tu Chung-yüan. Nor were the religious and nationality groups unaffected. Uighur participants included Abutu, Reconstruction Affairs Commissioner, and

Kuerpan Niaz, Vice-Director of the Police Department. Kazakhs such as Sarifuhan, Administrator of the Altai Region, and Prince Buhart were implicated. Moslem participants included Lan Yen-shou, a vice-commissioner of the provincial government. Even the White Russians, long loyal to my administration, were represented by Biakdiyev, Director of the Bureau of Highways.

I was in a quandary. Sinkiang remained dependent on the Soviet Union for military and economic assistance. The public declaration of co-operation between the Chinese Communists and the Kuomintang remained in effect. If I were to move boldly against the conspirators, what would prevent them from denouncing me as a traitor to the anti-imperialist cause? Better to move slowly, nip the uprising in the bud, and await a more propitious moment for smashing all the conspirators. Thus, of the 481 participants in the abortive insurrection, only 59 were sentenced to death. These included those I knew to be the ringleaders and the chief Soviet spies.

It is interesting to note that, coincidental with my move against the conspiracy, new rumors swept the province to the effect that, "The Chinese traitor, Wang Ching-wei, has sent agents into Sinkiang to stage riots and uprisings." The primary purpose of this rumor was to mask any possible identification of the conspiracy with the Reds. In fact, Tu Chung-yüan in a later interrogation, falsely confessed during his preliminary trial, to being "an agent of Wang Ching-wei." It was only after he stood trial before a committee participated in by representatives of the central government, such as Wang Te-fu, Chu Shu-sheng, Chi Yuan-fu, and Cheng Ta-lung, that he finally admitted he had been ordered by Chou En-lai to wipe out my government by assassination and insurrection.

A second rumor paralleled the familiar tactic employed during the 1937 plot, alerting officials to the allegation, "Commissioner Sheng will soon start a purge against high-ranking persons in the provincial administration." As before, this rumor alarmed many who might otherwise have been counted upon to give me unswerving support. They resigned lest they become victims of this "purge."

Tension mounted. The attitudes and activities of the Soviet military advisers, instructors, and technical experts called for increasing attention from my surveillance corps. Representatives of the Soviet Eighth Regiment stationed at Hami were in constant contact with officials in the Soviet consulate. Soviet aircraft appeared in increasing numbers over the border regions of Aqsu, Ili, Tacheng, and Altai. Although one uprising had been quelled, reports of spreading unrest came in from all points along the Soviet border.

I did not have long to wait before the Kremlin tried to tighten the noose still another notch around my neck. In November three Soviet emissaries arrived in Tihua, headed by one Bakulin. Their purpose was to extract my agreement to a fifty-year lease of Sinkiang's tin mines for Russian exploitation. The terms were so absurd and unreasonable as to confirm my worst fears of Russian intent and, after reading the document over carefully, I decided to exert all effort to stop this aggressive move against Sinkiang at the earliest opportunity.

The means at my disposal were few, however. All I could hope to do was to stall for time and hope that at some later date circumstances might turn in my favor. Therefore, I planned to call a conference of the high officials in the provincial government, in co-ordination with the Commission of Foreign Affairs. Such a meeting would surely reject this imperialistic document, and we could then submit the document to the central government for consideration. In effect, this would table the matter indefinitely.

Two days after their arrival, Bakulin and his associates called at my office. After the usual polite preliminaries we settled down to the business at hand. I told them that, while I had read the document several times, I could not affix my seal to it because it concerned the mining interests of Sinkiang and therefore would require the approval of the members of the provincial government. In addition, it involved another country and thus necessitated the consent of the Commissioner of Foreign Affairs. Finally, this was a matter transcending the prerogatives of the provincial authorities and would have to be submitted to the central government for approval. Only then could I place my signature upon the document.

Bakulin studied me a moment, impassively. We both knew that relations between Sinkiang and Soviet Russia were at a turning point, although they had not yet arrived at an impasse. I had been careful in my moves against the conspiracy directed from Moscow and Yenan to save face and in no way publicly implicated either Communist center with the plot. My comments about the document were in perfect legal order and on the surface followed the most correct of diplomatic protocol. Yet the substance of both instances indicated I was unwilling to become a helpless pawn in the hands of the Communists. I remained a Chinese, loyal to the central government, and this was a fact which neither side was capable of forgetting for a moment.

Bakulin broke the silence abruptly and in curt, clipped delivery declared, "When we were preparing to leave Moscow for Sinkiang, Comrade Stalin told us that the contents of this secret agreement on the Soviet lease of tin mines must not be revealed to anyone except Commissioner Sheng, who is to put his signature on it. The document should not be referred to any other provincial government members nor submitted to the central government. Both contracting parties must sign the agreement tomorrow, or the day after tomorrow at the latest. Meanwhile, the Soviet Consulate in Tihua will have Chinese and Russian copies typed."

I restrained my rising temper and began quietly. "Let us not be in such a hurry," I suggested. "You may type copies after we have discussed certain revisions. For instance, in the preamble it states that, 'In order to assist in the development of productivity in the territory of Sinkiang, the Government of the U.S.S.R. agrees to undertake the work of prospecting, investigation, and exploitation of tin mines and ancillary minerals in the territory of Sinkiang.' Now, how could this clause stating 'the Government of the U.S.S.R. agrees . . .' accord with the facts since neither the Sinkiang provincial government nor I knew anything about the agreement before it was addressed to me. This clause apparently gives the impression that the Sinkiang government initiated negotiations and the Soviet government agreed. Such clearly is not the case."

Bakulin listened but took no notes. Moving on to more important points, I continued, "Furthermore many items in the fifteen articles need reconsideration. First, the agreement should be valid for three years instead of fifty years as stipulated in the original text. At most, it should terminate with the conclusion of the Second World War. Secondly, the original agreement stipulates that the trust, known as 'Sin-tin' to be established for the prospecting and exploitation of tin mines, shall, during the first five-year period, pay the Sinkiang government five per cent of the tin and ancillary useful metals mined in Sinkiang. Although my government is making no investment in the trust, I deem it necessary that the payment of five per cent be changed to 'not less than twenty per cent.' Thirdly, the article stipulating that 'the Government of Sinkiang shall not inspect, supervise, investigate, or audit the various operations of production, finance, and commerce of Sin-tin' should also be revised."

Before I had finished my argument Bakulin rudely interrupted, "Although it is our wish to hear your opinions on the agreement we must call your attention to the fact that when we were given our mission Comrade Stalin said that Commissioner Sheng must sign the agreement as it is and not a single word of it is alterable."

I could restrain my temper no longer and I spoke from my heart. "This agreement is comparable to Japan's infamous Twenty-One Demands forced on the late president Yuan Shih-k'ai. I have always believed that the Soviet Union is not a Red aggressor as some charge but a Marxist socialist state, fighting for the liberation of the oppressed throughout the world. If no word in this agreement is alterable, I shall have to write to Comrade Stalin directly and ask him if the Soviet Union is a nation of aggression or one of socialism, dedicating herself to assisting the backward peoples of the East. I wonder if Comrade Stalin has read this agreement which is so insulting in its aggressive tone. I wonder if he really said that it must be signed as it is and that not a word of it is alterable. As a believer in Marxism it is my wish to bring the Chinese revolution and the world revolution to a successful completion through the practice of Marxist ideology. I want the oppressed peoples of the world to unite under the Marxist banner for their own liberation. Now, if Comrade Stalin takes such an attitude toward Sinkiang, how can the people of China and of the world continue to put faith in the principles of Marx and Lenin? If the people lose their faith in Marxism-Leninism, how can the Chinese revolution and the world revolution succeed? For these reasons, I must negotiate directly with Comrade Stalin and ask him these questions. Meanwhile I hope you will wait at the Soviet consulate for my final reply."

Karpov, another of the trio, tried to placate me. "Commissioner Sheng, you have misunderstood the whole matter," he said. "The U.S.S.R. is not an aggressive nation. The purpose of the Soviet Union's leasing the Sinkiang tin mines is to fight fascist aggression. Furthermore, you are a member of the All-Union Communist Party and therefore should obey the orders of the party. Finally, you ought to remember that during the rebellion of Ma Chung-ying, much Soviet blood was shed in Sinkiang for which the Soviet Union has not yet been compensated."

"You have just said that the Soviet Union is not an aggressor," I retorted. "The other aggressive countries have leased many Chinese ports for periods up to 99 years. Now the Soviet Union is trying to set the period of this agreement at 50 years. I would like to ask the difference between 99 years and 50 years. If this is not aggression, what would you call it? You said that the purpose of leasing the tin mines is to fight fascism. I would like to ask if the war against fascism will last five decades. You also said that the orders of the All-Union Communist Party must be obeyed by its members. I would like to know how you could have said that. As a true believer of Marxist ideology, I regard your comment on this particular point as an insult to me. I have faith in Marxism because I believe it will bring about the liberation of China and of all the oppressed peoples in the world. Because of my faith in Marxism, I joined the Communist Party so that I could fight for the liberation of China and of the oppressed peoples of the world. I did not join the party with the purpose of betraying Sinkiang and selling out the interests of my country to another country. You said that during the rebellion of Ma Chung-ying, much Soviet blood was shed in Sinkiang for which the Soviet Union has not yet been compensated.

"Yes, the four million people of Sinkiang and I are grateful to the Soviet Union for the presence of the Red Army in Sinkiang during the rebellion. It was due to Soviet bloodshed that the rebellion was suppressed and the siege of Tihua lifted. However, I must call your attention to the fact that the Red Army entered Sinkiang with the purpose not only of suppressing the rebellion but also of protecting Russia's own interests. The Soviet Union dispatched her troops to Sinkiang to liquidate the armed forces under Ma Chung-ying, the running dog of the Japanese war lords, and thus to offset Japan's aggressive influence in the province and remove Japan as a threat to the Soviet border. Furthermore, the Red Army entered Sinkiang of its own free will and without the previous approval of the Sinkiang authorities. Sinkiang never made a request for this assistance."

At this point, Bakulin interrupted in an angry and proud voice, "It is superfluous to talk about ideology. Comrade Stalin did not send us here to debate ideology. We are here to solve practical problems. Otherwise the theoreticians would have been with us. Solution of practical problems means settling all problems connected with the lease of Sinkiang's tin mines. As to the reasons for keeping the agreement secret, maintaining its present wording, setting its provision for fifty years, and all that, you will understand better when you see Comrade Stalin yourself or when you write to him later on."

Before I could voice my objections to this abrupt dismissal of my argument, Bakulin continued in a more ominous tone. "It seems you are too ignorant of the actual conditions in the Soviet Union to believe that Comrade Stalin actually read the text of this agreement. It seems that you have not realized the position and prestige of Comrade Stalin. Important affairs of state, particularly those that concern foreign relations, are decided by Comrade Stalin himself. Who else dares to put forward in the name of the Soviet Union this agreement? This was handed to us by him personally. Everything that he decides is correct. No one dares to criticize or question him on ideological grounds. You are the only person I know of who dares to do this."

Bakulin paused, choosing his words carefully not only for my benefit but undoubtedly to impress upon his cohorts his loyalty to the Kremlin. The threat was unmistakably clear in his concluding remarks. "You are not an easy person to deal with; this we know. Before we left Moscow, we asked Comrade Stalin what we should do in case you refused to sign as ordered. 'If Commissioner Sheng refuses to sign, you just return home,' was Comrade Stalin's reply, given with a quick wave of his hand. Your request that we wait at the Soviet consulate while you negotiate with Moscow directly cannot be accepted under any circumstances. We shall give you another night to consider. At two o'clock tomorrow afternoon we shall call on you again with the typewritten copies. It is up to you to decide whether to put your signature on the agreement or not. If your decision is 'no,' we only request that you put this on the original document so that we may hand this back to Comrade Stalin. We have nothing more to say today. We hope you will make a wise and cautious decision on a matter which affects not only the future of Sinkiang but also yourself."

With this grim warning, Bakulin and his colleagues turned and left my office.

This was the final proof of Soviet intent, if Bakulin were representing Stalin's views honestly. Now I could see the consequences Stalin hoped would follow from his generous policy of assistance to Sinkiang. Now I could see where the oppressed peoples of backward countries would gain Russian support against one oppressor only to be saddled with another. As I reviewed in my mind Soviet foreign policy of the previous months and years, the pattern suddenly came into sharp focus. By concluding the nonaggression pact with Nazi Germany and the agreement with Japan settling the Manchukuo-Mongolian border disputes, Stalin had shrewdly turned the fascists against the other imperialists. But he had not rested with this purely defensive goal. In addition, Russia had attacked Finland, partitioned Poland with Germany, and had incorporated the Baltic states of Estonia, Latvia, and Lithuania into her domain.

Small wonder Stalin smacked his lips over Sinkiang, a tempting morsel which seemed to rest on his plate, simply awaiting his pleasure. I knew that the central government was even less in a position to help than earlier, now that it had taken refuge in Chungking. Moreover, the situation in the province was deteriorating rapidly, thanks to the constant conspiracies hatched from Moscow and Yenan. The Altai rebellion seemed about to break out again and rumors of new uprisings in the Aqsu and Ili regions reached my office. One of the Kremlin's most trusted agents, Miss Liu Yun, had become personally enamoured of me and politically loyal to my politics. As a result, she was acting as my informant, unbeknown to Moscow. She instructed my agents to prepare for a series of outbreaks following a pattern laid down by Moscow after the unsuccessful attempts of September. The Soviet consul general was to organize groups in the Altai, Ili, and Aqsu regions for uprisings against the government. The Red troops along the Soviet border would then disguise themselves as guerrillas and infiltrate into the ranks of the rebels. An "All-Union Revolutionary Army" would then be formed after success in the Altai-Ili-Aqsu area. During the second stage, the main force of the "All-Union Revolutionary Army," the Soviet Eighth Regiment at Hami, and the garrison forces of the "Agricultural Implements Manufacturing Factory" (the aircraft assembly plant), would converge on the capital of Tihua from north, east, and west. Soviet plans would provide the crucial support by bombing the Office of the Border Defense Commission and dropping leaflets urging me to surrender with my troops.

I knew that Moscow was capable of such tactics in view of what it had done in Poland. I also knew that it had the force to carry out such a scheme. If I were to turn down the Soviet proposal and run the risk of war, only one fate lay ahead for Sinkiang as well as for myself. With only a meager defense force of 10,000 men, counting infantry and cavalry, Sinkiang would soon become a Soviet satellite. My troops were scattered throughout the wild terrain of the province. With one rebellion in Altai in the making, additional outbreaks would overtax our strength. The outside world would learn of our demise only as a *fait accompli*, when the grim tales of refugees reached New Delhi and Chungking.

That evening my deliberations were interrupted by a message from Liu Yun, the Red spy. She reported that Bakulin had telegraphed Stalin for instructions covering the possibility that I might refuse to sign the document. She predicted Bakulin would refrain from seeing me until further instructions had arrived. No sooner had I received her message than a secretary of the Soviet consulate telephoned to say that Bakulin had caught cold and therefore would be unable to see me on the next day. At least I had gained a momentary reprieve from my dilemma.

The additional time meant little, however, for I could find no escape except subterfuge. I resolved to avoid battle and marshal my forces for another day. Therefore, when Bakulin and his companions called on me shortly thereafter I addressed them with honeyed words and placed my signature upon the document. After I had laid the brush aside, Bakulin asked me to affix the seals of the Sinkiang Provincial Government as well as of the Border Defense Commissioner's Office. This I refused on the grounds that these two seals represented the authority of the central government and no person could affix them without specific authorization from Chungking.

Bakulin paused, uncertain as to the necessity for such seals and anxious to return with the demanded prize for Stalin. Finally, he agreed, and the group departed with victorious and proud smiles. They did not realize that by refusing to affix these seals I had made the agreements null and void. They must have considered their mission successful, perhaps warranting personal decorations from Stalin upon their return. Little doubt could have crossed their minds; yet within two years I was to make my successful counterthrust, and their efforts would be proved to have been in vain.

Thus, through covert conspiracy and open dictation did the Soviet Union reveal her true motives in Sinkiang during 1940. Disguised as the guardian of socialism and the friend of backward peoples in Asia, Stalin, by means of coercion and subversion, plotted to exploit them for his own benefit. No more explicit evidence of the imperialistic goals held by the Soviet Union can be found than the terms of this lease for the Sinkiang tin mines which I have included in the Appendices to this book. Although I had no choice but to sign this agreement, I determined to destroy its consequences at the earliest moment and to break Sinkiang away from the ever-tightening grip of the Kremlin.

8

Trouble with Yenan

HAVING SETTLED, at least temporarily, my relations with Moscow, I turned to the difficult task of preparing for the moment of breaking loose from the net being woven around me by Soviet and Chinese Communist advisers. The next months proved to be the calm before the storm, offering a welcome respite from the pressures of 1940 and at the same time marking a continual buildup of conspiratorial activity directed against my administration.

Both Mao Tse-tung and Chou En-lai cunningly plotted to wrest control of Sinkiang from my hands. Their dilemma lay, paradoxically enough, in the fact that my power rested largely upon arms and assistance rendered by the Soviet Union. Therefore, their problem was to divide Sinkiang from Russia, to alienate me from Stalin and thereby leave me without any means of outside assistance. Although my relations with Stalin gradually worsened as a direct consequence of his own aggressive ambitions, I learned later that additional trouble had come from the interference of agents from Yenan.

Virtually all persons sent into Sinkiang by the Chinese Communist Party acted under directions from Mao or Chou to create cleavages between the province and the Soviet Union. By 1940 it was clear that the plotting of Tu Chung-yüan, Chang Chung-shih, and Shen Yen-ping followed orders from Chou En-lai. After this abortive uprising I instructed my investigators to gather all evidence systematically so that when the opportune moment came, I would be able to smash back openly and lay the proof before those who had been duped by the Communists.

As early as 1938, after my return to Tihua from Moscow, information reached me that Fang Lin (Teng Fa), representative of the Chinese Communist Eighth Route Army, was engaged in various activities detrimental to the interests of Sinkiang. I therefore telegraphed Mao Tse-tung, requesting that Fang Lin be replaced and that a confidant of Mao be sent to Tihua so that I could relate to him all of the "errors" of Fang. At that time Mao replied that he was in no position to recall Fang independent of concurring approval from Moscow, inasmuch as Fang was appointed by both party centers to act as their joint representative. I accepted this in good faith although I was disappointed at being overruled in this matter.

After the events of November, 1940, and the signing of the "Sin-tin" agreement, Chou En-lai and his wife, Teng Ying-ch'ao, passed through Sinkiang en route to Moscow. Chou ostensibly was going for medical treatment, although naturally I wondered what additional political matters underlay his trip. Staying in Sinkiang for more than ten days, he seemed quite anxious to talk with me and to improve relations between Tihua and Yenan. With reference to recent correspondence, Chou said, "Chairman Mao has received your telegram and your letter. You have raised for the second time the question of Fang Lin and I am interested in conveying to Chairman Mao your report on Fang's errors."

Always on my guard, and especially anxious after discovery of the plot in September in which Tu Chung-yüan had acted as an agent for Chou, I decided to tell of Fang's less significant activities and see what reaction Chou gave. In this way I could preserve appearances, while letting Yenan know that I was not entirely in the dark as to the plotting against my life.

Not too long before, I had seen the galley proofs of Mao's writings on "Dialectics." After reading through the first section, I had told Fang I was interested in seeing additional parts. Fang had turned aside my request for having Yenan send part two, saying, "You had better not read it. From the theoretical point of view, Chairman Mao's 'Dialectics' is full of errors." I wondered whether Fang was trying to organize a conspiracy against Mao or was he trying to test my loyalty, so had said nothing beyond asking him to point out the errors to which he had alluded. Fang had refused to make any further comment.

In telling this episode to Chou En-lai, I knew that any term of disrespect toward Mao on my part would only be used against me. Therefore, I took extreme pains to place all critical comments in Fang's mouth. Chou surprised me, therefore, when he replied, "Since Chairman Mao was too busy with his official duties at the time, he might have missed some of the theoretical points which he should have included in the book. It is very difficult for anyone to study philosophy, and errors can creep in without the writer's knowledge."

Was Chou also testing me? I determined not to fall into the trap and interrupted, "But even if Chairman Mao had made some errors, it is improper for Fang Lin to criticize them in public. Instead of attacking the theoretical concepts of his leader before others, he should suggest to Chairman Mao directly where corrections might be made."

Chou quickly retreated from the implications of his previous comment. "You did quite right and I agree with you fully," he replied. "Chinese Communist Party members, especially top-ranking ones, should not criticize political or theoretical errors of Chairman Mao in public. They should first discuss the matter privately with Chairman Mao himself."

To prove my confidence, I suggested that Chou check with Fang to verify my account of the conversation. The next day Chou returned and said, "Comrade Fang Lin admitted that what you told me yesterday is true." "I am glad," I replied, "that Comrade Fang has frankly admitted his errors. This is proof of the success of practicing self-criticism by members of the Chinese Communist Party."

Secretly, however, I resolved to press further for Fang's replacement and to test Mao's willingness to give me disinterested assistance, free of any complications and under my supervision. Therefore, I sent several thousand fur coats to Yenan as token of Sinkiang's willingness to co-operate in the struggle against Japanese imperialism and followed this, in late 1941, with a detailed list of demands for advisers and assistance.

Mao's reply was not long forthcoming. While he seemed to maintain a cordial and co-operative tone on the surface, beneath his friendly phrases I felt the thin edge of hostility. The letter read in part as follows:

February 4, 1942

Dear Commissioner Sheng:

Comrades T'eng Tai-yuan and Chou Hsiao-chou have brought me your letter dated December 21, together with your picture and the fur coat which you so generously sent me. My deep gratitude for your kindness is beyond my power of expression.

The position of Sinkiang has been consolidated following the realization of the six great policies under your indispensable leadership. Your fortitude and courage have helped you weather many a storm and bring the province once again from peril to safety. You have done a great service, not only to Sinkiang but also to the whole nation now at war with our enemy. I hope you will continue in your efforts to stabilize Sinkiang and to solve its racial problems so that we shall be one step nearer to victory in our war against Japan.

In compliance with your request, I am trying my best to pick out those party workers who can be of help to you when they are sent to Sinkiang. You probably have realized that we are also in short supply of personnel. Among those who have been to Tihua, Hsü Meng-ch'iu has received my permission to stay on there while Chung Tsi-ping is willing to place himself at your service. I hope you will discuss with Comrade Teng Fa their problems.

Part of your generous donation of several thousand fur coats has reached Yenan. I express again my heartfelt thanks . . . I am glad to report that we have scored victory after victory over the enemy, but, upon the request of our friendly party, we give ourselves no publicity. It is my wish that we can fight with united effort toward final victory. The Japanese invaders are attempting to attack the Border Region and Ninghsia province. If these two areas should fall, the land route between Kansu and Sinkiang would be cut off. With concerted efforts Sinkiang and Yenan must by all means protect this communication line.

Your letter to Comrade Chu Teh has been duly forwarded. It is rather difficult to find a theoretician for you, but I promise to try my best. I hope you will take good care of yourself.

Very sincerely yours,

(signed) MAO TSE-TUNG

As evidence of his apparent sincerity, Mao had dispatched his brother, Mao Tse-min, to act as my personal adviser and assistant. I knew this act could be a two-edged sword, however, which might eventually strike against me as well as for me. Mao Tse-min seemed to sense my growing suspicion and shortly after this letter arrived, he came one day to my office with a request to be granted a leave of absence. As he put it, he felt a growing lack of interest in his work, and perhaps a respite in Yenan might be mutually advantageous.

This seemed to be the Chinese way of expressing discontent, and I tried to press him further on this matter. Obviously, his departure would not augur well for my relations with Mao Tse-tung. Furthermore, I suspected he might be trying to escape before something happened, perhaps something which he himself was engineering against me.

After considerable hesitation and evasion, he said, "It was always my intention to contribute my humble share in the building up of a new Sinkiang. You have treated me most kindly since my arrival a year ago. Therefore, this is nothing personal. All this time, however, I have had the disquieting feeling that there is a misunderstanding between Sinkiang on the one hand and the Soviet and Chinese Communists on the other. It is my belief, therefore, that my presence here will do no good for the parties concerned.

"I plan to return to Yenan for a short rest," he continued. "I shall be most glad to return here if my service is needed in the future. I remember that when I left Yenan for Tihua, Chairman Mao told me that you are our distinguished comrade. In fact, you have been very kind to me and have shown this by your permitting me to see all the letters addressed to you by my brother. After I reach Yenan I shall explain to Chairman Mao the reasons for my leaving Sinkiang. What I would like to say today, however, is that although Comrade Fang Lin was a representative of the Eighth Route Army in Tihua, what he has said and done in Sinkiang could not be construed as representing the views of the Chinese Communist Party. Moreover, I would like to call to your attention the fact that although the All-Union Communist Party and the Chinese Communist Party are brotherly parties, their policies are by no means identical. The acts of one cannot be construed to mean the will of the other."

At this point Mao Tse-min paused, dropping his glance

downward as though moved at the thought of departure, and asked quietly if I had any instructions for him before his leaving. When I replied negatively, he then asked if I cared to comment on his remarks.

Perhaps here was a man I could trust, for his intimate relationship with Mao Tse-tung certainly should have placed him in a unique position to talk with the leader of the CCP, and his family ties should make him an honest bearer of my message. Speaking quite frankly, I said, "I think you are correct in pointing out the misunderstanding between Sinkiang and the Soviet and Chinese Communists, but I personally believe it is up to the Chinese Communist Party, rather than the Sinkiang authorities, to clear up this misunderstanding. At least the responsibility of the CCP in this respect is greater than that of Sinkiang. So far as Fang Lin's past words and deeds in Sinkiang, that is a matter of the past. Moreover, it is my understanding that the Yenan authorities have already criticized Fang Lin for these errors.

"I think that since it is your wish to visit Chairman Mao, I have no objections to your trip," I added, hoping thereby to dispel any feeling of ill-will or suspicion of distrust on my part. "But on one point I wish to be quite clear. It is correct to say, as you did, that the relationship between the All-Union Communist Party and the Chinese Communist Party is one of brotherly parties. However, while they may have different views on matters of minor importance, I am convinced that they always take the same stand on outstanding problems of the moment."

Mao Tse-min said that he concurred fully in my opinion. I believed at that time that his words were spoken sincerely, although his manner was somewhat disconcerting. I attributed this to his embarrassment at asking for a leave, as well as to the difficulty of discussing such delicate matters. I hoped that

by expressing myself openly I had conveyed to him my willingness to work co-operatively with Yenan and Moscow and
my absence of ill will. At the same time I wanted to convey
a warning that honeyed words could not conceal malicious
intent and I wanted all to be aware of my concern over past
actions.

My hopes were short-lived. Only two days later Hsü Chieh,
Eighth Route Army representative in Tihua, called on me with
the news that he intended to go to Moscow for medical treatment. He added that he would probably have to remain there
for at least six months and, therefore, he had already requested
the Soviet government to send a replacement for him. Hsü
thanked me for his kind treatment and the courtesies shown
by the Sinkiang authorities. He declared that since he had
succeeded Fang Lin as Eighth Route Army representative,
he had been getting along quite well with those in Yenan.
However, Hsü added, it was very difficult to deal with the
Soviets. Frankly speaking, he concluded, he doubted his presence in Tihua could be beneficial much longer and, while he
was going for "reason of health," he had already petitioned
Moscow through "Chairman Mao" for another replacement.

Hsü's words sounded strangely similar to those I had heard
from Mao Tse-min only forty-eight hours before. I decided to
lay the cards on the table and therefore spoke bluntly. "Well,
just two days ago Commissioner Chou (Mao Tse-min) asked
leave of absence to return to Yenan. Now you also want to
leave Sinkiang on grounds that you are ill, or really on
grounds that you are no longer useful. I wonder if all my
friends are mistreated here."

"Oh, please do not think that way," Hsü declared, with some
emotion. "The Chinese Communists here are deeply grateful to
the Sinkiang authorities and particularly to Commissioner Sheng

for all that has been done for them. In fact, it is out of gratitude that we feel we may not be able to meet Sinkiang's future needs and expectations."

"The Chinese Communists in Sinkiang have rendered us a great service. In no way have they disappointed us," I replied.

"When I said that we may not be able to meet Sinkiang's expectations," Hsü responded, "I indicated this was for the future and not the present or the past. Frankly speaking, I have entertained the belief for several months now that there is a misunderstanding between Sinkiang, on the one hand, and the Soviet and Chinese Communists, on the other. At the same time, differences of opinion also exist between the Chinese Communists and the Soviet Communists. If the present situation remains unchanged, all parties concerned will be gravely affected. It is for this reason that I have made up my mind to leave Sinkiang."

"It seems that all the Chinese Communists here have taken note of the present unhealthy situation," I remarked with thinly veiled sarcasm. "If you and Commissioner Chou hope that this misunderstanding will be cleared up and relations improved all around, then you should continue to help us and not leave us."

He agreed that I was right, but explained that the Russians were hard to deal with. "They are biased and all of them have a strong personality," Hsü said, watching me carefully for my reaction. I remained impassive, determined to show no feeling but to inscribe his words deep upon my memory for later examination. Surely something strange was afoot, but exactly what? Hsü continued, "According to what I have heard, the former Soviet Consul General Apresoff was not on friendly terms with you because he was a Trotskyite disguised as a member of the All-Union Communist Party."

"Yes," I answered, "but this is a matter of the past. Besides

Apresoff was sentenced to death by the Soviet Government. I do not believe such a case will arise again."

"It is very hard to say," Hsü remarked quietly, "for the Trotskyite remnants are still very active amongst the Russians."

I was not going to be trapped into any provocative comments and matched his move by suggesting that if he or his colleagues knew of any Trotskyites, they should certainly point them out and accuse them before the proper authorities. Hsü dodged, "It is pretty difficult to identify them, because they always conceal their identity. Besides, we cannot accuse them without evidence. However, I think it is time for you to rest now. I shall call on you again some other time."

With these words, he left. I weighed his comments carefully, turning them over in my mind in search of some clue, but I could find nothing. Although Hsü acted suspiciously at times and his statements paralleled those of Mao Tse-min, yet I could not discover any motive in his asking for a leave. My conclusion then was that they [Hsü and Mao Tse-min] were dealing quite frankly with me, that they sensed the growing tension and therefore wanted to leave for more fruitful work elsewhere.

Suddenly, the fatal hand of the assassins moved once again, as they had moved so often in Sinkiang's bloody and turbulent history. This time the deadly bullet struck at my family. On the night of March 29, 1942, my younger brother, Brigade Commander Sheng Shih-ch'i, was shot and killed in the south garden behind the Border Defense Commission. When my servants broke into my darkened rooms with the tragic news, I knew that my province and I faced our grimmest hours of trial. So desperate were the plotters they would kill one of Sinkiang's most able leaders of the future. Where would they strike next?

My grief over the loss of my brother was professional as well as personal. Less than six months before, he had graduated from the Red Military Academy in Moscow. Young and energetic, he had contributed much in training Sinkiang's motorized force, in consolidating our administration, and in strengthening border defenses. His death was a loss to all, not merely to me.

Was this the reason for so many Chinese Communists asking for leave? Was another great conspiracy afoot to break out on the occasion of celebrating the original April Uprising? My investigators immediately set to work, rounding up suspects and grilling potential informers. In the meantime, I tried to check matters for myself.

I did not have long to wait, for immediately after the murder of my brother, one of the persons uppermost in my mind, Mao Tse-min, called to express his condolences. He suggested that I cable Mao Tse-tung, asking that all the three hundred or more Chinese Communists in Sinkiang be transferred to Moscow for indoctrination. I told him that while I had no objections to their leaving Sinkiang, I was in no position to ask Yenan for their transfer. If they wanted to go to Moscow for indoctrination, they could bring forward the matter themselves. Mao argued that it was not proper for the Chinese Communists personally to raise the point and insisted that I do this on their behalf.

"If I do this," I retorted, "do you not think a misunderstanding on the part of Yenan and Moscow might result?"

"I do not think so," Mao replied, "besides, I am going to make a report to Chairman Mao explaining the background of the situation. I shall let him know that it is they themselves who want to go to Moscow for indoctrination."

I was in a troubled state, not knowing whether this was providing an escape for conspirators or co-operating with potential friends. I finally agreed to his request, because I did not wish to keep any persons in the province who really desired to be elsewhere. Their dissatisfaction might only lead to more trouble. Therefore, I telegraphed Yenan along these lines, and awaited the reply with considerable curiosity. Much to my surprise, no word came from Mao Tse-tung.

Meanwhile, the Sinkiang Trial Committee was uncovering startling evidence pointing to the most widespread conspiracy yet unearthed in the province. Any personal motives behind the murder were ruled out almost from the start when political plotting appeared certain in terms of the persons involved. Particularly after the trials of Tsang Ku-feng and Li I-ou, both high in the provincial government, was the committee convinced that this network had penetrated every organ of government and was directed jointly from Moscow and Yenan. Almost simultaneous with the discovery that Mao Tse-min and Hsü Chieh were implicated came a telegram from Mao Tse-tung, agreeing to the requested transfer of all Chinese Communist Party members in Sinkiang to Moscow. In fact, while the Sinkiang Trial Committee was petitioning the Border Defense Commission and the Sinkiang Provincial Government to issue a warrant of arrest against these two persons, Mao Tse-tung was urging me to send them to Moscow at the earliest opportunity. Now it was my turn to ignore a telegram. This was the time to smash the conspiracy once and for all!

The ultimate objective of the plot, designed to break out in assassination and rebellion, was to overthrow the existing regime and set up an entirely new government, independent of Chungking. Among those proved to have taken part in the plot, according to the confessions of key conspirators, were Bakulin, Soviet Consul General in Tihua; Latoff, Chief Soviet Military Adviser of the Border Defense Commission; Tsang Ku-feng, Finance Commissioner of the Sinkiang Provincial Government; Li I-ou, Education Commissioner; Mao Tse-min, Civil Affairs Commissioner; P'an P'o-nan, Garrison Commander of Hojen and member of the CCP; Lu Yu-ling, Administrator of the Hojen Region; Ch'en Fan-po, Administrator of the Karashar

Region; Yu Teh-yi, Administrator of the Yenchi Region; Chao Chien-feng, Administrator of the Tacheng Region; Liu Hsi-p'ing, Administrator of the Hami Region and member of the CCP; Wang Pao-ch'ien, publisher of the Sinkiang *Daily* and member of the All-Union Communist Party; Meng Yi-ming, chairman of the Sinkiang Translation and Compilation Commission and member of the CCP; Wang Tsi-hsiung, chairman of the Sinkiang Finance Supervisory Commission; Kuo Teh-chi, Chief of Staff of the Sinkiang Military Academy; Ma Chiao, general manager of the Sinkiang Local Products Company; Hsiao Tso-hsin, assistant general manager of the same company; P'eng Huan-shu, Chief of Staff of the Motorized Brigade; and Chao Ching-tang, regimental commander of the same brigade.

Of the 656 participants in the plot, only 88 were eventually sentenced to death, but these included the key figures. Among them were Mao Tse-min and Hsü Chieh.

No words of mine could describe adequately the perfidy and treachery of these plotters manipulated from Moscow and Yenan. The reader need only turn to their confessions, which are reproduced in full in the Appendices to this book, exactly as transcribed by my investigators during the interrogations of April and June, 1942. Perhaps there is no more fantastic story in fiction than the true tale of how my brother was murdered by his own wife, acting upon instructions from her Soviet and Chinese Communist comrades. Herein lies the final degradation of the soul brought about by the Reds!

After reading these confessions and examining all the irrefutable evidence, I wondered anew about the events that had preceded my brother's murder and the abortive uprising. It was clear that both Mao Tse-min and Hsü Chieh knew while they were speaking with me of their proposed departure that a vast plot was about to unfold. Their strategy was twofold. In the first place by appearing not to follow the course of the All-Union Communists, they hoped to implant in my mind confidence in Yenan's representatives and to poison it against those from Moscow. Secondly, by requesting leave they wished to prove their lack of ulterior purpose or ambitions in Sinkiang. Finally, by suggesting the presence of Trotskyites among the Soviet Communists in Sinkiang, they hoped to pin all blame on "Trotskyites" in case the plot should be uncovered.

As for Mao Tse-min's request that all Chinese Communists be transferred after the murder, two thoughts presented themselves. First, as a conspirator in the plot, he was in fear of discovery and simply wanted to leave the province as soon as possible. Secondly, he wished to reassure me as to any future ambitions of the CCP in Sinkiang.

Mao Tse-tung, on the other hand, apparently hesitated to reply to my request for transfer of the CCP representatives because he probably did not fear for their safety, being certain that the provincial government would never dare to move against such prominent Communists even if the plot were uncovered. Furthermore, a unilateral quitting of Sinkiang by Yenan might disturb Moscow, whose representatives remained at their posts.

As usual, a wave of rumors, fantastic in their extent and content, followed in the wake of my moves against the conspirators. One current story held that, "A feud for political power has been going on between Commissioner Sheng and his brother, resulting in the death of the younger Sheng." Another story claimed, "Commissioner Sheng has shifted his allegiance from Moscow to Chungking because the Nazis have besieged Moscow and the collapse of the Soviet armies seems imminent."

Nevertheless, the confessions provided proof positive that whatever others on the outside thought, I and my loyal supporters saw the handwriting on the wall. Its message was clear.

Either we remained in terror under perpetual threat of Communist overthrow, or we exerted every energy to oust the conspirators and cement relations with Chungking. I knew that such a reversal of Sinkiang's previous course, which had lasted almost ten years, would be difficult and most certainly would be misunderstood by many of my compatriots. However, I felt confident that when the story was finally and fully told, my motives would be applauded and our record would stand without criticism.

9

Pressure from Moscow

I KNEW THE DIE was cast. My moves against the Communist conspiracy clearly marked me as a threat to the Moscow-Yenan plot. Although I held off executing Mao Tse-min and Hsü Chieh, I knew this could only delay, not prevent, an eventual showdown. It seemed unlikely the Reds would rely upon plots any longer. My police had proved too effective at smashing these underground movements. Now it would be open political warfare, employing all the tactics familiar to those who have felt the wrath of the Communists.

The first move came from Bakulin, Soviet Consul General in Tihua. When it became generally known that Mao Tse-min and Hsü Chieh had been placed under arrest, Bakulin paid me a special visit. He warned that I was acting against the brother of Mao Tse-tung, whose Chinese Communist Party was destined to win control of all China. Were I to execute this man, I would gain little and have no future except certain death or constant refuge. As for Hsü Chieh, Bakulin claimed that any move against him would arouse the entire army against me. His final gambit was to remark that both the Soviet government and Marshal Stalin personally hoped that the two men would be freed soon.

I answered quite formally and without hesitation, "First, Mao Tse-min and Hsü Chieh conspired to overthrow the local government and therefore should be punished in accordance with the law of the state. Second, both Mao and Hsü instigated their accomplices to murder my brother, Sheng Shih-ch'i. They must bear the burden of the law. Furthermore, since Mao Tse-tung had my brother killed, why should I not kill his brother? You may tell all this to Marshal Stalin. As for my personal future, I do not care."

In July, 1942, Stalin sent Dekanozov, vice commissar for foreign affairs, to act as the Kremlin's personal pressure agent in Tihua. His presence indicated the importance Stalin attached to Sinkiang and to my relations with the Communists, as well as with Chungking. Stalin knew that he had gone too far, and only slim hope remained for retaining the Soviet grip on Sinkiang. I awaited Dekanozov's initial visit with no little anxiety.

Stalin's envoy began by attempting the familiar tactic of the honeyed word. "These worsening relations between Sinkiang and Soviet Russia and the unpleasant relationship between Marshal Stalin and your honorable self in the past all arose out of misunderstanding. We should forgive each other, forget what is bad and remember what is good. We should particularly recall the aid and assistance Stalin rendered Sinkiang and your honorable self in the past. Moreover, as you are a member of the All-Union Communist Party, you should continue to have faith in Marxism and should never waver in your faith."

These tactics had been used before by Apresoff, Bakulin, and others. I replied politely, but with firmness, "What Stalin has done for my people and for me will never be forgotten. He helped to lift the siege of Tihua by Ma Chung-ying. He helped crush the aggressive designs of Hitler and Tojo to build a Moslem state under Ma's leadership. He gave us much military and economic assistance. But, while I will never forget these good things, I will never forget the bad ones either unless you can prove they arose out of misunderstanding."

Then I spoke as I had never spoken before. "As for my faith in Marxism, I must tell you in all frankness that this is no longer valid. I no longer believe as I did before that Stalin is the leader of the world revolution and Mao the leader of the Chinese revolution. Why did this happen? Because as a member of the All-Union Communist Party and as a candidate whose membership was unanimously approved by the Politburo of the Chinese Communist Party, I was responsible to both centers and more particularly to both Stalin and Mao. Why did they not tell me directly if they were displeased with my work? Why did they plot to murder my family and me? Why did their emissaries attempt to pressure me? Why did they force the tin mine lease upon me without even prior consultation? Is this the so-called comradely relations of party members? Is this Stalin's treatment of backward peoples? Or has Lenin's policy of aiding the peoples of Asia turned into a policy of aggression? Does Marxism aim at emancipating the peoples of the world or enslaving them? No, with these tragic events on my mind, I could no longer claim to believe in Marxism and to follow the leadership of Stalin and Mao Tse-tung."

Dekanozov tried to maintain a calm appearance, but his eyes revealed his shock and amazement at my words. Probably this was the first time in his life he had witnessed such a denunciation of communism and its leaders. Lest he think I was nothing but a selfish and proud person, I told him of my past loyalty to the revolution and recounted my contribution to the anti-fascist struggle. "Remember, when Mao Tse-tung sent his representative Chou Hsiao-chou to tell us of the difficulties besetting the Eighth Route Army during the winter of 1940, we sent money and donated fifty thousand fur coats without asking any compensation. I can show you the receipt of this gift, signed by the Commander-in-Chief, Chu Teh. Not long thereafter when Moscow was besieged by the Nazis, Sinkiang raised funds for Russian relief and we sold fifty thousand horses to the Soviet Government for a nominal sum, to help in the hour of need.

"And while I was doing all this, what was being done in return? Ouyanjak and Bakulin, Mao Tse-min, Hsü Chieh, and Tu Chung-yüan all were conspiring against my people and my life. I cannot feel anything but betrayal. If this is the result of Marxism, then I must look elsewhere for inspiration. That is why I have begun study of *San Min Chu I* (Three People's Principles). The more I learn of democratic ideology, the more mistakes I discover in the materialistic interpretation of history. My conclusion is that the Marxist interpretation of class struggle is essentially cruel and callous. Thus, the callousness with which Stalin and Mao treated me and my comrades is not accidental."

Dekanozov, though obviously infuriated at my words, replied as casually as if we were discussing the weather. Dismissing my charges as "misunderstanding," he attributed the problem to "our common enemy who tries by every means to drive a wedge between us. Even among your followers and your agents, particularly those in the organ responsible for the trial of political prisoners, there are our common enemies," he warned. He gave the stock defense of the tin mines agreement as necessary for the "anti-fascist struggle." After a brief defense of communism as a doctrine, he pleaded fatigue and suggested we resume our discussions on another day. Before he left, however, Dekanozov sounded a thinly veiled threat, the first such tactic he had used. "I sincerely hope you can think this over carefully before you make any final decision. It is of extreme importance to you and you should not act through the impulse of the moment. My present visit to Sinkiang has much to do with your future and that of your province. It is the final chance for restoring friendly relations between Sinkiang and

Soviet Russia on the one hand, and Stalin and your honorable self on the other."

Despite his ominous tone, he shook my hand warmly and left.

The next day our meeting was rather brief. Dekanozov did little but listen. He was clearly awaiting further instructions from Moscow. I took this opportunity to repeat, for his benefit, as well as for the record he might be keeping, my charges of Soviet aggression in the tin mines agreement and Communist conspiracy. Opening my inner self to him on the question of ideology, I remarked, "I am very grateful for the deep concern you have shown over my faith. I became a devoted disciple of Marxism in my school days, believing in it for its own sake with neither political nor personal motives of any kind. Now I have changed. Although this change takes place when I am an official of the government of the Republic of China, it is prompted by my faith and love of truth without a shred of opportunism or personal advantage involved. To be a government official takes only a short span of one's life. It is soon over. Faith and truth are the very foundations upon which the conduct of one's whole life is based, however. Only by taking a doctrine which embodies truth and by joining a political party which fights for fulfillment of truth is there any prospect of realizing the welfare of the people, the country, and humanity. Only then will a democratic world based upon equality, mutual help, freedom, and happiness come into being."

At this point, Dekanozov pleaded fatigue once more and departed, again shaking my hand before leaving. After two such talks, given the degree of "deviationism" shown on my part, I knew that whatever orders Dekanozov received from Moscow could only instruct him to follow a harsher line. In short, the tea ceremony was past; now we would see what type of an ultimatum Stalin had in mind.

Our next discussion dispensed with the preliminaries and moved quickly to the give and take of bargaining. Dekanozov asked whether I intended to scrap the entire program of my previous administration and how ruthless I intended to be against those whom I felt guilty of creating dissension between myself and others. I seized upon his reference to "our common enemies" to declare, "If Marshal Stalin and Mao Tse-tung both admit that the persons I have named as guilty of conspiracy against me are the 'common enemies' you refer to, I will change my opinion immediately. They must all be arrested and purged. As for the policies of my administration, I can only say that as a devoted advocate of the Three People's Principles I intend to construct democratic rule in Sinkiang. However, the provincial authorities are still willing to co-operate with both Moscow and Yenan, provided the latter are willing to give up their aggressive designs. After all, China and the Soviet Union are military allies, standing shoulder to shoulder against fascist aggression. Furthermore, the Kuomintang and the Chinese Communists are co-operating with one another in resisting Japanese invasion. I can assure you that any genuine 'common enemies' will be relentlessly pursued and purged if they are maliciously sowing seeds of discord between Sinkiang and Soviet Russia."

Dekanozov then gave vent to his anger at my words, which he considered impudent in the extreme. Marshaling the full vigor of his resources, he resorted to open threat and blackmail. "As you seem to have made up your mind to give up your faith of many years and to take up another belief, I can say with certainty that all who change their political belief midway can only meet with difficulty. Furthermore, the Marxists throughout the world, particularly the Soviet and Chinese Communists, will not let one of the party members—and in this case, an important one—forsake his party membership of his own free will and attack Marxism with freedom and impunity."

Dekanozov coupled this threat with implications of blackmail, citing what he thought to be incriminating evidence which purported to prove I had passed the point of no return so far as my affiliations with Chungking were concerned. "I remember that back in 1934 you suggested the communization of Sinkiang. You supported Chang Hsueh-liang in 1936 at the time of the Sian Incident. Furthermore, you proposed setting up a full-fledged Soviet regime in Sinkiang in 1941. All these will prove to be serious predicaments for your political future if you change sides. Now that you are at the bewildering crossroads in life, you need more than ever to use your best wisdom and judgment so as to choose between light and darkness." Before I could make any response, Dekanozov left.

I had a feeling that the next talk would be our last. I had made clear my unwillingness to reverse my position and Dekanozov had played his final card with his threat of blackmail. Sinkiang still had Soviet troops, military advisers, and instructors, not to mention the prospecting and drilling teams exploiting our minerals. I decided to make our final interview as formal yet as frank as possible so that if there were any possibility of retaining businesslike relations without submitting completely to the Kremlin I could do so. At the same time I determined to answer explicitly Dekanozov's threats so that Stalin would know I had no fear of whatever he might do to ruin my reputation and my future.

Dekanozov's mild manner on our next encounter was in sharp contrast to the bombast and bluster he had used at the end of our previous conversation. I took advantage of his subdued approach to speak of something I knew would interest Stalin, my philosophical basis for breaking with Marxism. "As you know," I pointed out, "Communists believe that politics and all party activities are based on philosophical foundations, on ideological understanding. Thus, the future of the political worker is determined primarily by the correctness of his political philosophy. Momentary successes must not mislead us, for if they are based on incorrect understanding they will be short-lived victories. For instance, in saying that Hitler will fail sooner or later, we do not mean that Hitler is in any way inferior to Roosevelt or Stalin in intellect and ability. What we mean is that the incorrectness of fascism which has brought about aggression dooms his efforts to failure.

"I believe that communism is right in this emphasis upon the philosophical foundations and that is why I fear no attacks against my new political faith and the party which I am now joining, because if attacks proved successful then my decision would be proved wrong. I have faith that the decision is correct. So far as my personal plan for the next thirty years or so is concerned, I expect to devote most of my time to the study of philosophy."

At this point, Dekanozov interrupted with a look of suspicion and almost a smile of sarcasm, "Do you mean to say that you are giving up your political career to become a philosopher?"

"Yes," I replied, quietly, "a philosopher can contribute more to mankind than either a statesman or a soldier. Chancellor Bismarck, of Germany, left a glorious page in German history for his manifold achievements when Hegel was only a scholar. This philosopher's contribution to Germany was nothing extraordinary, but his contribution to academic learning, particularly to philosophy, has exercised tremendous influence upon the mind of mankind. He was a far greater man and truer genius than Bismarck, whose achievements influenced only a small sector of humanity.

"In the course of my study of philosophy in the future, I earnestly hope that all my former Marxist comrades will let me have the benefit of their free criticism on the works that

I may publish. I hope further that I shall be able to debate with Marxist philosophers on the material interpretation of history versus democracy, so as to clarify the confusion in present philosophical thought and to deliver mankind from peril."

I paused to see the effect of my words upon Dekanozov. His silence signified nothing; I was not even certain he was able to comprehend my remarks. But I did know he was duty bound to repeat them to Stalin and that was my intent.

Having disposed of the theoretical question, I moved on to take up systematically the statements he had made about my past so as to dispel any illusions Stalin might have about their possible use as blackmail. "With respect to the statements of my past actions, both alleged and true, I would like first of all to deal with them as matters of principle, then as matters of fact. I realize that your motive in telling these things to me is twofold. In your capacity as my former comrade you hope talking with me this way will bring me back into the Marxist fold. At the same time you think you can intimidate me into submission so as to prevent my joining any other political grouping. I respect your former motive and reject the latter as hopelessly useless.

"The reason it is useless is that you cannot hope to sell this story to the Republic of China. The reason is quite simple: before my conversion to The Three People's Principles, I was a devoted Marxist. What could have been more natural in terms of principle than my suggesting to Stalin setting up a Soviet regime in Sinkiang? As a disciple of communism and a member of the All-Union Communist Party it would have been a matter of course for me to hope to communize Sinkiang. Stalin knows this but hopes that by bringing up these charges he can discredit me in the eyes of another party and make it lose its confidence in me. As a matter of fact, the leader of the party to which I have pledged my allegiance has long since known that I was formerly a Communist. Furthermore, he does not care what I said or did before my change of faith. What he and that party care about now is my conduct after joining them and whether I obey orders and observe party principle."

Dekanozov betrayed not a flicker of emotion at this information of my having formally affiliated with the Kuomintang and personally communicated with Generalissimo Chiang Kai-shek. Either he had intelligence information on this from agents earlier or else he was an excellent actor, disguising his disappointment and surprise.

I continued, "As for the facts of the matter, some of your charges are downright absurd. In light of Sinkiang's social conditions, practicing communism as such would be highly undesirable. Such a change could take place only after the six great policies had been effective. When Tihua was besieged by Ma Chung-ying in 1934, Soviet Consul General Apresoff raised the question of practicing communism in Sinkiang. I told him that conditions were not ripe for communism at that time. Only when the peoples of all tribes were ready to accept its new forms could this system be brought into Sinkiang. Apresoff then asked me to make my views known to Stalin.

"The next time this particular matter came up according to your charges was after the conspiracies of 1940. I discovered that according to confessions of various agents their chief motive had been to overthrow my regime and to set up a Soviet government. I could not tell whether this was false testimony of Trotskyites designed to alienate me from Stalin or true confessions. Therefore, to test their story I made a proposal to Stalin that communism be introduced in Sinkiang and that the government be made a Soviet one. Knowing well my motives behind such a proposal, Stalin did not reply nor have I heard from him on this matter to the present day. I thus concluded that his evasiveness proved that the conspiracies had been plotted by Moscow. Naturally this was a key factor in causing unfriendliness between the two of us.

"Finally, you raise the question of my relations with Chiang Hsueh-liang at the time of the Sian Incident in 1936. Your account does not correspond with the facts. My cable to the Sinkiang representative in Nanking and my reply to Chang Hsueh-liang at the time eloquently proved that Sinkiang was neither sympathetic with the Sian Incident nor had any intention of taking part in it. Even had I supported it I could not be held responsible, because I was a Communist, at least in sympathy at the time. Since the incident was instigated by the Communists and the Third International, it would only have proved my subordination to the All-Union Communist Party."

I concluded by drawing upon my people's history to show Dekanozov why such malicious stories would cause me no harm in my new relationships with Chungking. "The tradition of Chinese society is to pardon one's enemy. We not only forget the wrongs done to us by our enemy, but even trust and give him heavy responsibilities if he has proved himself worthy of such a trust. All he must do is give up his former political stand and join ours. Such examples are many in the centuries of Chinese history. Kuan Chung had shot the Duke of Chi Huan with an arrow. Subsequently, Kuan changed his political stand and gave his wholehearted support to the Duke of Chi Huan. The latter not only forgave him but also appointed him as his prime minister."

Dekanozov remained quiet after my lengthy statement and slowly sipped his tea. Perhaps this allowed him to compose himself and conceal whatever anger my words may have caused, for he rose, bade me farewell in a cordial manner, and said he would see me "at some later date." The vagueness of his leave-taking increased my feeling that our talks had reached an impasse. Thus, it came as no surprise to learn a few days later that he was preparing to return to Moscow.

Just before his departure, Dekanozov called on me for the last time. In a remark that I was to puzzle over often thereafter, he said in a sincere tone, "Whenever you need me, I can come to Sinkiang any time." Although this caught me off guard, I attempted to respond in kind, and replied, "I wish you a bon voyage. Please pay my respects to Marshal Stalin."

10

The Final Break with Moscow

AS THE SUMMER MONTHS passed, nothing untoward happened except the arrival of a new Soviet consul general, Pushkin, in Tihua. His appointment signified the failure of all previous missions. Now had come the time for me to take the final, decisive step against Moscow. I was anxious, however, even though it seemed there was little Russia could do against me now. I knew that forebearance and vigilance on my part had acted in the interests of my province, my people as well as myself. This was no time for giving in to impulse.

All the burden of breaking with the Soviets was borne by me as governor of Sinkiang. I did not feel that the diplomatic negotiations leading to the withdrawal of Soviet troops and the liquidation of Soviet political and economic interests in Sinkiang were the responsibility of the Commissioner for Foreign Affairs of the Chinese Foreign Office. China and Russia were still allies in the war against the Axis powers. Every precaution had to be taken to ensure "friendly relations" between the two countries. Therefore, I had the delicate and onerous task of confronting the Russians singlehandedly.

On October 5, 1942, I sent a memorandum to the Soviet government through the consul general in Tihua demanding the general withdrawal of Soviet military and technical personnel from Sinkiang. According to my note, "Aside from Soviet diplomatic officials who are granted freedom of residence in

Sinkiang, all Russians in Sinkiang, including military advisers, military instructors, advisers in the employ of the Departments of Finance and Reconstruction, technical experts, engineers, medical doctors, the rank and file of the Eighth Regiment of the Red Army stationed at Hami, and the tin miners and explorers in the Altai and Ili regions, should leave the province within three months."

Upon receipt of the memorandum, Consul General Pushkin immediately demanded an appointment with me. Storming into my office, he protested in an angry voice, "Why do you demand withdrawal of the Russians? These advisers, instructors, and the like are in the employ of the Sinkiang government. The Red Army is here to help you quell rebellion. Finally, the tin miners and workers enjoy the right of residence in Sinkiang as stipulated by the lease agreement."

"I demand their withdrawal because they are not here to help Sinkiang," I retorted. "On the contrary, they are here to engage in subversive activities, to instigate riots and uprisings, and to bring destruction to Sinkiang."

"What evidence have you to offer in proof of your statement?" asked Pushkin.

I recited the dreary record of plots and uprisings, highlighting those of 1940 and 1942, and concluded, "The Provincial Government has submitted all facts and data concerning these plots and assassination attempts to the Soviet Government through Adviser Sarnin of the Border Affairs Department."

"I know nothing of what you have just told me," Pushkin replied, perhaps in truth, for the Soviet Government has seldom let its right hand know what the left hand was doing. "However, I shall forward your demands to the Soviet People's Commissariat for Foreign Affairs and give you my reply as soon as I receive instructions from my government. Regarding the questions of withdrawal of the Soviet Army, you had better talk with Chief Adviser Latoff, as I am not in a position to touch on the military aspects of the problem."

No further word came from Pushkin. As the days stretched into a week, I realized that unless I showed firmness, Moscow might stall indefinitely, hoping that a more fortunate turn of events locally or internationally might permit it to oust me from power. Therefore, on October 11, I informed the Soviet consulate of my desire to speak with Pushkin the next day. As soon as he entered, I asked for word of reply to my ultimatum.

"Nothing yet," Pushkin answered curtly.

"Can you not send Moscow an urgent message, asking for an early reply?"

Pushkin promised to press for instructions but added he was not responsible for military matters, that being Latoff's area. "As to the other personnel which came to Sinkiang at your request, they are not to be dismissed at a moment's notice. Those here under provisions of the secret agreement concerning the lease of Sinkiang's tin mines are legally present. This agreement cannot be unilaterally abrogated."

I decided to bear down hard, and informed him bluntly, "Your statement that you have nothing to do with military affairs can only be construed to mean shirking responsibility on your part. As a representative of the Soviet government, you are responsible for the conduct of the Soviet military personnel here. You are also responsible for forwarding to your government our demand requesting the withdrawal of the Red Army from Sinkiang. I admit that the other Soviet advisers and technical experts are here at our request, but it must be remembered that Sinkiang has no specific agreement with Russia regarding their employment."

"All Soviet advisers, technical experts, and engineers," Pushkin interrupted, "are to serve here for at least two years."

"That may be what you think," I countered, "but Sinkiang has never signed any agreement to this effect with the Soviet government. I am free to dismiss them at any time. As for the secret agreement on the tin mines, it was forced on me in 1940 by Bakulin and two other emissaries of Stalin. I did not sign willingly. Dark clouds hung over Sinkiang; rejection of the Soviet demand would certainly have meant Russian seizure of the province."

"How can you say that?" demanded Pushkin. "The Soviet Union is not an aggressor and has never taken advantage of the weakness of others!"

"It was the beginning of the period of Soviet territorial aggrandizement on weak and small nations," I reminded him. "First, the Soviet Union signed a nonaggression pact with Germany in 1939. Then, she conquered Finland by sheer might of arms, while partitioning Poland with Hitler. Next, she incorporated the Baltic states of Estonia, Latvia, and Lithuania into her territory. What could I have expected from Moscow?

"On the other side of my province, what help could I have received from Chungking, already hard pressed by Japanese invaders? And within Sinkiang itself, what were the conditions at the time of this lease agreement? Moscow was secretly instigating the Kazakhs to rebel in the Altai region. The Eighth Regiment of the Soviet Red Army was busily repairing and strengthening bridges along the Tihua-Hami highway, preparatory to attacking the capital. The Soviet garrison of five hundred officers and men, together with eight tanks and dozens of airplanes stationed within the compounds of the so-called Agricultural Implements Manufacturing Factory at T'out'ungho posed an additional threat to Tihua. Finally, the province was seething with general unrest because my troops were dispersed against the rebellions in the north, while elsewhere fear prevailed as my investigators sought to round up the conspirators led by Tu Chung-yüan."

Pushkin seemed to forget his role in the negotiations. Apparently out of genuine curiosity, he asked, "How were the men in the 'Agricultural Implements Factory' able to threaten Tihua?"

"Very easily," I replied. "On the pretext of holding maneuvers, they frequently created disturbances around the capital and when the uprising was to have taken place, their unit would have played a pivotal part.

"In these circumstances, I had no choice but to swallow my pride and cater to the wishes of Stalin by signing the secret agreement. But since it was clearly concluded against my will and without the approval of the central government, it must be abrogated and the miners and explorers must leave the province."

Pushkin exploded at this point, claiming he would "report your false charges against my country to Moscow." I did not cower before his wrath, but answered in kind. "I am not pouring forth false charges. My accusations are based upon facts. Your disguise as a friend and helper of backward peoples of Asia can deceive only Mao Tse-tung and Chu Teh for a time. It has no effect on me because after struggling with Stalin for many years I have discovered the depths of his treachery. This treachery, as well as the true nature of communism, may eventually be discovered even by Mao and Chu and Communists the world over."

"Your judgment is completely wrong," replied Pushkin. "This, together with your insulting remarks on Comrade Stalin, will be fully reported to Moscow."

"You need not try to scare me," I retorted. "Do what you like. I hope Stalin will learn of this because he should not only ponder but accept with his whole heart the sincere criticisms from an Asian member of the All-Union Communist Party."

At this, Pushkin's face flushed deeply, and he snapped back, "All Communists are not to criticize Comrade Stalin but only to obey him."

"Those Communists who are submissive to him are his slaves, not his comrades!" I replied. "Since I am not his slave, I am free to criticize him."

Pushkin instantly contained his anger and changed his tone. After looking at me quietly for several minutes, he asked, "You are leaving soon for Hami and Chensi for an inspection, correct?"

"Yes, I intend to."

"I learned that construction work on air-raid shelters in and around Tihua has been going on day and night since some time this summer. Is Sinkiang preparing for war?"

"Yes," I responded calmly, "Sinkiang is preparing for war."

"I have further learned that Sinkiang is planning to organize a guerrilla unit comprising 100,000 men. Is this preparatory to large-scale guerrilla action?"

"Yes, if necessary." I knew that only a show of force and a willingness to defend ourselves to the death would convince Moscow that this time I meant business. I doubted that things would come to so extreme a pass, especially since Russia was deeply involved in a death struggle with Nazi Germany. Nevertheless, I was prepared for any eventuality.

After repeating our earlier exchange concerning the question of Pushkin's responsibility over the military personnel, he left my office. I felt secure, secure in the knowledge that I had made no concessions to his demands and secure in the conviction that Moscow was helpless.

On October 16 Pushkin returned for our third parley. According to his instructions from Moscow, two points were to be flatly rejected and the third accepted only conditionally. Specifically, (1) all military personnel, including the officers and men of the Soviet Eighth Regiment at Hami, were not to withdraw; (2) all those connected with the tin mines agreement were also to remain at their posts; and (3) only those Soviet advisers, technical experts, and doctors who had served two years in the province could withdraw and their vacancies would not be filled.

"Such a reply typifies the aggressive and oppressive policy of the Soviet Union," I replied. I recapitulated in brief my arguments concerning the absence of any agreement covering most of the Soviet personnel, as well as the lack of validity of the tin mines lease. I concluded by reiterating my three-month ultimatum for the complete evacuation of all Soviet citizens other than those with diplomatic immunity.

"But it is the decision of our government not to withdraw these people," said Pushkin, firmly and somewhat arrogantly. "What can you do if we refuse to leave?"

"If you are deaf to reason, we will take all steps necessary to protect the sovereignty and territorial integrity of Sinkiang," I said. "Tell Stalin that the four million people of my province, particularly the Commissioner and the armed forces under his command, will not hesitate to fight to the bitter end against any foreign aggressor."

"I shall report every word of yours to Moscow," Pushkin answered angrily.

"That is exactly what I expect of you," I snapped. "I wish Stalin to read every word of your report and then make a wise decision on the Sinkiang problem."

Five days later Pushkin returned with a partial concession. I was familiar with the Asian way of bargaining and resolved to stick it out as long as it took to win my points. This time he began, "The Soviet People's Commissariat for Foreign Affairs has given its reply. First, it makes clear that the nonmilitary advisers, technical experts, engineers, and doctors are here to help Sinkiang. If their service is no longer necessary, they should of course withdraw from the province.

"Secondly, the Commissariat has not yet received sufficient information from the authorities in charge of the tin mines to express its views on this problem. Thirdly, the Commissariat is in no position to make any decision regarding the problem of the withdrawal of military advisers and instructors, including the officers and men of the Soviet Eighth Regiment."

One step forward, two steps marking time; such was the thought in my head. Therefore I stood my ground, saying, "All Soviet nationals, be they military personnel or civilians, miners or doctors, must leave before the time limit. These are mere pretexts to play for time. If the tin miners and explorers refuse to comply with my demand, the provincial government will deny them all facilities and will accord them no protection. If the military advisers and instructors refuse to comply, they will be stricken from the rosters and go without further compensation. If the Soviet Eighth Regiment is not withdrawn, the Border Defense Commission will deny them all necessary services and order the people of Hami to stop supplying them with foodstuffs and fodder. The Sinkiang Provincial Government will assume no responsibility for any untoward incidents which may occur regarding the Soviet military advisers and instructors. We will hold you personally accountable for the consequences. Finally, we intend to make known to the peoples of China and of the world all the facts concerning Soviet aggression in Sinkiang."

Pushkin blanched upon hearing my warning. Stammering with anger at the thought of little Sinkiang threatening citizens of the mighty Soviet Union, he sputtered, "This is an insult to the government of the Soviet Union. I shall report every word of yours to Moscow. As for the responsibility of any incidents, it must rest with you. I am leaving for the resort of Paiyankou near South Mountain to recuperate from some recurring illness."

I was not to be put off by this ruse. "As a Soviet representative in Sinkiang, you are to be fully responsible for anything happening to or caused by Soviet nationals within the borders of this province. At the same time you cannot leave now for Paiyankou. The climate there at this season does not suit your health."

Now I was threatening to add injury to insult. Pushkin almost shouted his question, "What, do I not even have the freedom to leave Tihua?"

"I am not denying you freedom of movement," I explained tactfully, "I am only asking you to stay in Tihua because at a critical moment when all Soviet nationals in Sinkiang are in poor spirits and the people here are living in a state of uneasiness, both you and I should take great responsibility upon ourselves."

The implicit threat was not lost upon him, and Pushkin left, agreeing to report everything to Moscow, "including your restraint upon my freedom of movement." Needless to say, he did not leave the capital, but returned on October 26 for our fifth discussion, this time bearing good news so far as I was concerned. In addition to conceding the immediate withdrawal of all the tin mines personnel, Moscow agreed to pull out its troops within six months. Now that I had this much, I would settle for nothing less than total victory and demanded full compliance with my three-month limit, adding, "Following the departure of the Soviet nationals connnected with the tin mines, the secret agreement concerning the lease shall be abrogated in full."

Pushkin countered, "The message from Moscow mentioned only the withdrawal of nationals working in the mines and said nothing about abrogation of the agreement. If this is to be done, further procedures must be explored."

My proposal was direct and, I felt, reasonable. "No further steps are necessary. All the buildings of the various enterprises of the tin mines shall be purchased by the provincial government. Similarly, we shall buy all the engineering equipment and material which the Soviet Government does not wish to ship back to Russia. Your government will sustain no loss."

At this encouraging moment in the deliberations, my telephone rang. To my dismay, the Staff Office of the Border Defense Commission reported that more than twenty Soviet medium tanks had crossed the border in defiance of the Ili border garrison and were ready to advance toward Tsingho. I immediately ordered the Ili garrison to remain on the alert and to keep me informed of all developments.

I turned to Pushkin, barely able to control my emotions in the face of such perfidy. "If these Soviet tanks should continue to advance and should clash with the local defense units," I warned him, "I shall hold you personally responsible. You have not only refused to withdraw the Eighth Regiment from Sinkiang but now you bring in new reinforcements. This proves your malicious intent."

Pushkin pleaded ignorance, claiming it was a matter of the Soviet Commissariat for War. Earlier he had attempted to explain the stalling on the Eighth Regiment by claiming the commissariats for war and for foreign affairs had separate responsibilities in Sinkiang and had to consult before acting on such matters.

"Your argument is no different from that used by the Japanese following the outbreak of the Mukden Incident," I replied. "When the Mukden authorities protested against the attack of the Kwantung army upon the city, the Japanese consul general in Mukden denied all responsibility."

Pushkin felt the sting of my comparison and protested, "The Soviet Union is an anti-aggression and anti-imperialist socialist state. The diplomatic officials of the Soviet Union are different from those of the fascist countries." After several exchanges of this type, he finally said, "I shall submit a report to Moscow regarding the incident and ask Chief Adviser Latoff if he knows anything about it."

"I must call your attention to the fact," I reminded him, "that I have ordered the defensive forces along the western border to stop the advancing tanks and to destroy the bridges if necessary. The Sinkiang Provincial Government will bear no responsibility for any incident which may arise."

The hours after Pushkin left my office were anxious ones. Was Moscow about to test my position by force of arms? Or was this merely a bluff to frighten me into submission? I knew there was no turning back, regardless of Stalin's intent and resolved to stand firm whatever the cost might be.

That evening Pushkin telephoned to say that the tanks "were merely replacements of the units in the Eighth Regiment at Hami." So weak was this argument he had refused to confront me with it personally! I answered brusquely, "The Soviet Union should not send any replacements to the Eighth Regiment since it has already agreed to withdraw it soon. Furthermore, any replacements wishing to enter the territory of Sinkiang must gain prior approval from the authorities concerned. Also the old tank units of that regiment must first withdraw before replacements can enter Hami, the exchange point being Ili. According to my information, the intruders have passed Tsingho and are now on their way to Wusu. A clash seems inevitable unless you take effective and immediate steps to stop the advance of these Soviet tanks!"

"I shall send the chief Soviet military adviser to the spot to stop them," was Pushkin's reply.

"Very well, but you must be prompt," I answered. "Meanwhile, please inform Moscow that I hold to my demand that all Soviet military personnel withdraw within three months, not within six months."

"And if Moscow refuses, then what?"

"Then Sinkiang will take measures to effect such a withdrawal."

After some additional haggling, Pushkin finally saw that I was resolute and hung up. His promise to halt the tanks proved genuine. By the next morning, my reports showed no further advance and tension along the border immediately subsided. Victory seemed almost in hand.

On November 14 Pushkin called, beaming with friendliness and chatting most amiably. In a generous manner he informed me that Moscow had made the following decisions: "First, all military advisers, instructors, technical experts, engineers, doctors, and Soviet nationals connected with the tin mines shall be sent back to the Soviet Union. Secondly, the regiment of Soviet troops maintained at Hami shall be withdrawn within the period fixed by the Sinkiang Government. Finally, the newly arrived tank replacements are to leave the territory of Sinkiang immediately."

"This was a wise decision on the part of Marshal Stalin," I commented. "Regarding the withdrawal of the Eighth Regiment, the Border Defense Commission shall fix the evacuation route and the time for its passing through Tihua so that no incidents or accidents may take place."

"I shall ask Chief Adviser Latoff to give orders to the Soviet regiment that the rules for its evacuation as set by the Border Defense Commission must be observed," replied Pushkin. "By the way, may I ask the reason for your demanding the withdrawal within three months of all Soviet nationals? Could it be because of the forthcoming establishment of the Kuomintang headquarters in Tihua?"

"It has something to do with this, but that is not the main reason."

"What is the main reason then?"

"My policy in the past was to be friendly to the Soviet Union, but now I must follow the anti-Russia course," I answered frankly. "I was the friend and comrade of Stalin and Mao Tse-tung, but now I am their enemy. All concerned know my reasons full well, and they are especially clear to Marshal Stalin and Mao Tse-tung."

Thus ended by negotiations with Pushkin, breaking once and for all the grip of Stalin on Sinkiang. Thus ended my ten years as a Red war lord.

11

In Conclusion

In presenting this record to the world, I have omitted much evidence of Soviet and Chinese Communist plots against my people and against myself, so that the reader may more easily grasp the main lines of Communist strategy. Were I to have told of the final attempt to overthrow my regime in 1944, engineered by Stalin in Moscow, and by Chou En-lai and Panyushkin in Chungking, were I to have included the incredible story of attempts to break up my family on the part of Miss Liu Yun and of her becoming a double agent because of admiration for me, were I to have recounted the numerous plots to poison me at the Soviet consulate and in my own home, the reader would have faced twice as much reading as I now offer.

However, I believe that even the bare account contained in these meager pages can alert the free world to the strategy and tactics of international communism. The fact that ten years of plotting failed to win Sinkiang can be taken to heart, for therein lies the formula for successfully combating this world menace. My efforts in this direction were several, the more important of which bear close attention by those faced with a similar threat.

First, the importance of good government and a loyal populace cannot be overstressed in thwarting the Communist terror. Maladministration and starvation open the door to Communist instigation of uprisings. In their plots against the Sinkiang government, Soviet Russia and the Chinese Communists did not attempt to win over the masses in the rural districts. They knew that good administration and prosperity made these people immune to Red blandishments. Instead, they focused upon the leftists, young students, adventurers, and ambitious political and military leaders of dubious loyalty. The failure of the plots lay in their inability to win the backing of the people, a prerequisite to overthrowing the existing government and seizing political power. This fact is true, not only for China, but for all countries.

Secondly, countermeasures play a critical role in preventing infiltration, particularly into the armed forces. The Sinkiang Border Defense Commission established a dual secret service system, operated jointly by the Commissioner's office and by the department of police. The advantages were twofold. It enabled the government to check reports from two sources, thereby preventing secret agents from supplying forged information to mislead the authorities. In addition, it facilitated detection of enemy spies, infiltrating our network and made it impossible to penetrate the apparatus through bribery or threats.

This is especially important in the armed forces. Even should the enemy win over sympathizers and conspirators in the higher ranks, the security system prevents the troops from engaging in rebellious activity. The dual secret service apparatus worked closely with a system of political officers, whose duty was to raise the general standard of ideology and understanding among the soldiers. By indoctrinating the troops with patriotism to their country and obedience to their superiors, they were made immune to subversion. The importance of this may be readily seen from the treacherous role played by commanding generals, division commanders, and even brigade commanders in the plots against Sinkiang. Nevertheless, the mass of the armed forces remained loyal to the government throughout the plots.

Third, all persons must remain constantly alert to the menace of Communist subversion. "Peaceful coexistence" is a dangerous myth, propagated by Moscow to lull the unsuspecting free world into complacency. Once the democratic peoples become isolated from one another, apathetic in their attention to politics, and unwilling to bear the burden of counterattacking communism, the enemy will strike the main blow. Evidence of this lies in my ten years of fighting communism in Sinkiang. Whenever I fell prey to my dreams of coexistence and of working harmoniously for the good of the people, my regime almost fell under the weight of the enemy's attack. Fortunately, my alert reaction to the first signs of danger saved both my people and myself from destruction.

Finally, a clear understanding of differentiating between the Communists and their dupes must produce a magnanimous policy toward the culprits which will permit repentance and conversion among the victims of Communist propaganda. Only in this way can the free world divide the Soviet bloc, and demonstrate its humanity and civilized superiority. During my regime, all conspirators were arrested, but those who confessed their crimes were, with only a few exceptions, excused from the death penalty. The following table proves this point.

YEAR	ARRESTS	EXECUTIONS
1933	. . .	3
1934	142	30
1937	435	33
1940	481	59
1942	656	88
1944	220	0*

* I left my post before the trial was completed for a new assignment in Chungking. No person was sentenced to death as a result.

In addition to these main trials, there were two small plots. One, engineered by the Soviet consulate in Karashar, ended in 114 arrests, with only 20 executions. The second, organized by the Soviet consulate in Tihua, led to only 21 arrests, with 7 persons receiving the death penalty. Thus, of all those arrested during my regime, only a little more than ten per cent were executed.

The handling of these conspiracies was prompted by two factors. On the one hand, prompt arrests and secret trials were called for by virtue of Sinkiang's isolation from China proper and its accessibility to Soviet Russia. Only quick action could seize the culprits before they made good their escape across the border, or before they received help from the Russian and Chinese Communists.

On the other hand, magnanimity was both practical and wise. By giving the criminals assurance of safe treatment, they produced sincere confessions which named all important accomplices. By recognizing that many of them were merely dupes of Communist deception, they became true believers in the superiority of the provincial government. In truth, only Stalin and Mao Tse-tung were the real enemies of Sinkiang. Some of the accomplices belonged to the All-Union Communist Party, and had no alternative but to take orders from their superiors. Others were either public functionaries with no deep understanding of Marxism-Leninism, or those who feared Soviet strength. These joined through bribery and coercion. Finally, there were the Trotskyite remnants and political adventurers. If these confessed their crimes, they were capable of being pardoned. Through this combination of speedy but magnanimous trials, all the important conspirators were captured and none of the plots proved successful. The lesson bears study throughout the free world.

Of a different order is the problem posed by Soviet policy, as distinct from Soviet Communist plotting. It should be noted that my affinity with Soviet principles was used, whenever possible, to bring destruction to Sinkiang. All the Russian advisers, instructors, experts, and technicians, employed by the provincial government, became fifth columnists. Stalin never genuinely followed Lenin's dictate to render aid and assistance to the backward peoples of the East. On the contrary, his dealings with those peoples were aggressive in character, as are those of his successors.

In Sinkiang the Soviet consulate in Tihua acted as the nerve center of plots and conspiracies. Only the preponderance of Russian power compelled Sinkiang, through self-protection, to adopt the pro-Soviet policy. Once the weight was lifted, however, that policy was scrapped. Only the fact that China and the U.S.S.R. were allies in war against the Axis powers, necessitating "friendly relations," compelled my government to negotiate politely for the exclusion of Soviet power in Sinkiang.

But stripped of diplomatic niceties, the harsh truth behind Soviet policy is the strategy of "one step backward and two steps forward." Thus, when the "revolutionary tide" was on the ebb in Sinkiang, the Soviet Union would beat a hasty retreat and adopt a weak and soft policy. But when the revolutionary tempo was rising, she would instantly adopt the "two steps forward" policy. In 1940, when Stalin sent Bakulin and his accomplices to force upon Sinkiang the "Tin Mines" agreement, I found the foreign policy of Moscow firm and strong. In 1942, when I made a showdown with Stalin by demanding withdrawal of the Red Army and the liquidation of Soviet political, economic, and military interests in Sinkiang, the foreign policy of the U.S.S.R. proved soft and weak.

Confronted with a constantly changing policy, Sinkiang at times had to bear the disgrace brought upon it by Stalin. At other times it could counter him with drastic measures. But the free world today need not take the same line in dealing with the Soviet Union. It need not bear the disgrace of dealing with the Communists. Meeting the "two steps forward" policy with firmness, and drastic measures if need be, will force communism to a hasty retreat. Should it then adopt the "one step backward" tactic, the free world must take advantage of the opportunity to break through the Iron Curtain and crush the Communist conspiracy.

Until the final battle, however, the Communists will follow the policy of peaceful offensive and subversion. The best method to defeat this is by infiltration and countersubversion. Only by constantly detecting the Communist penetration of government organizations, armed forces, and the vital nuclear laboratories, can the free world guarantee its security during the so-called "cold war."

In addition to undermining national security, Communist plots aim at the assassination of leaders throughout the free world. The innumerable attempts upon my life provide dramatic proof of this. Thus, the four steps to power must be clearly understood and countered. As evidenced in Sinkiang, these are: (1) providing official support on the supposed basis of friendship, so as to introduce agents into the target area; (2) developing underground organizations and infiltrating the government; (3) instigating riots and co-ordinating these with assassination of key figures; and (4) seizing the existing apparatus through the police and the armed forces.

If my experiences have served in any way to alert the free world and to show it the way to combat communism, my life shall not have been in vain. Only in this way can we work toward the day when not only my own people but the hundreds of millions behind the Iron Curtain will know freedom, happiness, and prosperity under the democratic way of life.

Appendices

Appendix A

GLOSSARY

Apresoff, Garegin A.: Soviet consul general in Urumchi, 1933-37. Specialist on Central Asian affairs. As consul in Meshed, Persia, Apresoff had worked closely with Persian Communists and affiliated minority groups in the 1920's. He was executed in Soviet purges of 1937 for "Trotskyite plotting."

CCP: Chinese Communist Party.

Chen Hsiu-ying: Wife of Sheng Shih-ch'i and member of All-Union Communist Party, who according to her confession in the Appendices assassinated her husband.

Chin Shu-jen: Governor of Sinkiang, 1928-33. Won power through a coup in which his predecessor, Yang Tseng-hsin, was assassinated, though uncertainty remains as to Chin's role in the coup. Lost power in the local revolt of April, 1933, when Chin's White Russian mercenaries ousted him in dissatisfaction with maladministration and poor prosecution of pacification in province. Later imprisoned by Nanking for illegal signing of commercial treaty with Soviet Union in 1931.

Huang Mu-sung: Emissary from Nanking sent to Sinkiang in 1933, ostensibly to ascertain state of affairs and to verify competence of Sheng Shih-ts'ai. Believed by Sheng and others to have headed coup against Sheng; therefore, placed under house arrest and three alleged conspirators were executed.

Ining Affair: See Kuldja revolt.

Kuldja revolt: Also referred to as the Ining Affair, Ining being an alternate name for Kuldja. Revolt broke out November 7, 1944, under apparent Soviet direction, and spread to the three districts of Ili, Tacheng, and Altai under the banner of the "East Turkistan Republic." The cease-fire occurred in September, 1945, followed by armistice agreements in January and June, 1946, which resulted in complete autonomy of the rebel districts until the Chinese Communist seizure of Sinkiang in 1949-50.

Liu Wen-lung: Commissioner for Education in Sinkiang, who was named acting governor after the April, 1933, coup. Ousted by Sheng within a year.

Li Yung: Installed by Sheng Shih-ts'ai as acting governor of Sinkiang in 1934, replacing Liu Wen-lung. Li's extreme age and rumored deafness suggested to observers his role as a figurehead, with Sheng wielding actual power.

Ma Chung-ying: Young warrior of famed Ma family in Kansu province, in northwest China. Known as Tungans because of their conversion to Islam, the Ma family ruled as independent war lords throughout much of the twenties and thirties. Warriors on horseback, they resisted outside authority and formed temporary alliances with Moslem minorities in Sinkiang, Chinghai, and Kansu. Ma Chung-ying laid siege to Urumchi in 1932 and was defeated by Sheng Shih-ts'ai. Regrouping his forces, he again besieged the capital in 1933-34 and was beaten off by Soviet airplanes and troops assisting Sheng. After retreating southward, he won sanction in the Soviet Union, where he stayed in isolation from outside contact. He was apparently executed during the 1937 purges.

Mao Tse-min: Brother of Mao Tse-tung, named Minister of Finance in the Sinkiang government from 1937 to 1942. Arrested and executed by Sheng in 1942 on charges of plotting against his government.

Sheng Shih-ch'i: Fourth younger brother of Sheng Shih-ts'ai. Schooled in Moscow military academies; returned to Sinkiang in the winter of 1941-42 and named commander of motorized brigade in Urumchi. Died under mysterious circumstances in March, 1942. Not to be confused with another brother, Sheng

Shih-yi, who negotiated with Chungking on Sheng Shih-ts'ai's behalf in 1941-42.

Sovsintorg: Soviet-Sinkiang Trading Company (name abbreviated from Russian title), created by agreement with Chin Shu-jen, and active until Soviet withdrawal in 1943. Exercised near-monopoly control of trade with Sinkiang, with diplomatic immunities granted to offices throughout the province and preferential position with respect to competing trade from China proper or India.

Tu Chung-yüan: Childhood friend of Sheng Shih-ts'ai. Generally thought to be a member of a group known as "Progressives" rather than a member of CCP, but extremely favorable to Sheng-Soviet *entente*. Author of only firsthand book on Sheng's rule, *circa* 1937. Executed by Sheng on charges of plotting in 1943, after having directed educational activities as director of Sinkiang College, 1937-42.

Tungan: Name given to Chinese converts to Islam.

Uighur: Turkic people, comprising slightly more than half of Sinkiang population. Predominantly sedentary people, settled around the oases of southern Sinkiang.

Wu, Aitchen K.: Emissary from Nanking, who attempted to mediate between Sheng Shih-ts'ai and Ma Chung-ying in 1933. Author of several books on Sino-Soviet relations and Sinkiang.

Wu, Chaucer H.: Special Commissioner for Foreign Affairs in Sinkiang, appointed by Chungking in August, 1942, and active in negotiations with Russians in 1942-43.

Wu Chung-hsin: Governor of Sinkiang, appointed by Chungking as successor to Sheng Shih-ts'ai in October, 1944.

Yakub Beg: Moslem adventurer, who led rebellion in Sinkiang and ruled as a self-styled potentate from the late 1860's until his defeat and death in 1875.

Yang Tseng-hsin: Governor of Sinkiang, 1912-28. Won power through coup and lost it through assassination. Ruled independently of central government, concluding agreements with Soviet authorities and appointing consul generals in neighboring Russian cities.

Appendix B

AGREEMENT OF CONCESSIONS SIGNED BY THE REPRESENTATIVES OF THE GOVERNMENT OF U.S.S.R. AND GOVERNOR OF SINKIANG

IN ORDER to assist in the development of productivity in Sinkiang territory, the Government of the U.S.S.R. agrees to undertake the work of prospecting, investigation and exploitation of tin mines and its ancillary minerals in the territory of Sinkiang in accordance with the following provisions:

ARTICLE 1. The Government of Sinkiang agrees to extend to the Government of the U.S.S.R. within the territory of Sinkiang exclusive rights to prospect for, investigate and exploit tin mines and its ancillary minerals.

ARTICLE 2. The Government of the U.S.S.R. will enjoy in the territory of Sinkiang the following rights:
- (a) To exploit and investigate deposits of tin and its ancillary minerals and to make adequate geological and geographical surveys and carry on other work;
- (b) To exploit tin mines and its ancillary useful minerals and, through the application of appropriate productive processing to the ores mined, to produce concentrates and products;
- (a) To build and equip mine shafts, washeries, foundries, machine shops, godowns, houses, dormitories, offices, hospitals, schools, etc.;

(d) To utilize all natural resources to obtain power, with the right to install hydraulic power and other plants;

(e) To construct power stations, including hydraulic power stations, and to erect networks of transmission lines, transformers, etc.;

(f) To supply the needs of the concessions, the right to make use of all existing means of transportation in the territory of Sinkiang, the right to construct roads and necessary building equipment for the roads, including railways, and to organize and utilize all kinds of means of transportation of its own;

(g) To make use of all kinds of means of communications and, to suit the needs of the concessions, to install telephone lines, telegraphic lines and to construct radio stations;

(h) To import without hindrance into the territory of Sinkiang all necessary engineering equipment and material, to repair and rebuild all machines and equipment and parts thereof, and to transmit the same from one enterprise to another;

In the first ten-year period of validity of the present Agreement, imports of equipment and material into the territory of Sinkiang shall be free of customs duties and other imposts and taxes. Thereafter, imports of equipment and material for these concessions shall be liable for the payment of current customs duties of the territory of Sinkiang, provided that the sum of the customs duties and other imposts does not exceed twenty per cent of the value of the equipment or material.

The equipment and material imported may be re-exported to the U.S.S.R. at any time and shall be free from customs duties and other imposts and taxes.

(i) To supply the needs of the concessions, the right to procure local building materials (bricks, stones, lumber, limestone, etc.), coal and fuel wood, and to purchase and store all materials needed by the mining concessions;

(j) To employ laborers in Sinkiang and to employ engineers, technicians and workers from the U.S.S.R.; the Government

of Sinkiang shall without hindrance grant them permits of
entry into Sinkiang and freedom of residence in various places
in Sinkiang;

(k) To supply the needs of the workers and staff employed by
the concessions, the right to import into Sinkiang territory
provisions and articles for normal daily use which are to be
distributed through the trade network of the concessions.

ARTICLE 3. The Government of the U.S.S.R. shall have the right to
export without hindrance from the production centers in Sinkiang
free from customs duties and other imposts and taxes the manu-
factured products or finished products of the tin mines and its
ancillary useful minerals.

ARTICLE 4. For the implementation of the provisions of this agreement on Concessions, the Government of the U.S.S.R. will establish
a trust to prospect for and exploit tin mines and their ancillary
minerals, to be known as "Sin-tin," enjoying all the rights and
privileges of an independent juridical person.

The operations of "Sin-tin" will be regulated by a constitution
which will be enacted in accordance with the legislative procedures
of the U.S.S.R. "Sin-tin" shall have the right to establish without
hindrance branch offices, sub-branch offices, and agencies within the
whole territory of Sinkiang.

ARTICLE 5. During the period of validity of the present Agreement,
the Government of Sinkiang shall guarantee the acquisition of lands,
including the felling of timbers, the mining of coal and areas for
the procurement of building materials which may be necessary for
the carrying on of the various kinds of works referred to in this
Agreement. The Government of Sinkiang shall remove all the
population residing in such areas as may have been allotted to "Sin-
tin."

Such areas of land shall be allotted on the application of "Sin-tin."
In the allotment of such areas of land, there shall be no delay and

shall be in strict conformity with the terms of the applications. The rental for such allotted areas shall be paid with the product of "Sin-tin" as provided for in Article 7.

"Sin-tin" shall pay the Government of Sinkiang the value of the buildings and abutments left on the areas of land allotted to "Sin-tin," the amount and conditions of such payment to be agreed upon between "Sin-tin" and the Government of Sinkiang.

ARTICLE 6. In addition to the areas of land allotted to "Sin-tin" in accordance with the provisions of Article 5 of this Agreement, "Sin-tin" shall have the right to purchase or to rent houses, buildings and godowns; and to supply the needs of the various enterprises of "Sin-tin" and the needs of provisions of the workers and staff of such enterprises, the right to rent land for agricultural and pasturing purposes. "Sin-tin," its workers and its staff, shall enjoy the right to fish for their own consumption in the rivers and lakes of Sinkiang.

ARTICLE 7. During the first five-year period, commencing from the day of the signature of this Agreement, "Sin-tin" shall pay the Government of Sinkiang five per cent of the tin and its ancillary useful minerals mined in Sinkiang. Thereafter, during the period of validity, the rate of payment shall be six per cent. The time of payment shall be the first quarter of the ensuing solar calendar year after production. On the other hand, the products to be paid to the Government of Sinkiang in accordance with paragraph 1 of this Article shall be sold to the Government of the U.S.S.R.; at the price of delivery at the Soviet-Sinkiang border, the said price to be at par with the average annual (the year preceding the sale) price of the principal centers of the world market for tin and its ancillary useful materials.

In accordance with the wish of the Government of Sinkiang, the Government of the U.S.S.R. shall pay for the products sold to it by the former with commodities in kind; the price of such commodities in kind shall be the price of delivery at the Soviet-Sinkiang border of the respective commodities when imported into Sinkiang.

The Government of the U.S.S.R. shall have the right to have the tin and other useful ancillary minerals, sold to it by the Government of Sinkiang, exported without hindrance from Sinkiang, free of customs duties and other imposts and taxes.

ARTICLE 8. In compensation for its privilege of exemption from customs duties, "Sin-tin" shall contribute annually to the Government of Sinkiang a sum equivalent to two per cent of the price of the products exported by "Sin-tin," the price to be fixed in accordance with the provisions of Article 7 of this Agreement.

The contribution due in any one year shall be paid in January of the ensuing year.

Except the said contribution, "Sin-tin" shall not be liable to the payment of any imposts or taxes.

ARTICLE 9. The Government of Sinkiang shall assist "Sin-tin" in the attainment of its objectives as stated in this Agreement; and shall not interfere in the operations of "Sin-tin"; especially the Government of Sinkiang shall not inspect, supervise, investigate, or audit the various operations of production, finance and commerce of "Sin-tin." The administrative technical personnel of "Sin-tin" shall have the right of movement without hindrance through Sinkiang territory in the performance of their duties.

The various enterprises, buildings, houses, means of transportation, products and other properties of "Sin-tin" within the scope of this Agreement shall not be subjected to conscription. The means of transportation of "Sin-tin" shall not be subjected to any mobilization order of the Government of Sinkiang. The workers and staff of "Sin-tin" who are citizens of the U.S.S.R. shall be exempt from personal labor service; their property shall not be subjected to conscription.

ARTICLE 10. "Sin-tin" shall have the right to deal with all its capital, to raise loans, to have current accounts with banks in either local or foreign currencies, to carry on within or without the territory of

Sinkiang remittance and exchange operations; to exchange foreign currencies into Sinkiang currency, *et vice versa*.

ARTICLE 11. "Sin-tin" shall have the right to sell in the territory of Sinkiang, after fulfilling the needs of its basic enterprises, the surplus products of its auxiliary enterprises.

ARTICLE 12. For the protection of its houses, buildings, factories, plants, godowns, etc., and to ensure the security of its transport service, "Sin-tin" shall have the right to establish armed guards.

ARTICLE 13. Any damages suffered by the "Sin-tin" trust as a result of the violation of any provision of this Agreement on the part of either the provincial or the local political authorities of Sinkiang or, as a result of illegal acts of the said political authorities, shall be compensated for by the Government of Sinkiang.

ARTICLE 14. The Government of U.S.S.R. agrees to train a skilled cadre from amongst the citizens residing in the territory of Sinkiang, the number and types of technical skill to be agreed upon between the representatives of the U.S.S.R. and the Government of Sinkiang.

ARTICLE 15. The period of validity of this Agreement shall be fifty years, commencing from the date of signature.

On the expiration of the period of validity of this Agreement, all the buildings and equipment of the various enterprises of the concessions shall be transferred without compensation to the Sinkiang Government. The products, materials, commodities, provisions, supplies, cash, capital and claims against third parties shall remain the assets of "Sin-tin" and shall be exportable or transportable without hindrance from Sinkiang.

The Government of Sinkiang agrees to be responsible not to transfer or alienate the buildings and equipment of the various enterprises to any foreign person, natural or juridical, and not to permit under whatever conditions foreign capital to participate in the exploitation of the tin mines and its ancillary minerals in Sinkiang.

ARTICLE 16. This Agreement shall enter into force immediately upon its signature.

ARTICLE 17. This Agreement is signed in quadruplicate. two in the Russian language, two in the Chinese language, all equally authentic.

DONE on the Twenty-Sixth Day of November, One Thousand Nine Hundred and Forty at Tihua (Urumchi).

Representatives of the Government of the U.S.S.R.

(signed) BAKULIN

(signed) KARPOV

Representative of the Government of Sinkiang

(signed) SHENG SHIH-TS'AI

Appendix C

CONFESSION OF MAO TSE-MIN

BEFORE I WRITE my confession, I must offer my apology to Commissioner Sheng who has been very kind to me and the other Chinese Communists.

I believe it is the Soviet Union, rather than Sinkiang and the Chinese Communist Party, who should be chiefly responsible for the worsening of Sinkiang-Soviet and Sinkiang-Yenan relations. It is my firm belief that Commissioner Sheng is a faithful follower of Marxism-Leninsm. His book entitled *The Six Great Policies* is proof of his profound understanding of the ideologies of Marx and Lenin. His policy of kinship to sovietism and his aid and assistance to the Chinese Communist Party is proof of his ability to put these ideologies into practice.

Two reasons accounted for the worsening of the relations between Sinkiang on the one hand and the Soviet and Chinese Communists on the other. First, Moscow and Yenan thought that Commissioner Sheng distrusted the Soviet Union and the Chinese Communist Party. Second, Commissioner Sheng thought that the policy of the Soviet Union and the Chinese Communist Party was to undermine Sinkiang. When I was in Moscow under medical treatment, I had more than once advised the Soviet policy-makers to give up temporarily their policy of undermining Sinkiang. I suggested that they should instruct Miss Liu Yen to take every possible means to win the Sinkiang authorities over to the Communist side. I told them that the policy of "undermining" and the policy of "persuading" are contradictory to each other. If both policies were adopted at the same time, they were doomed to failure. They concurred with me in my opinion, but they never took my advice in practice.

Two other errors have been committed by the Soviet Union. First, she insisted on leasing the Sinkiang tin mines for a period of fifty years. This was considered by Commissioner Sheng as an act of aggression. Second, she prevented Commissioner Sheng from becoming a member of the Chinese Communist Party and insisted that he could only join the All-Union Communist Party, thus creating the impression that she has territorial ambitions toward Sinkiang. Because of these mistaken policies on the part of the Soviet Union, Commissioner Sheng lost his confidence in Stalin and in Marxism-Leninism.

The Chinese Communists had no other alternative but to follow the course of the Soviet Union. The idea of assassinating Brigade Commander Sheng Shih-ch'i originated not from Yenan, but from Moscow. Moreover, it was the errors of Comrade Fang Lin alone, and not the errors of the Chinese Communist Party, that made Commissioner Sheng distrust the Chinese Communists. Comrade Fang Lin intended to make a hero of himself by getting rid of Commissioner Sheng and taking the political power into his own hands. The mistakes committed by Fang Lin had put the Chinese Communist Party at a great disadvantage.

Fang Lin had also brought me into serious trouble. He first created a dissension between me and my wife, resulting in our divorce. Then he caused Miss Chu Tan-hua to marry me. Through Miss Chu, he attempted to win me over to his side—a fact which I did not find out until after our marriage. He wanted to win me over to his side because he knew that I was the one who reported his misdeeds to Commissioner Sheng and who suggested that he should be replaced. (I made the suggestion because I believed at that time that Fang Lin's leaving Sinkiang would help to maintain Sinkiang-Yenan relations and enhance the personal friendship between Commissioner Sheng and Chairman Mao Tse-tung). Fang Lin also knew that Commissioner Sheng once advised me not to marry Miss Chu Tan-hua in order to avoid the criticism of others. For this reason Fang Lin always entertained the suspicion that Commissioner Sheng and I were on very intimate terms. Apparently he wanted to drive a wedge between me and Commissioner Sheng by urging me and Miss Chu Tan-hua to unite in matrimony. I deeply regret that I ignored Commissioner Sheng's kind advice and allowed myself to be allured into a snare.

The Chinese Communists should be sorry for Tu Chung-yüan's subversive activities in Sinkiang in 1940. However, Tu was not instigated by my brother, but by the well-known conspirator, Chou En-lai, to undermine Sinkiang. On the surface, Chou's purpose of undermining Sinkiang was to control the land route to Russia. As a matter of fact, his real motive in seizing Sinkiang was to expand his own influence. It must be noted that Tsou Tao-feng and Hu Yü-chih of the Life Book Store were Chou En-lai's intimate friends. It was through the recommendation of Tsou Tao-feng and Hu Yü-chih that Tu Chung-yüan and Kao Tsung-ming became members of the Chinese Communist Party. In the end, Tu Chung-yüan was closely connected with the Chou En-lai clique. My brother always said that Chou En-lai was one of few Communists who like to create dissension among his fellow party members. He was chiefly responsible for the strifes within the party during the early period of the Communist movement in Kiangsi.

The policy of the Chinese Communists toward Sinkiang was carried out in three stages. During the first stage, every possible means was taken to win Commissioner Sheng over to the side of the Communists and to help him build up a New Sinkiang. During the second stage, the Communist position was consolidated and preparations were made to undermine the local government. During the third stage, all measures were taken to overthrow the existing administration that advocated the six great policies and to replace it with a Soviet regime independent of the Chinese government.

I was always of the opinion that the policies of both the Soviet Union and the Chinese Communists toward Sinkiang were mistaken. As a member of the Chinese Communist Party, however, I could not raise objections to them. Both the Soviet and Chinese Communists have failed to understand the character and the extraordinary tact of Commissioner Sheng. The more Moscow and Yenan attempted to undermine Sinkiang, the closer was the province to the Kuomintang and farther away from the Soviet Union and the Chinese Communists. I knew long ago that if the situation remained unchanged, grave consequences would follow. It was for this reason that in the past I often asked leave of absence from Commissioner Sheng and went to Moscow for medical treatment. It was also for this reason that in the past I often advised Commissioner Sheng to join the Chinese Communist Party and then either to leave Sinkiang for Yenan or bring his army to the interior part of China and make it a strong anti-Japanese force. I also told him that if his troops could leave Sinkiang, I would be willing to work in the political department of the army under his command. Unfortunately, I could not tell him the reason for my giving such advice and thus incurred his suspicion against me. As a matter of fact, in giving Commissioner Sheng the advice, I had no other purpose than to protect him.

There is nothing more I want to put down in my confession. In a word, as a member of the Chinese Communist Party, I had to obey its orders and to take part in the plot prepared jointly by the Soviet Union and the Chinese Communists against Sinkiang, no matter how strongly I was opposed to it. If the Sinkiang court should pronounce the death sentence on me, I would die a martyr to Marxism-Leninism. If Commissioner Sheng should commute the sentence in consideration of our past friendship as well as his political future, I would strive to requite his kindness.

(signed) MAO TSE-MIN, alias CHOU PING

June 25, 1942

Appendix D

CONFESSION OF TU CHUNG-YÜAN

ACTING ON the orders of Chou En-lai, the Chinese Communist Party's chief representative in Chungking, I came to Sinkiang to seek an expansion of the Communist organization here by taking full advantage of my personal relations with Commissioner Sheng. According to Chou's instructions, my work was to be carried out in two stages. During the first stage, every means were to be taken to win Commissioner Sheng over to the side of the Chinese Communists. If this proved a success, Commissioner Sheng and I were to join hands in making Sinkiang a Chinese Communist base for the sovietization of China. If this proved a failure, I should proceed to the second stage of my work. During this stage, a revolutionary force was to be secretely organized and a Communist regime was to be instituted at the opportune moment to replace the administration headed by Commissioner Sheng.

When Chou En-lai dictated his orders to me, I told him that I would try my best in carrying out the mission of the first stage. But it seemed improper for me during the second stage to plot against Commissioner Sheng, who was not only my friend but also my former schoolmate and a compatriot of my native province. I therefore begged him to send another person to carry out the mission of the second stage. Chou was very much displeased with my request. "It is a surprise to me that you are still full of feudalistic thoughts," he said. "How can you neglect the orders of the party? If you are a faithful follower of the teachings of Marx and Lenin, you should absolutely obey the orders of your party. If it is the order of the party, you can even plot against your brother, and certainly against your friend or schoolmate or a compatriot of your native province."

"Please don't be angry at my words," I said. "As a member of the Party, I shall obey its orders. I must admit that I am not a well-trained member of the party. Therefore I beg your pardon for making the request."

At this point Chou En-lai changed his tone and spoke softly to me. "I am glad that you have realized that a party member must obey the orders of the party. You should know that you are sent by the party for this specific mission because of your intimate relations with Commissioner Sheng."

I then told Chou En-lai that I was a cultural worker and had no experience in instigating riots and uprisings. I asked for instructions as to how to proceed to the second stage of my mission in case the first proved a failure.

"The difficult and dangerous mission of organizing the rioters and instigating the uprisings does not rest with you alone," Chou said. "There will be others to help you. Comrades Shen Yen-ping, Shih Mei, Sa Kung-liao and Chang Chung-shih will come to your aid. Moreover, the experienced staff members of the Soviet Consulate will give you all the necessary assistance."

After I arrived in Sinkiang, I found out that Commissioner Sheng is well versed in political theories and philosophy and therefore I did not dare to persuade him to go over to the side of the Communists. Upon the pressure of the Chinese Communists and the staff members of the Soviet Consulate, I skipped over the first stage of my mission and proceeded at once to the second stage. I regret having done such a thing to my old friend. If Commissioner Sheng should commute the sentence in consideration of our past friendship, I would strive to requite his kindness.

(signed) TU CHUNG-YÜAN
June 20, 1942

Appendix E

Member of the All-Union Communist Party and Wife of Sheng Shih-ch'i

AFTER HIS graduation from the Red Military Academy in Moscow, Sheng Shih-ch'i originally planned to return to China together with me and our children. As he could not leave within a short period, he asked me to return to Tihua first with our children. I made the acquaintance of Mr. and Mrs. Latoff in Moscow, and we were on very good terms. After my return to Tihua, our relations were even closer. There was no news of Sheng's homecoming three months after my return. One day Latoff told me that the reason for Sheng's lingering in Moscow was his love for a Russian girl. I was seriously perturbed at the time. I learned that the Commissioner had cabled his brother urging him to return; yet he still did not come. I thought he must have lingered in Moscow because of that Russian girl. I was not only angry but also hated him. Once Latoff said, "As your husband is in love with somebody else, your future is quite hopeless. Your husband is a college graduate, while you have not even graduated from a middle school. So wide a gap exists between you with respect to your education that he would eventually take a college graduate to be his wife, even if he does not bring the Russian girl back to Sinkiang. He would never want you again." On hearing Latoff's words, I was very much disheartened, believing that my future was all over. I wept for a whole day and slept two days.

On another occasion Latoff asked me whether I knew anything that had happened recently. I replied that I did not, and asked him what he had heard. He said that he had better keep his mouth shut for fear that I might either tell other people or report to the government. I said that I would not do this. He replied that, if I could keep a secret, he would take me into his confidence. "As a young Communist in the All-Union Communist Party, I have to keep secret whatever a Russian has to say to me," was my reply. Then Latoff laughed and said, "I can tell you now." He added that within Sinkiang all peoples as well as government and military officials were against Commissioner Sheng, while both the Soviet Union and the Chinese Communists were dissatisfied with him. There was a plan afoot to unite all the forces, both internal and external, to overthrow Commissioner Sheng. "You know well that I am deeply concerned over your welfare," Latoff said. "However, no matter how bright is the future of Commissioner Sheng and your husband, it makes very little difference to you. The brighter is their future, the higher will be your husband's position and the more anxious will he be to marry a girl of higher education. From this perspective, the future of Sheng's family has nothing to do with you. On the other hand, if everything does not go well with Sheng's family, you will be involved. As you are a member of the Sheng family, those who are against the government will never forgive you. For this reason, I hope you will plan everything beforehand for yourself." I was seriously agitated and could not go to sleep that night.

Since then I did not take good care of my children but spent my time in riotous living. It was in this period of great anxiety that Sheng Shih-ch'i returned to Tihua from Moscow. He did not bring home his Russian wife and was as kind to me as he had ever been. Gradually, I became my normal self, taking good care of our children. Everything went on well until after quite a while after my husband's return, when my sister-in-law, Shih-tung, spoke ill of me to him. He began to get angry with me, accusing me of having neglected the children and having fooled around most of the time. I was very unhappy and could not help deluding myself into thinking that he must have become tired of me and planned to take a college graduate to be his wife.

Seeing that I was in very good mood since the return of Sheng Shih-ch'i, Latoff, whenever I saw him, did not say anything more to me. When I said that my husband did not bring home the Russian girl, he replied that it was not because he did not want to bring her home but that the Soviet Union would not let him. One day he saw that I was very much depressed. Taking advantage of this opportunity, he said, "Everything is not going on well. You should make your own plans. Or you will simply sacrifice yourself for the Sheng family."

"Did you hear something bad recently?" I asked.

He replied, "I cannot tell you, because you will tell your husband."

"I shall not, because our relations now are far from good. Please tell me!" I entreated.

Then he said that on the occasion of the April Uprising anniversary, the revolutionary organization which had among its supporters all important government and military officials both within and without the province would assassinate Commissioner Sheng and seize the political power of the province. At the time of the riot the Eighth Regiment of the Red Army stationed at Hami and the Red forces at the aircraft factory, assisted by formations of Red airplanes from Alma-Ata, would participate in the fighting. In the light of the present situation, there was a fair chance for the revolution to succeed. The fate of members of the Sheng household was doomed.

I then said, "I am scared. As a young Communist in the All-Union Communist Party, can you and Consul General Bakulin help me?"

To this he answered, "Of course, we can find ways and means to save your life, but it is very difficult. You being the wife of the Commissioner's brother, people would not believe you, even if you tell them that you are against Commissioner Sheng."

"What can I do then?"

"If you obey the order of the All-Union Communist Party and do something for the cause of the revolution, then the consul General may be able to say something on your behalf and help you."

"What can I do?"

"What I am afraid of is that you may not have enough determination and courage. You women cannot be trusted. If I tell you, you will tell your husband. Then everything would be finished."

"Please tell me. I only care for my own safety and shall not tell my husband what you say."

He then said, "If the party orders you to kill Commissioner Sheng and your husband, can you do that?"

To this I answered, "I cannot. First, I have no such courage. Secondly, how can I be so hardhearted as to do so?"

"If so, you have no way for salvation, and you are not even a member of the All-Union Communist Party. You have to take the order of your party, even if it were to kill your own parents and brother. Only then are you a good and devoted party member. You had better think it over and we shall discuss it again. What I have said to you today should be kept as an absolute secret from your husband. If you tell him tonight, that means the end of your life by tomorrow."

"I shall not tell him. Don't worry. Please think over if there is any other way to save my life," was my answer.

Ke Mo was then sick and lay on bed crying. It further depressed my gloomy mood. One day, just after my husband had gone to office, Hsiao Tso-hsin came to see me, saying that Latoff wanted me to go to his house at once. He warned, "I cannot think of a good way to save your life. The All-Union Communist Party, with a view to saving your life, orders you to assassinate your husband." I readily said, "I cannot take this order. First, I have no such courage to kill him. Secondly, even if I could kill him, his brother would surely beat me to death. Should I sacrifice my life just because I try to save it?"

Latoff, in obvious displeasure, replied, "If you would not do so, we have no way to save your life. If you disobey the order of the party, it will also wash its hands of your affair." Seeing that I was frightened, he continued, "The party has thoroughly considered your case, trying to save your life in every conceivable way. Because of your close connection with the Sheng family, it cannot save your life unless you render some meritorious service for the cause of the revolution. If you can carry out your mission as directed, there is no danger whatsoever for the following reasons. First, Commissioner Sheng and all your family members would never suspect that you are the culprit, causing the death of your husband. Secondly, even if Commissioner Sheng suspected that you had killed your husband, he could not beat you to death on the spot and would probably send you to the court for trial. The uprising would have broken out at the time of trial. The first thing for the revolutionaries to do would be to release all political prisoners. The time of assassination would be in close co-ordination with the revolutionary uprising on April 12. In other words, even if you were arrested and tried, the time of trial would not be far away from that of the uprising."

"Furthermore, your father-in-law, mother-in-law, and sister-in-law may possibly let you live to take care of your children—one boy and two girls—even after the death of your husband. They would not put you to immediate death. In view of the above, you will not run danger of any kind. So I advise you to take the order of the party. As to the details of your mission, I shall tell you later. If you obey the order of the party, it will be responsible for the protection of your life. Otherwise, it can do nothing for you."

Under the inducements and threats of Latoff, I accepted the mission to kill my husband. Latoff then said that he would report to the party authorities my acceptance of this order. I regretted having promised to take the order of the party after returning home, and felt very sad. When my husband came home for lunch, seeing that I was fidgeting, he asked me what was wrong. I replied that I did not feel well because Ke Mo was sick. In the evening he asked me where I went during the day. To this I answered that I had been to Latoff's home. He advised me to stay at home to look after the children and not to go to see Latoff so often. I could not go to sleep that night when I thought of that terrible mission. I was dejected and prone to beating and scolding the children. For almost one week I did not go out. One day Hsiao Tso-hsin called on me, saying that Latoff wanted to see me immediately for some important matter. Next day, when I saw Latoff he told me that the situation was getting tense and that the revolution would come around after one month. He further said that I should do the preparatory work for the mission I had promised to carry out. I begged him to reconsider whether it was possible to have a man to undertake this task. Being a woman, I was not fitted to do this work. Should it fail, to sacrifice my own life would be quite immaterial, but it would upset the whole plan of the party.

Latoff did not try to conceal his displeasure. He said, however, that he had already reported to the party authorities regarding my acceptance of the mission. Should I fail to carry out the order, the party would expel me. Furthermore, it would notify my husband in this connection. As both my husband and Commissioner Sheng did not know that I had joined the All-Union Communist Party, it would be very bad for me, because I had joined without the permission of my husband. Furthermore, my husband was not a member of the All-Union Communist Party. I replied that everything would not be so serious as it might seem. In fact, I had not disobeyed the party's order. What I had said was simply to ask him to report to the party authorities on my behalf that I was not a suitable person to carry out this mission. Should they insist on my doing the work, I would still do it. But I would not be held responsible, should I fail to carry out the mission.

Latoff then said, "This is not at all necessary, because the party believes that you are the most suitable person to do the work. Now that you are willing to undertake this task, you just go ahead and do it." He asked me further whether I had had the experience of shooting a pistol. My reply was in the negative. He then said, "This is what I think. Ask your husband for a pistol under the pretext that Ke Mo is afraid of ghosts—that with a pistol placed under his pillow he would sleep more peacefully." I told him that I doubted whether he would give me the pistol. Then Latoff said that in this case he would give me one. He said further that if my husband consented to give me the pistol, I had to have it tested to see whether it was good. Finally, he again warned me to make due preparations for the mission I had undertaken and at the same time to be as submissive and kind to my husband as I could, so that members of my family would not suspect me. He also told me that my brother Chen Yu-chang had joined the All-Union Communist Party and taken active part in the revolutionary organization headed by Bakulin, Hsü Chieh, and Chou Ping. The revolutionary strength was very great.

I immediately called on my brother and asked him if he knew what Latoff has asked me to do. His reply was that he had known it long ago. Bakulin had told him that he would give me such a work. He did not quite agree with it, for fear that I might not be equal to such a task. Now that I had promised to take it, he advised me to go ahead and do it. I asked him whether they would save me should I be arrested and put into prison. My brother answered, "The revolutionary strength is tremendous. The uprising scheduled to take place on the April 12 Anniversary is bound to succeed. Even if you were unfortunately imprisoned, they will surely do everything possible to save you." With such an assurance given by my brother, I was greatly encouraged.

I went ahead with my preparations exactly in accordance with the instruction given by Latoff. Hsiao Tso-hsin called on me after a few days, asking me how far I had gone with my preparatory work. I pretended not to understand him. He then said, "Don't conceal it from me. I know everything. Both your brother and I have taken part in the revolutionary organization." I asked him who sent him here to make the inquiry. He whispered that he was sent by Consul General Bakulin. I frankly told him that I had completed all necessary work. He wished me success, but cautioned me that I should carry out my mission two weeks before the April 12 Anniversary.

As soon as I had completed my preparatory work, I reported to Latoff. He was very much satisfied but said, "You should best carry out your mission either in late March or early April. When you shoot, shoot right through the head of Commander Sheng. In case it is discovered by your family members, you may say that it was an accident caused either by the children when they played with a pistol or by your husband when he taught the children how to shoot. If you are unfortunately placed under arrest, you should under no circumstance make a confession. If this cannot be avoided, you can give any other reason you can think of than that you are ordered to do so by the revolutionary organization through me. If you can hold out until April 12, you will be saved from the very moment of the outbreak of the uprising." He paused for a while and continued, "If Commissioner Sheng comes to the South Garden, you can kill him first, if possible." I replied that I dared not shoot him.

Everything was then set in readiness to carry out the plot at the end of March. My husband did not suspect me, because I was particularly good to him and did everything as he told me. However, I overheard a talk exchanged between my mother-in-law and sister-in-law one day. The latter said, "It is funny that Chen Hsiu-ying has entirely changed in the past two weeks. She is no longer her former self with respect to her conduct. She is particularly good to my fourth brother." The old lady replied, "The younger people are always like that. When they have patience, everything would be all right. I have the same feeling about my fourth daughter-in-law. She is more amiable now."

Hsiao Tso-hsin came again on March 27 and said in an undertone, "I am instructed by Consul General Bakulin and Adviser Latoff to inform you that you should carry out your mission within three days." Thus, I assassinated my husband at around 8 o'clock at night on March 29.

Being an ignorant woman, I was victimized by Latoff under his dual tactics of inducement and pressure. I am deeply grieved at having committed such an unpardonable sin. If the government and Commissioner Sheng would not sentence me to death, in consideration of the fact that I committed the crime not on my own free volition but through the insinuation and pressure of others, I would henceforth take good care of my children, and be filial to my father-in-law and mother-in-law. When the children grow up, I shall together with them wreak my vengeance on Bakulin and Latoff for my husband, so that he may lay in peace. If the government and Commissioner Sheng cannot forgive me and sentence me to death, it is what I deserve and I have no grudge against anyone. All that I ask of Commissioner Sheng is to give a copy of my written confession to my children, so that they will know that I killed my husband, because I had been intimidated, and cheated by the Soviet Communists, Bakulin and Latoff. When they grow up, I hope they will kill the enemies of my husband and myself. If so, even if I die, I can rest in peace.

However, the root of all mistakes was my having joined the All-Union Communist Party in Moscow, and my belief in communism, thus giving them a chance to exercise their pressure over me, and leaving me no other alternative than to take their orders. I hope with all my heart that my children will be anti-Communist and take upon themselves the duty to extinguish the Communists.

CHEN HSIU-YING

April 14, 1942

Bibliography

OFFICIAL ARCHIVES AND PUBLICATIONS

REPUBLIC OF CHINA

Ministry of Foreign Affairs archives, Taipei, Taiwan: selected documents in paraphrase and translation; no file number or title.

Report on Geological Investigation of Some Oil Fields in Sinkiang, T. K. Huang, C. C. Young, Y. C. Cheng, T. C. Chow, M. N. Bien, and W. P. Weng, published by The National Geographic Survey of China under the Ministry of Economic Affairs, Nanking, February, 1947.

Su lien tui Sinkiang ti ching chi ch'in Lüeh (Soviet Economic Aggression Against Sinkiang), Ministry of Foreign Affairs, Taipei, Taiwan, 1950.

JAPAN

Ministry of Foreign Affairs Archives, Tokyo, Japan: *Sinkiang seiji oyobi ji jô kankei zasson* (Miscellaneous Documents Relating to the Political and General Situation in Sinkiang), 8 vols., official file number A.6.1.3:4.

UNITED STATES

Foreign Relations of the United States, Diplomatic Papers, 1942: China. Washington, D.C.: State Department, 1956.

Institute of Pacific Relations, Hearings Before the Subcommittee to Investigate the Administration of the Internal Security Act and

Other Internal Security Laws, Part 7a, Appendix II, 82d Congress, 2d Session. Washington, D.C.: Judiciary Committee, United States Senate, 1952.

Military Situation in the Far East, Hearings Before the Committee on Armed Services and the Committee on Foreign Relations, United States Senate, 82d Congress, 1st Session, to Conduct an Inquiry into the Military Situation in the Far East and the Facts Surrounding the Relief of Douglas MacArthur from His Assignments in That Area, Part 5. Washington, D.C.: Senate Armed Services Committee, 1951.

United States Relations with China, with Special Reference to Period 1944-49, Based on Files of Department of State. Washington, D.C.: State Department, Far Eastern Series, Item 913, 1949.

PRIVATE PAPERS

Henry R. Lieberman
Frank Robertson
General Sheng Shih-ts'ai

BOOKS AND ARTICLES

An Ning-chu, *Sinkiang nei mu* (Behind the Scenes in Sinkiang). Hong Kong: 1952.

Barmine, Alexandre, *One Who Survived, The Life Story of a Russian Under the Soviets.* New York: G. P. Putnam's Sons, 1945.

Beloff, Max, *The Foreign Policy of Soviet Russia, 1929-1941.* London: Oxford University Press, 1947-49, 2 vols.

————, *Soviet Policy in the Far East, 1944-1951.* London: Oxford University Press, 1953.

Byrnes, James, *Speaking Frankly.* New York: Harper & Brothers, 1947.

Chang Chih-chih, *Sheng Shih-ts'ai tsen yang t'ung chih Sinkiang* (How Sheng Shih-ts'ai Controlled Sinkiang). Taipei, Taiwan: 1954,

Chang Ta-chün, *Szu shih nien tung luan Sinkiang* (Forty Years of Turmoil in Sinkiang). Hong Kong: 1956.

Cheng Tien-fong, *A History of Sino-Russian Relations*. Washington, D.C.: Public Affairs Press, 1957.

Chiang Chun-chang, "Reflections on T. V. Soong's Moscow Discussion" (in Chinese), *Chung Kuo I Chou*, No. 100, March 24, 1952, pp. 14-16.

Chiang Kai-shek, *Soviet Russia in China: A Summing-Up at Seventy*. New York: Farrar, Straus and Cudahy, Inc., 1957.

Dallin, David J., *Soviet Russia and the Far East*. New Haven, Conn.: Yale University Press, 1948.

Degras, Jane, ed., *Soviet Documents on Foreign Policy, 1917-1941*. London: Oxford University Press, 1953, Vol. 3.

Fedyshyn, Oleh S., "Soviet Retreat in Sinkiang? Sino-Soviet Rivalry and Cooperation, 1950-55," *American Slavic and East European Review*, Vol. XVI, No. 2, April, 1957, pp. 127-45.

Feis, Herbert, *The China Tangle; The American Effort in China from Pearl Harbor to the Marshall Mission*. Princeton, N.J.: Princeton University Press, 1953.

Fleming, Peter, *News from Tartary: A Journey from Peking to Kashmir*. New York: Charles Scribner's Sons, 1936.

Hedin, Sven Anders, *The Flight of "Big Horse,"* New York: E. P. Dutton and Co., Inc., 1936.

————, *The Silk Road* (translated from the Swedish by F. H. Lyon). New York: E. P. Dutton and Co., Inc., 1938.

Lattimore, Owen, *High Tartary,* Boston: Little, Brown and Co., 1930.

————, *Inner Asian Frontiers of China*. New York: Capital Publishing Co. and the American Geographical Society, 1931, 2nd ed.

————, *Nationalism and Revolution in Mongolia*. New York: Oxford University Press, 1955.

————, *Pivot of Asia*. Boston: Little, Brown and Co., 1950.

Lenczowski, George, *Russia and the West in Iran, 1918-1948; A Study in Big-Power Rivalry*. Ithaca, N.Y.: Cornell University Press, 1949.

Liu, F. F., *A Military History of Modern China, 1924-1949,* Princeton, N.J.: Princeton University Press, 1956.

Norins, Martin R., *Gateway to Asia: Sinkiang.* New York: The John Day Co., 1944.

North, Robert C., *Moscow and Chinese Communists.* Stanford, Calif.: Stanford University Press, 1953.

Schwartz, Benjamin I., *Chinese Communism and the Rise of Mao.* Cambridge, Mass.: Harvard University Press, 1951.

———, "On the 'Originality' of Mao Tse-tung," *Foreign Affairs,* Vol. 34, No. 1, October, 1955.

Shabad, Theodore, *China's Changing Map; A Political and Economic Geography of the Chinese People's Republic.* New York: Frederick A. Praeger, Inc., 1956.

Shapiro, Leonard, *Soviet Treaty Series.* Washington, D.C.: Georgetown University Press, 1949, 2 vols.

Sheng Shih-ts'ai, *Liu ta cheng ti chiao ch'eng* (The Six Great Policies Study Manual). Tihua (Urumchi): 1942, Vol. 1.

Sherwood, Robert, *Roosevelt and Hopkins, an Intimate History.* New York: Harper & Brothers, 1948.

Smedley, Agnes, *The Great Road; The Life and Times of Chu Teh.* New York: Monthly Review Press, 1956.

Snow, Edgar, *Red Star over China.* New York: Modern Library Edition, Random House, 1944.

Sun Fu-k'un, *O ti ch'in hua shih* (A History of Russian Imperialism in China). Taipei, Taiwan: 1953.

———, *Su lien lüeh tao Sinkiang chi shih* (A Record of Soviet Plundering of Sinkiang), Hong Kong: 1952, 2 vols.

Teichmann, Sir Eric, *Journey to Turkestan.* London: Hodder and Stoughton, 1937.

Truman, Harry S., *Memoirs.* New York: Doubleday & Company, 1955-56, 2 vols.

Tu Chung-yüan, *Sheng Shih-ts'ai yü hsin Sinkiang* (Sheng Shih-ts'ai and the New Sinkiang). Hankow, China: 1938.

Wei, Henry, *China and Soviet Russia.* Princeton, N.J.: D. Van Nostrand Co., Inc., 1956.

Wei Jung-t'ien, *Sheng Shih-ts'ai ju ho t'ung chih Sinkiang* (How Sheng Shih-ts'ai Ruled Sinkiang). Shanghai, China: 1947.

Whiting, Allen S., "Nationality Tensions in Sinkiang," *Far Eastern Survey*, Vol. XXV, No. 1, January, 1956.

Willkie, Wendell L., *One World*. New York: Simon and Schuster, Inc., 1943.

Women ti ti kuo (Our Enemy). Taipei, Taiwan: Chung Yang Jih Pao (Central Daily News), 1952, 2 vols.

Wu, Aitchen K., *China and the Soviet Union: A Study of Sino-Soviet Relations*. New York: The John Day Co., 1950.

———, *Turkestan Tumult*, London: Methuen, 1939.

PERIODICALS

Hsin Hua Yüeh Pao

Pravda

Sinkiang Jih Pao (in files of Union Research Institute, Hong Kong)

Index

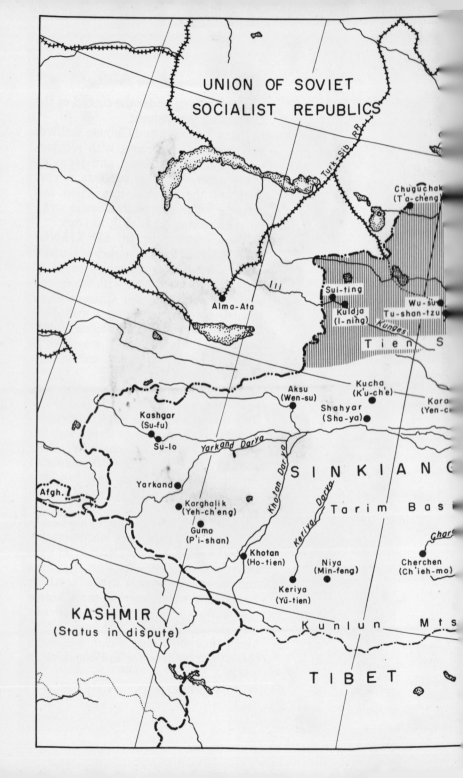